SHAKESPEARE'S FUGITIVE POLITICS

EDINBURGH CRITICAL STUDIES IN SHAKESPEARE AND PHILOSOPHY
Series Editor: Kevin Curran

Edinburgh Critical Studies in Shakespeare and Philosophy takes seriously the speculative and world-making properties of Shakespeare's art. Maintaining a broad view of 'philosophy' that accommodates first-order questions of metaphysics, ethics, politics and aesthetics, the series also expands our understanding of philosophy to include the unique kinds of theoretical work carried out by performance and poetry itself. These scholarly monographs will reinvigorate Shakespeare studies by opening new interdisciplinary conversations among scholars, artists and students.

Editorial Board Members

Published Titles

Rethinking Shakespeare's Political Philosophy: From Lear to Leviathan
Alex Schulman
Shakespeare in Hindsight: Counterfactual Thinking and Shakespearean Tragedy
Amir Khan
Second Death: Theatricalities of the Soul in Shakespeare's Drama
Donovan Sherman
Shakespeare's Fugitive Politics
Thomas P. Anderson

Forthcoming Titles

Making Publics in Shakespeare's Playhouse
Paul Yachnin
Derrida Reads Shakespeare
Chiara Alfano
The Play and the Thing: A Phenomenology of Shakespearean Theatre
Matthew Wagner
Shakespearean Melancholy: Philosophy, Form, and the Transformation of Comedy
J. F. Bernard

SHAKESPEARE'S FUGITIVE POLITICS

◆ ◆ ◆

THOMAS P. ANDERSON

EDINBURGH
University Press

Edinburgh University Press is one of the leading university presses in the UK. We publish academic books and journals in our selected subject areas across the humanities and social sciences, combining cutting-edge scholarship with high editorial and production values to produce academic works of lasting importance. For more information visit our website: edinburghuniversitypress.com

Edinburgh University Press Ltd
The Tun – Holyrood Road, 12(2f) Jackson's Entry, Edinburgh EH8 8PJ

Typeset in 12/15 Adobe Sabon by
IDSUK (DataConnection) Ltd, and
printed and bound in Great Britain by
CPI Group (UK) Ltd, Croydon CR0 4YY

A CIP record for this book is available from the British Library

ISBN 978 0 7486 9734 2 (hardback)
ISBN 978 0 7486 9735 9 (webready PDF)
ISBN 978 1 4744 1743 3 (epub)

CONTENTS

CONTENTS

ACKNOWLEDGEMENTS

I would like to thank Michele Anderson for sharing in this project with me from inception to completion. Without her patience, indulgence and support over the years, this book would not have been finished. I have received financial support from many institutions during the writing of *Shakespeare's Fugitive Politics*. At Mississippi State University, Richard Raymond in the Department of English supported my many trips to libraries and conferences as this project took shape; Dean Greg Dunaway of the College of Arts and Sciences, along with the Office of Research and Economic Development, supported my research substantially, investing in visits to the Folger Library and to Vanderbilt University and enabling my participation in annual meetings of the Shakespeare Association of America. Caroline Baker Smith was my research assistant early on when radical politics was just a search term. My colleagues in the Department of English are remarkable resources. Peter DeGabriele read nearly every word of the manuscript and offered timely criticisms. I only wish my responses to his comments were half as smart as his interventions. Eric Vivier read the book's introduction, asking for clarity and precision at a time when I needed his gentle encouragement. My other Renaissance colleagues – Lara Dodds and Greg Bentley – made the book better simply by modelling what it means to be a scholar and teacher. Dean Christopher Snyder and my colleagues and students in the Judy and Bobby Shackouls Honors College supported my research, giving me a forum to share portions of it in private conversations at MSU and with honours students at the University of Oxford.

Outside of the intellectual community at Mississippi State University, I received valuable support from several institutions and colleagues. The Marco Institute for Medieval and Renaissance Studies at the University of Tennessee invited me to Knoxville as a Lindsay Young Fellow in the summer of 2013, giving me time to research and write the chapter on *Coriolanus*. I want to especially thank Heather Hirschfeld, the Director of the institute in 2013, for supporting my scholarship. Julia Reinhard Lupton was convinced that my musings on fugitive politics were a book long before I thought they were. Although the book's faults are completely my own, the fact that it appears in print at all is a tribute to her intellectual generosity. Like Julia, Kevin Curran supported the book when it was only an idea in a seminar in Toronto in 2013. I hope that the book's final form does justice to his thoughtful comments about it since then. At the press, Cathy Falconer's collaboration on revisions to the manuscript proved invaluable. I can only hope to have her as an editorial partner on a future book. The best parts of *Shakespeare's Fugitive Politics* have been made that way through many conversations with Ryan Netzley over the years, all of them filled with my laughter and his insight. Finally, *Shakespeare's Fugitive Politics* belongs to my daughters Olivia and Elizabeth, whose presence at home with family, while I was away yet again, gave my writing and research purpose. They are my imagined audience – someday.

A section of Chapter 4 originally appeared as '"Legitimation, Name, and All Is Gone": Bastardy and Bureaucracy in Shakespeare's *King John*' in *Journal for Early Modern*

Cultural Studies 4.2 (2004). I would like to thank the University of Pennsylvania Press for permission to reprint that material here. A revised version of Chapter 2 appears as '"Here's Strange Alteration!": Hospitality, Sovereignty and Political Discord in *Coriolanus*' in David Goldstein and Julia Reinhard Lupton (eds), *Shakespeare and Hospitality: Ethics, Politics, and Exchange* (Routledge, 2016), and a section of Chapter 5 appears as '"Ay, me. This object kills me!": Julie Taymor's Cinematic Blazon in *Titus*' in Deborah Uman and Sara Morrison (eds), *Staging the Blazon in Early Modern English Theater* (Ashgate, 2013). I would like to thank the Taylor & Francis Group for allowing me to reprint the material here.

SERIES EDITOR'S PREFACE

Picture Macbeth alone on stage, staring intently into empty space. 'Is this a dagger which I see before me?' he asks, grasping decisively at the air. On one hand, this is a quintessentially theatrical question. At once an object and a vector, the dagger describes the possibility of knowledge ('Is this a dagger') in specifically visual and spatial terms ('which I see before me'). At the same time, Macbeth is posing a quintessentially *philosophical* question, one that assumes knowledge to be both conditional and experiential, and that probes the relationship between certainty and perception as well as intention and action. It is from this shared ground of art and inquiry, of theatre and theory, that this series advances its basic premise: *Shakespeare is philosophical.*

It seems like a simple enough claim. But what does it mean exactly, beyond the parameters of this specific moment in *Macbeth*? Does it mean that Shakespeare had something we could think of as his own philosophy? Does it mean that he was influenced by particular philosophical schools, texts and thinkers? Does it mean, conversely, that modern philosophers have been influenced by *him*, that Shakespeare's plays and poems have been, and continue to be, resources for philosophical thought and speculation?

The answer is yes all around. These are all useful ways of conceiving a philosophical Shakespeare and all point to lines of inquiry that this series welcomes. But Shakespeare is philosophical in a much more fundamental way as well. Shakespeare is philosophical because the plays and poems actively create new worlds of knowledge and new scenes of ethical encounter. They ask big questions, make bold arguments, and develop new vocabularies in order to think what might otherwise be unthinkable. Through both their scenarios and their imagery, the plays and poems engage the qualities of consciousness, the consequences of human action, the phenomenology of motive and attention, the conditions of personhood, and the relationship among different orders of reality and experience. This is writing and dramaturgy, moreover, that consistently experiments with a broad range of conceptual crossings, between love and subjectivity, nature and politics, and temporality and form.

Edinburgh Critical Studies in Shakespeare and Philosophy takes seriously these speculative and world-making dimensions of Shakespeare's work. The series proceeds from a core conviction that art's capacity to think – to formulate, not just reflect, ideas – is what makes it urgent and valuable. Art matters because unlike other human activities it establishes its own frame of reference, reminding us that all acts of creation – biological, political, intellectual and amorous – are grounded in imagination. This is a far cry from business-as-usual in Shakespeare studies. Because historicism remains the methodological gold standard of the field, far more energy has been invested in exploring what Shakespeare once meant than in thinking rigorously about what Shakespeare continues to make possible. In response, Edinburgh Critical Studies in Shakespeare and Philosophy pushes back against the critical orthodoxies of historicism and cultural studies to clear a space for scholarship that confronts aspects of literature that can be neither reduced to nor adequately explained by particular historical contexts.

Shakespeare's creations are not just inheritances of a past culture, frozen artifacts whose original settings must be expertly reconstructed in order to be understood. The plays and poems are also living art, vital thought-worlds that struggle, across time, with foundational questions of metaphysics, ethics, politics and aesthetics. With this orientation in mind, Edinburgh Critical Studies in Shakespeare and Philosophy offers a series of scholarly monographs that will reinvigorate Shakespeare studies by opening new interdisciplinary conversations among scholars, artists and students.

Kevin Curran

CHAPTER 1

THE EMBODIED WILL IN *JULIUS CAESAR*: AN INTRODUCTION TO SHAKESPEARE'S FUGITIVE POLITICS

But let the world rank me in register
A master-leaver and a fugitive.
                    Antony and Cleopatra, 4.10.20–1[1]

Who then but English Henry will be lord,
And thou be thrust out like a fugitive?
                    1 Henry VI, 3.7.66–7

'fugitive': Of immaterial things: Evanescent, fleeting, of short duration [. . .] One who flees or tries to escape from danger, an enemy, justice, or an owner.
                    Oxford English Dictionary

Despite the title's use of the word 'fugitive', which evokes a sense of dislocation, boundary and place, *Shakespeare's Fugitive Politics* is not about a particular location of politics in Shakespeare's plays. The word 'fugitive' might imply a place for politics in Shakespeare that his plays and their characters somehow escape, a boundary or proper scene for the political – and that Shakespeare's radicalism is his rejection of this proper place for a world elsewhere. In this

understanding of the word 'fugitive' in the title, Shakespeare is a refugee from the properly political that defines
and polices civil bounds. This book, however, is not necessarily interested in the proper place of politics in Shakespeare's plays – its policing and policed boundaries, its
parameters and its institutions. *Shakespeare's Fugitive Politics* is, instead, about how the political is experienced in his
plays. The book's central premise is that much of the political radicalism in Shakespeare is indifferent to politics – that
is, indifferent to legitimised and public contestation that is
'continuous, ceaseless, and endless' in a civil society[2] – and
predicated instead on the possibility of dramatic subjects
becoming political beings. In this formulation, as Sheldon
Wolin has argued in the context of modern democracy, the
political articulates not a form of civic engagement but a
'mode of being' that appears only temporarily. Wolin writes
that 'Democracy is a political moment, perhaps the political
moment, when the political is remembered and recreated'.[3]
The democratic political persists as long as the memory of
its past expression survives. The promise of fugitive politics is in a rebellious moment rather than a form; it appears
as an occasional presence or evanescence 'that may assume
revolutionary, destructive proportions, or may not'.[4]

The unpredictable promise of Shakespeare's fugitive politics is perhaps best illustrated in the ritual events surrounding
Caesar's funeral depicted in *Julius Caesar*. As this introduction unfolds its argument about the way Shakespeare archives
the political in his plays, *Julius Caesar* will serve as a touchstone, establishing and amplifying dimensions of the political that are explored more fully in chapters on *Coriolanus*,
Henry V, *King John*, *Titus Andronicus* and *The Winter's Tale*.
Julius Caesar is a play that has at its centre (3.3) a flash mob
occupying the marketplace and rendering a form of wild justice on Cinna – the poet who unfortunately bears the same
name as one of Caesar's conspirators. Roman plebeians

randomly come across the poet on his way to Caesar's funeral and promise to '[t]ear him to pieces' (34) and to '[p]luck but his name out of his heart' (32–3). The contingency of the event of Cinna's murder and its fleeting yet absolutely essential political nature[5] are the culmination of events in the play informed by early modern concerns about sacred sovereignty, friendship and body politics that are the themes of *Shakespeare's Fugitive Politics*.

In the moments leading up to Caesar's funeral, as the plebeians make clear, everything and everyone becomes political. Cinna's twice-repeated defence that he is 'Cinna the poet' (28) and 'not Cinna the conspirator' (31) is met with indifference. 'It is no matter, his name's Cinna,' says the plebeian (32). In this encounter, bodies become political despite themselves, and friends of Caesar are indistinguishable from his enemies. Cinna's exchange with the plebeians before he is assaulted illustrates the collapse between friends and enemies that defines the politics of the scene:

CINNA. Directly, I am going to Caesar's funeral.
FIRST PLEBEIAN. As a friend or an enemy?
CINNA. As a friend.
SECOND PLEBEIAN. The matter is answered directly.
FOURTH PLEBEIAN. For your dwelling, briefly.
CINNA. Briefly, I dwell by the Capitol.
THIRD PLEBEIAN. Your name, sir, truly.
CINNA. Truly, my name is Cinna.
FIRST PLEBEIAN. Tear him to pieces! He is a conspirator.
(3.3.19–28)

Shakespeare infuses this scene with a violent antagonism collapsing the friend-enemy distinction. In this new political dispensation, dissensual politics usurps the politics of consensus informed by amity and concord. In this moment, Cinna embodies the logic of friendship in the play more broadly. That is to say, just as Brutus and Antony can be both friend and enemy to Caesar, the nature of politics in this scene makes Cinna both a friend and an enemy.[6]

Cinna's fate unintentionally highlights the volatility of dissensual politics, foregrounding the concept that will be central to a reading of *Coriolanus* that follows this introduction. In act 4 of the play, Coriolanus enters Aufidius's home and is questioned by servingmen. The servingmen's reaction to their guest illustrates the tension between friends and enemies that frames the scene of Cinna's murder in *Julius Caesar*. Using the language of friendship in their address to Coriolanus, both servingmen express the ambivalence that is at the core of a concept of friendship that makes antagonism foundational to its political framework.[7] The First Servingman says, 'What would you have, friend? Whence are you? Here's no place for you. Pray, go to the door' (4.5.7–9), followed by the Second Servingman, 'Whence are you, sir? Has the port his eyes in his head, that he gives entrance to such companions? Pray, get you out' (12–14). Both servants describe Coriolanus in terms common to the rhetoric of friendship in the period, yet both reactions suggest that there is an aspect of Coriolanus that is not knowable: 'Whence are you?' The question posed by both servingmen lingers as the play's acknowledgement that friendship's divisibility prevents it from being co-opted by sovereign absolutism in service of the state. Even as the ambiance of the scene – its music, its food and its wine – intimates unity in plenitude, Coriolanus introjects division, insulting the servingmen by ordering them to '[f]ollow your function. Go, and batten on cold bits' (31–2), and saying to another, 'Thou prat'st, and prat'st. Serve with thy trencher. Hence!' (47–8).

The scene's ambivalence toward friendship and hospitality in the moments before the portrayal of the alliance between Aufidius and Coriolanus helps to shape how we are to understand their strategic union. Coriolanus rejects consensus as a form of politics even before he aligns himself with his rival. His reluctance to show his wounds and to participate in the ritual of the gown of humility in the presence of Roman citizens points to his refusal to engage in a politics defined by consent, compact or compromise. 'Would you have me / False to my nature?' asks Coriolanus of his mother Volumnia. 'Rather say I play / The man I am' (3.2.14–16). Coriolanus's wounded body becomes a trope in this scene. In the ritual of the humility gown, his wounds earned alone in battle for Rome become invitations for community and consent. They, in short, invite political collaboration at the expense of the dissensual force that Coriolanus's politics demands.

Shakespeare's Fugitive Politics makes the case that scenes such as these illustrate rebellious moments that exceed any singular and sustained political form. As an occasional presence or evanescence, the political in Shakespeare appears most often in relation to sovereign power as moments that recall and recreate a political past – a past in which the subject comes into being as a form of life in relation to sovereign power, retaining, however, the agency of its own sovereign subjectivity. The emergence of the political comes with some risk to the subject, whose civic life in relation to sovereignty is not guaranteed. In 'Transgression, Equality, and Voice', Wolin writes, 'The demos exists as striving, but that may be directed not at assuring duration to its existence but at challenging its own finitude. The tangible expression of that problematic would be the leap from polis to empire.'[8] Once the subject exists as a form of life, its struggle to be – to survive – is seen as a threat to sovereignty and, ironically, to the demos's own existence outside of the form of power that immediately seeks to contain it. Elsewhere, Wolin describes democracy as an 'ephemeral phenomenon rather than a settled system', arguing that it

should be about forms rather than *a* form or constitution; and, instead of an institutionalized process, it should be conceived as a moment of experience, a crystallized response to deeply felt grievances or needs on the part of those whose main preoccupation – demanding of time and energy – is to scratch out a decent existence. Its moment is not just a measure of fleeting time but an action that protests actualities and reveals possibilities.[9]

While the idea of democracy as a form of government was not available to Shakespeare and his contemporaries, I want to suggest that democracy is one form that the political takes on stage in early modern England, not as a coherent political formation in response to the structure of sovereignty, but as a mode of political being registered in encounters with and, as this book will show, more critically within sovereign absolutism. Henry S. Turner has shown how, despite the fact that the political category 'democracy' was 'little more than a distant philosophical' concept, the early modern period was fascinated with problems that 'would eventually become central to the notion of a democratic polity'.[10] He cites David Wootton's observation about how linguistic translation eliminated the word 'democracy' from the early modern lexicon in favour of the idea of the republic or commonwealth.

> The Romans had no word for democracy, but since they read the Greek philosophers they paraphrased the concept into Latin as government by the people [. . .] In the late fifteenth century, in the Florence of Savonarola, a remarkable linguistic revolution took place: the only real republic, it was argued, was a popular government (which was understood to be a way of paraphrasing the Greek term democracy into Latin) [. . .] Thus a history of the concept of democracy needs to take seriously the idea that republic (or, in English, commonwealth) was for a long time . . . a synonym for democracy, and, since there was a strong preference for Latin over Greek . . . the word 'democracy' was rarely needed.[11]

If democracy is not a form, but a mode of being without linguistic register, then, according to Wolin, 'small scale is the only scale commensurate with the kind of power that democracy is capable of mobilizing'.[12] He describes the 'modest sites' of democratic articulation, including 'the ingenuity of ordinary people in inventing temporary forms to meet their needs'.[13] For Wolin, the essence of the political is a democratic encounter – fleeting and unpredictable, subject to failure as well as success. In this way, fugitive politics is both modest and grand. On one level, the modesty of the political encounter (exemplified, for example, in the scene of hospitality between Coriolanus and Aufidius) means that the ordinary political subject does not 'magically' come to possess the time and energy to become a full-time political actor in response to the sovereign absolutism that defines the early modern subject. With Wolin's account of democracy as a model for the political on Shakespeare's stage, the fugitive condition of politics does not 'stand for pent-up revolutionary fervor waiting for an opportunity to wreak havoc'[14] in an epic battle with absolutism. As Wolin writes, 'Given the material condition of the demos, the actuality of democracy is necessarily episodic and circumstantial.'[15] On another level, fugitive politics as a type of encounter is grand and ambitious. Fugitive politics, as I am conceiving it in the chapters that follow, describes characters – including the sovereign in a new theo-political dispensation – who are 'provocateurs whose passionate commitments can arouse self-consciousness in the public, stimulating the latter to become aware of what they believe and of the mixed legacies that compose a collective inheritance'.[16] The broad aim of the book, then, is to give shape, if only fleetingly, to fugitive politics in early modern drama, articulated through the contours of theories of sovereignty, which raise questions about the period's understanding of forms of republicanism, democracy and tyranny. I contend, *pace* Wolin, that the controversies explored on stage and examined in *Shakespeare's Fugitive Politics* are critical to the 'cause of anti-totality and its vitality'.[17]

Fugitive Interventions

In pursuing fugitive politics in several of Shakespeare's plays, this book addresses important questions about the relationship among subject, sovereignty and civil society. *Shakespeare's Fugitive Politics* explores the embodiment of dramatic political encounters – Henry V's royal touch, Catherine and Henry's kiss, Hermione's agitating body, Coriolanus and Aufidius's twinned body, Lavinia's veiled face, and the royal touch ratifying a sovereign alliance between England and France. In exploring scenes of political embodiment on stage, the book argues that the plays' investments in these affective moments increase the possibilities for modes of expressing new and resistant political forms of life in relation to sovereign power. Daniel Juan Gil turns explicitly to images of the flesh in Shakespeare to argue that the emerging nation-state 'energizes a life of the flesh that is rooted in the (shared) experience of the body abjectly exposed to sovereign power'.[18] The central argument of Gil's book is consonant with my own insistence in *Shakespeare's Fugitive Politics* that viable political agency is not eliminated with the production of bare life. Gil elaborates on this point in *Shakespeare's Anti-Politics*:

> the focus of Shakespeare's art is to bring this life of the flesh to the stage as the object of an audience's aesthetic experience; through Shakespeare's plays, readers and audiences are invited to take aesthetic pleasure in seeing and even fantasmatically participating in a life of the flesh that is an alternative to functional integration into the nation-state.[19]

In staging scenes of bare life in relation to the sovereign exception, Shakespeare's plays irreducibly link sovereign power to its own abject other, reconfiguring the political potential of both. I argue that Shakespeare's plays, in staging these intensely affective encounters, insist on the specificity of literariness – the archive that remembers and recreates – to challenge the coherence of early modern politics that sovereignty works to produce.[20]

Shakespeare's Fugitive Politics examines plays that stretch across the playwright's career – from *Titus Andronicus* in 1594 to *The Winter's Tale* in 1611 – and across dramatic genres, including histories, tragedies and romance. The chapter 'Friendship, Sovereignty and Political Discord in *Coriolanus*' reorients the way that we understand early modern political sovereignty by arguing that the relationship between Coriolanus and Aufidius is a friendship predicated on agonism and discord. The chapter's close examination of their alliance and eventual betrayal establishes the counter-politics of friendship that organises political relationships explored throughout the book. The fragile warrior-friendship established in act 4, I argue, links the two men in shared estrangement. In claiming that the two rivals embody a singular type of friendship with resonant political implications, the chapter revises early modern theories of friendship from Erasmus, Bacon and Montaigne, as well as friendship theory from their classical predecessors Cicero and Aristotle. Shakespeare's depiction of *amicitia perfecta*, I suggest, offers a critical point of intervention in contemporary accounts by Foucault and Derrida of the political potential inherent in a friendship characterised by dissensus, not amity. *Coriolanus* stages the possibility of radicalising the citizen/state binary, glimpsing the fragile grounds of a potentially new communal politics embodied in a fragile warrior-friendship.

In another chapter, 'Touching Sovereignty in *Henry V*', I extend the book's discussion of community by taking seriously the Chorus's avuncular description of Henry's presence in the camp at Agincourt as 'a little touch of Harry in the night' (4.0.47). I draw on early modern and modern understandings of the royal touch to make the case that tactility in the play becomes the vehicle for reconfiguring sovereignty, exposing its fractured condition as well as efforts to reconstitute its integrity. For Henry, to touch is to redeem sovereign authority. His contemplation of the ritual effect of the royal touch to cure his own diseased condition, however, demonstrates the impossibility of sovereign redemption through touch. To the multitude in the play, however – Falstaff, Williams, Bates, even Catherine – tactility is an expression of individual sovereignty that agitates institutional power through body politics. In Henry's quest for union between England and France, redemption and union are conjured, like magic, through his tactile encounter with Catherine. This magic does not serve a new politics of consensus; instead, it disavows what Henry knows too well – that his royal touch is powerless to make sensible the fugitive condition of a dissensual politics immanent at the core of his divided condition.

Divided sovereignty looks very different in *King John*, a play written and performed in between the first and second tetralogies. 'Sovereignty's Scribbled Form in *King John*' shifts the focus of community from the mobile and fleeting enunciations of political clusters found in *Coriolanus* toward a concept of the nation-state defined in terms of leagues, friendships and amity between England and France. The play consistently describes the evolving relationship between nations in terms of friendship and hospitality. Constance's desperate question 'France friend with England! What becomes of me?' (2.2.35), after the rival nations become momentary allies, captures the challenge that national sovereignty poses to a subject's liberty. In its depiction of this geopolitical friendship, *King John* interrogates the power-ful claims of an emerging bureaucratic network of author-ity exemplified by the Bastard's relationship with what the play calls 'borrowed majesty' (1.1.4) and 'perjured kings' (3.1.33). In arguing that *King John* makes explicit the politi-cal condition of friendship in depicting rival nation-states, I make the case that the Bastard's new sovereign relationship radically redefines a political subject as a bawd or broker in a bureaucratic network with radical, albeit unrealised, political potential. The Bastard – a bureaucrat with royal blood – is well aware that his fugitive survival and politi-cal efficacy are contingent on how he responds to the unin-tended contours of the sovereign decision, to its collateral effects that exceed ordered and absolute power, in other words, to that which allows him to act legitimately, with bureaucratic sovereignty, both inside and outside of the law.

In Chapter 5, I turn to female characters in *The Winter's Tale* and *Titus Andronicus* to show how Shakespeare's aes-thetics integrates performing objects and performing bodies in its depiction of powerful women. In staging the process of survival for Lavinia and Hermione, Shakespeare traves-ties the concept of the king's two bodies central to early modern sovereignty, redistributing agency between subjects to objects. Central to my reading of the female body in these two plays is Elizabeth Grosz's concept of corporeal femininity, which emphasises the tactility of the perform-ing body, its agitating power that poses problems for the way these plays and their critics attempt to make sense of the women's physical condition as an embodiment of frac-tured or incomplete subjectivity. Julie Taymor's film *Titus* (2000), with its cinematic expression of the power of the prosthetic, becomes a touchstone for a reading of these plays' explorations of the politics of vibrant matter. Both Lavinia and Hermione offer a form of corporeal feminism, exemplified in Taymor's film, which rediscovers feminine agency through the fragmented body as a social surface and the surface of inscription. In their parody of sovereignty's charismatic survival beyond death, these two plays to different degrees transform political theology into a feminist politics in which performing objects – Lavinia's body and Hermione's statue – evoke the phenomenon of non-sovereign agency that limits sovereign absolutism and enables fugitive politics in Shakespeare.

Common to each of these forays into Shakespeare's political archive is the belief that affirmative politics in Shakespeare – the process of transforming negative affect into political resistance – does not appear in a dialectical opposition to sovereignty, absolutism or tyranny, nor in some sort of inchoate form of republicanism on its way to becoming politically viable. Instead, the book views affirmative politics in his plays as events of dissidence outside dialectical opposition, beyond the presumption that political evolution leads ineluctably toward republicanism. In *Dorsality: Thinking Back through Technology and Politics*, David Wills defines controversion as a 'type of turning away, objection, or contradiction, which, instead of offering a cold shoulder, reveals the other side, another position, a nonconciliatory controversary dissidence'.[21] He explains that controversion is 'acceptance of the rupture of the integral subject via a relation with technology and participation with systematic forms of exteriority'.[22] Wills describes a political encounter as a moment that 'unsettle[s] relations of power by adding an element that asks to be contended with on different terms'.[23] Refusing the political efficacy of dialectical encounters, Wills endorses an affirmative form of political life imagined as a dorsal turn that 'concedes one's integral autonomy [. . .] by turning to an extrinsic construction of human relations, a particular articulation of the self to what is outside of it'.[24] *Shakespeare's Fugitive Politics* claims that the dorsal turn identifying affective, fugitive politics registers an antagonism or dissensus that the sovereign order always wishes to shut down in favour of submission or consensus. Wolin provides context for this claim: 'The central challenge at this moment', he writes in *Politics and Vision*, 'is not about reconciliation but about dissonance, not about democracy's supplying legitimacy to totality but about nurturing a discordant democracy – discordant not in the flashy but empty ways of latter-day Nietzscheans but discordant because, in being rooted in the ordinary, it affirms the value of limits.'[25] The central challenge of Wolin's late capitalist moment, I suggest, echoes the central challenge of Shakespeare's late sovereign moment. In other words, Shakespeare's plays reveal that there is always something more terrifying to the king than rebellion.

The book's sources include Montaigne, Cicero and Aristotle; modern writings on sovereignty by Giorgio Agamben, Sheldon Wolin, Michel Foucault and Carl Schmitt; and contemporary feminist accounts of the relation of the body to agency from, most prominently, Elizabeth Grosz, Ewa Ziarek and Sharon Krause. Thus, the book demonstrates the strong connection between early modern and modern discourses of sovereignty, sociability and agency.[26] Rather than simply celebrating the forms of equality and accord promised by friendship and hospitality characteristic of neo-liberal politics today, *Shakespeare's Fugitive Politics* emphasises dissensus and discord as affective responses that contribute to the politics of these encounters, often overlooked as democratic incubators.[27]

This portrait of dissident politics resembles that of Chantal Mouffe, Jacques Rancière and, as we have seen, Sheldon Wolin, for whom politics is not the logical extension of consensual desires that produce increasingly progressive civic policy, but the productivity of a politics of discord. In *Disagreement*, Rancière argues that the political is an interruption, a moment in which incommensurability becomes apparent in the fabric of an existing social order that exposes the process of subjectifica- tion. Mouffe calls political antagonism 'agonistic pluralism', and she argues that democratic institutions are characterised by agonistic conflicts that take on a form of 'conflictual consen- sus'.[28] For Mouffe, politics requires that others 'are not seen as enemies to be destroyed, but as adversaries whose ideas might be fought, even fiercely'.[29] Mouffe elaborates on the objective of dissensual, democratic politics:

> The prime task of democratic politics is not to eliminate
> passions or to relegate them to the private sphere in order
> to establish a rational consensus in the public sphere.
> Rather, it is to 'sublimate' those passions by mobilizing
> them towards democratic designs, by creating collective
> forms of identification around democratic objectives. [. . .]
> It is only when division and antagonism are recognized as
> being ineradicable that it is possible to think in a properly
> political way.[30]

Conflictual models of democratic politics in Shakespeare, represented as fugitive and contingent and that are the often ignored or misunderstood predecessors of the consensual politics of the neo-liberal democracy of late capitalism, ulti- mately change how we understand the practice of reading or experiencing the sovereignty in his plays, both in the early modern period and today. In exploring what Wills describes as dorsal encounters – affective, fugitive encounters regis- tering an antagonism or dissensus that the sovereign order always wishes to shut down in favour of submission or con- sensus – violated and volatile bodies in both their abject and sovereign condition become robust sites through which the political finds expression.

Caesar's Will, Caesar's Wounds

In order to help illustrate the political work that the abject body does, I want to fold this argument back into events surrounding Caesar's funeral in *Julius Caesar*. Caesar's body is subject to a form of ceremonial inscription. The events surrounding his dramatic funeral – with its emphasis on theatrical performance even as the ceremony illustrates an intense desire for ritual efficacy – raise questions about the sovereignty's theo-political authority and function at the end of the sixteenth century in England. The play depicts *funus publicum* in process, as Antony and others lead the ceremonial procession to the Forum, placing Caesar's body on the Rostra, or pulpit, while Brutus delivers his *laudatio* for the slain emperor. Brutus calls attention to the body as the funeral procession enters. 'Here comes his body, mourned by Antony' (3.2.38), he says, and he asks the plebeians to '[d]o grace to Caesar's corpse' (54) by attending to Antony's speech. With Caesar's body on the Rostra, Antony ascends to the 'public chair' (60) to deliver his *laudatio*. Also drawing attention to Caesar's body, Antony tells the crowd that his 'heart is in the coffin there with Caesar' (104). Antony then links the reading of Caesar's will to the corpse:

> [T]is his will.
> Let but the commons hear this testament,
> Which, pardon me, I do not mean to read,
> And they would go and kiss dead Caesar's wounds,
> And dip their napkins in his sacred blood,
> Yea, beg a hair of him for memory,
> And, dying, mention it within their wills,
> Bequeathing it as a rich legacy
> Unto their issue   (130–9)

In Antony's oration, the efficacy of the legal document is transferred to the efficacy of Caesar's wounded body as a sacred object.³¹ Antony's logic turns as if to bind the image of Caesar's sacred body in legal codes that guarantee its ritual efficacy. In the image, the bloody napkins and hair – charmed objects culled by the commoners from the dead body – are themselves objects included in their wills to be passed down to future generations of Romans. The power of Caesar's will seems to animate the bloody corpse, extending its efficacy through time guaranteed by legal testament.

In clamouring for the reading of the will that follows, the crowd is also asking to bear witness to Caesar's bloody body that Antony has brilliantly linked to the act of disclosure:

> FOURTH PLEBEIAN. We'll hear the will. Read it, Mark
>   Antony.
> ALL. The will, the will! We will hear Caesar's will!
> [. . .]
> FOURTH PLEBEIAN. Read the will! We'll hear it, Antony!
> You shall read us the will, Caesar's will!
> ANTONY. Will you be patient? Will you stay a while?
> I have o'ershot myself to tell you of it.
> I fear I wrong the honorable men
> Whose daggers have stabbed Caesar; I do fear it.
>
> (3.2.136–50)

In raising the spectacle of Caesar's wounded body in his response to the crowd – 'stabbed Caesar; I do fear it' – Antony again associates the inanimate body with the binding legal testament described by Antony as 'a parchment with the seal of Caesar' (130). He reinforces this link before descending from the pulpit to the Rostra:

> You will compel me then to read the will?
> Then make a ring about the corpse of Caesar,
> And let me show you him that made the will.   (155–7)

These three lines literalise the conceptual link between corpse and will. Antony's first and third lines end with the word 'will', encasing 'corpse of Caesar', which ends the second line of the passage. Like the plebeians who form a circle around Caesar's body after Antony descends from the pulpit to the Rostra – 'a ring; stand round' (162) – the 'will' in Antony's *laudatio* poetically makes 'a ring about the corpse of Caesar'.

The spectacle of Caesar's wounded body galvanises the crowd's attention for the remainder of the scene. The scene's complexity, however, as well as the play's sustained interest in the spectacle of bodies, both corporeal and inanimate, is made even more interesting in relation to questions about sovereignty if we take into account other sources about ancient Roman funerals. While Plutarch serves as Shakespeare's primary source for the history of Caesar's funeral, the way the funeral fed political unrest is more the subject of Appian's account of events.[32] Appian describes Antony delivering his famous oration from the pulpit and then descending to the Rostra with Caesar's body hidden. He stood close to the bier carrying Caesar's covered body. First bending over the body, Antony then straightened up, holding both hands up in witness to Caesar's divinity. He then uncovered the body of Caesar, lifting on the end of the spear the torn, bloody robe he wore during the assassination. According to Appian, the body had remained covered until this moment. In the play, the plebeians make room for Antony, ordering the crowd to '[s]tand from the hearse. Stand from the body!' (3.2.164), and Antony asks the crowd to 'press not upon me. Stand far off' (165), making room for as many in the crowd as possible to witness the spectacle that is about to transpire. All the plebeians follow Antony's request for space with the order to 'Stand back! Room! Bear back!' (166). The will or testament that poetically circles Caesar's body, having established its ritual efficacy earlier in the scene, is now the crowd that circles the corpse, and their reaction to the spectacle of Caesar's body is part of the transactional economy that gives value to Antony's oration. Daniel Juan Gil has noted that this moment

> refolds a social connection (his friendship with Caesar) into an eccentric shape that defines a new intersubjectivity. And this intersubjectivity spreads throughout the social world of the play by folding functional social solidarity into a new intersubjectivity mediated, first and foremost, by the body and bodily humors [. . .] What is left after the political field has been stripped of legitimacy is a radically bodily terrain in which fluids and humors seem to leap from body to body, weaving them together into new, radically extra-political networks.[33]

This form of agency – a combination of what appears to be ritualised sovereignty and the desire of commoners to bear witness to and accommodate it – is central to Shakespeare's fugitive politics.

Shakespeare explores the idea of intersubjective agency in plays before and after *Julius Caesar*, suggesting that it was at least a dramatic interest, if not a political preoccupation. The subject of Chapter 5, *Titus Andronicus* and *The Winter's Tale* depict the precarious, exposed and vulnerable body intimately woven into expressions of dissent that establish the parameters of the productivity of non-sovereign agency. Subjects of sovereign power, Lavinia and Hermione actively participate in the political even as their subjectivities are bound by the sovereign exception.[34] This expression of agency, as recent work by Sharon Krause argues, is 'non-sovereign'.[35] Lavinia's agitating body and her insistent presence demand a response from others on stage with her, even as her intersubjective agency threatens her interlocutors. As a sign of this affective power, Lucius claims that the sight of Lavinia's ravaged body kills him. In *The Winter's Tale*, Hermione's body is hidden from sight because, like Lavinia's body that was made vulnerable as the object of 'man's eye' (2.3.177), she and Paulina recognise the unpredictability of intersubjective agency in response to a volatile body. Non-sovereign agency differs from the neo-liberal form that links politically viable action or resistance to rational political subjects and, as Krause suggests, enables a critical position not limited to the disabling binaries – sovereign-subject, agent-victim, power-resistance – that tend to undermine minoritarian movements. If, as I am suggesting, the term 'fugitive politics' describes a divisibility of power disavowed by the sovereign exception as well as by the consensual politics of neo-liberalism, then *Titus Andronicus* and *The Winter's Tale* represent the spectrum of possibility for intersubjective agency at the expense of the integrity of the female body. Put otherwise, perhaps Shakespeare's most radical exploration of fugitive politics represents the female body as an object with an agitating force demanding a response to its fragile condition.

Folding this expression of political agitation registered in bodies back into a reading of *Julius Caesar*, the agency that inheres in Caesar's visible body in the funeral ritual is transferred to many different images of Caesar's body, each demanding a response. In Appian, Antony removes Caesar's bloody robe, revealing the fatal wounds smeared with sacred blood.[36] Shakespeare depicts this dramatic moment in the ritual this way:

You all know this mantle. I remember
The first time ever Caesar put it on:
[. . .]
Look, in this place ran Cassius' dagger through.

See what a rent the envious Casca made:
Through this the well-beloved Brutus stabbed,
And as he plucked his cursèd steel away,
Mark how the blood of Caesar followed it,   (168–76)

Antony's oration imparts grace on the drops of blood on the mantle, calling them 'gracious drops' (192), and asks the '[k]ind souls' in the crowd how much they will weep when they 'behold / Our Caesar's vesture wounded?' (193–4). At this point, Antony appears to reveal the body of Caesar himself to add final emphasis to the dramatic moment that incites mob violence. 'Look you here!' Antony says. 'Here is himself, marred, as you see, with traitors' (194–5).

It is worth pausing at this point to consider what exactly is being staged when Antony commands the plebeians to bear witness to Caesar himself. Certainly, he might be referring to the body of the slain emperor, but would he have pointed to the hearse already visible to the crowd? Would he have raised the body out of the coffin on the hearse to show the twenty-three fatal wounds? Does Antony's *laudatio* generate a new form of absolutism in the already visible wounds, re-signifying them as sacred and therefore efficacious in a way they were not moments before when a plebeian ordered the crowd away from the hearse and body? Plutarch is little help, writing in *The Life of Caesar* that 'they saw his body (which was brought into the market-place) all bemangled with gashes of swords, then there was no order to keep the multitude and common people quiet [. . .]'.[37] Given the problem in staging the dramatic moment, it is just as likely that the plebeian's response to whatever he witnesses, 'O piteous spectacle!' (196), is a reaction to something new added to this dramatic scene, not a response to a new evaluation of what was already on stage.

Sumi contends that the theatrical nature of the funeral was made more spectacular by Caesar's appearance at the event, attributing the intense dramatic quality to artificial Caesars – actors playing Caesar. Appian claims that 'Caesar himself appeared to speak', referring to a professional actor impersonating Caesar, 'transforming the funeral into a theatrical celebration'.[38] It is not hard to imagine a fifth actor impersonating Caesar, wounded, indicting his enemies, at Antony's direction. What sight would be surprising enough at this moment in the funeral to illicit the passionate responses from the crowd?

FIRST PLEBEIAN. O piteous spectacle!
SECOND PLEBEIAN. O noble Caesar!
THIRD PLEBEIAN. O woeful day!
FOURTH PLEBEIAN. O traitors! villains!
FIRST PLEBEIAN. O most bloody sight!   (196–200)

Although Shakespeare's stage directions provide little clue as to the theatrics that inform this scene, Appian records the use of another stage device that would have roused passions in the crowd – a funeral effigy of Caesar. Sumi notes that someone in the crowd 'raised above the bier a wax image of Caesar showing all twenty-three wounds over his body and face'.[39] The effigy was rotated during the funeral to give everyone in the crowd the chance to see the bloody spectacle. Appian's account describes Caesar's effigy:

While they were in this temper and were already near to violence, somebody raised above the bier an image of Caesar himself made of wax. The body itself, as it lay on its back on the couch, could not be seen. The image was turned round and round by a mechanical device, showing the twenty-three wounds in all parts of the body and on the face that had been dealt to him so brutally. The people could no longer bear the pitiful sight presented to them. They groaned, and, girding up their loins, they burned the senate-chamber where Caesar was slain, and ran hither and thither searching for the murderers, who had fled some time previously.⁴⁰

The appearance of the effigy recorded in Appian's history seems to have been coordinated with Antony's oration, making visible the wounds in spectacular fashion as Antony verbally narrates the event.

The appearance of Caesar's mechanical effigy amplifies the theatricality of the event. It allows us to raise questions about how absolute power is divided from the sovereign body and reallocated to other representational regimes. In the moment of reallocation – an event that the appearance of Caesar's effigy enacts – the absolutism of indivisible authority and of the sovereign decision is fractured and aestheticised. *Shakespeare's Fugitive Politics* explores these moments of reallocation, when sovereignty encounters its own limits and transforms into intersubjective agency. Antony's final reference to Caesar's body imagines the charisma of royal presence as intersubjective and non-sovereign – grossly material and collaborative:

> Show you Caesar's wounds, poor poor dumb mouths,
> And bid them speak for me. But were I Brutus,
> And Brutus Antony, there were an Antony
> Would ruffle up your spirits and put a tongue
> In every wound of Caesar that should move
> The stones to rise and mutiny.   (3.2.223–8)

Caesar's wounds invite collaboration; they encourage interpenetration and are mute without participation from others. If we believe that Caesar's artificial likeness appears on the early modern stage in some capacity at this moment, its dramatic appearance, with its display of Caesar's twenty-three wounds that invite touch to inspire mutiny, makes clear that a theatrical effigy is a body that animates the dead, providing an afterlife that renders ineffective attempts to memorialise the dead's passing and obscure the contradictions at the core of political power that constitute sacred kingship.[41] Contemporary critical accounts of the staged effigy suggest that the memorial figure had lost none of its theatrical power in the Renaissance.[42] Shakespeare recognises the power of this sublime effect and politicises it in his account of early modern sovereignty's immanent resistance to absolutism, turning sovereign power inside out, exposing and reversing the alienation that empowers political authority during the Renaissance.

The effigy that surprisingly appears in Caesar's funeral operates at the juncture of the body and body prosthesis, surpassing sacred kingship by exhuming the royal body before it has been properly interred and rendering it, paradoxically, a performance not of royal perpetuity but of perpetuity's failure, not a ritual that sutures time to guarantee sovereign stability, but an expression of the unsatisfied desire to do so.[43] As an expression of that unsatisfied desire to suture past to present, the crowd clamours for revenge. After witnessing the spectacle of Caesar's body, a plebeian shouts, 'We will be revenged!' (201), and the crowd joins in the call for retributive justice: 'Revenge! About! Burn! Fire! Kill! Slay! Let not a / traitor live!' (202–3). Taking up Caesar's body, the crowd takes control of the ritual at this point, leaving the Rostra to 'burn his body in the holy place / And with the brands fire the traitors' houses' (252–3). Enacting the paradox at the core of fugitive politics, sovereignty is transformed at this moment in the play; the ritual both reinforces and dilutes its power, reallocating it to the mob that murders Cinna, ironically, in a virtual defence of the civil bounds that sovereignty imposes on its subjects.

Shakespeare's Political Archive

Shakespeare's depiction of Caesar's funeral illustrates many of the themes that this book explores. It shows the fragile condition of the politics of friendship as it blurs the boundary between friend and enemy. The ceremony enacts the ritual of the king's two bodies so central to sovereign power and shows how the ritual that guarantees sovereign absolutism paradoxically enables political dissent. Caesar's body, exposed in some capacity in the ceremony as a stage prop, is shown to be vibrant and vocative matter, requiring social uptake to exercise any political potential. In depicting the vibrancy of matter, the ritual of Caesar's funeral in Shakespeare's play shows agency to be contingent, non-sovereign and fundamental to the forms of political life emerging in the early modern theatre.

In making these claims, *Shakespeare's Fugitive Politics* focuses on early modern and contemporary political theory and draws attention to how Shakespeare's political philosophy responds to the specific contours of the evolving nature of sovereignty in the early modern period. By placing Shakespeare in common with Thomas Hobbes and Jean Bodin on one level and Jacques Derrida, Giorgio Agamben and Chantal Mouffe on another, the book advances an understanding of Shakespeare's dramatic production of political forms of life, where consensus seems politically persuasive and effective, as moments that his plays work against themselves to mitigate the radical – and therefore vulnerable – political nature of an event. Paul Kottman describes encounters like these in Shakespeare as sites for 'the spontaneous emergence of futurity, without which politics would lose the very sense of its own drama'.[44] The evanescent, fugitive condition of the political explored in the chapters that follow produces a sense of its own drama.

Fugitive politics paradoxically understands sovereign absolutism as a necessary condition for community. In pursuing this counter-intuitive claim, the book makes the case for the impact of dissident politics in Shakespeare, even as his plays often stage the full and unfettered tyranny of sovereign authority. This intervention places *Shakespeare's Fugitive Politics* in conversation with, for example, Graham Hammill and Julia Reinhard Lupton's *Political Theology and Early Modernity*, Lupton's *Thinking with Shakespeare: Essays on Politics and Life,* and Hammill's *The Mosaic Constitution: Political Theology and Imagination from Machiavelli to Milton.* Each of these books understands early modern political commitment beyond notions of community formation predicated on consensus and agreement. In Hammill and Lupton's introduction to *Political Theology and Early Modernity*, they write that 'political theology [. . .] is neither a set of themes nor a particular form of government, but rather a scene of recurring conflict – both that which defines the early modern period as the attempt to resolve the challenges of the Reformation and that which continues to unfold today as the impossibility of the state to totalize politics'.[45] As imagined in their exploration of political theology, which according to Hammill and Lupton confronts readers as 'crisis and not content, as a recurrent question rather than established doxa',[46] the concept of dissensus in this study understands the political in Shakespeare as frustratingly incomplete. In *The Mosaic Constitution*, Hammill comments on the always incomplete project of the political, noting that 'instead of positing a public space based on national identity, [Renaissance writers] imagined a more fractured and fragile sense of community based on temporary political affiliations, divided between friend and enemy, and threatened by the tyrannical force of sovereign power – both real and imaginary'.[47] *Shakespeare's Fugitive Politics* hopes to add to the rich body of scholarship by showing how political disagreement and discord fundamentally alter dramatic figurations of sovereignty and the reading that such dramatic figures and metaphors require. Addressing the relationship between the early modern theatre and concepts of sovereignty, Philip Lorenz has trenchantly explored important aspects of this critical terrain. Plays about sovereignty, according to Lorenz, highlight the different logics of the tropes of sovereignty at the level of their linguistic and conceptual staging, thus exposing the mechanics of sovereign power. He calls these dramatic tropes exposure events: sovereignty's collapse, its reanimation, resistance, transformation and return.[48] The accounts of sovereignty developed in *Shakespeare's Fugitive Politics* offer a different approach to the political, suggesting that the drama of the political in Shakespeare – what Lorenz might describe as exposure events – is an incubator for the affective expression of dissident politics without the nostalgia for sovereign power that colours his insightful argument.

In dramatic moments explored in the following chapters, Shakespeare imagines the formation of fragile communities, clusters or polities with a political consequence that vanishes often as soon as it is realised. As in the reading of the ritual of Caesar's funeral enfolded into this introduction, the book recognises that in the scenes of the political, Shakespeare's plays condense these communities, sometimes into the body of a divided or dividing sovereign – Henry V, King John, Leontes; sometimes into the fleeting friendships between enemies – Coriolanus and Aufidius, King John and Philip; and sometimes into the volatile bodies of vulnerable, exposed women – Hermione, Lavinia, Paulina, Catherine. Although they are portrayed as intimate encounters beyond or outside of legitimate civil bounds, the political that informs these encounters is democratic in Wolin's sense of the term. That is to say, fugitive politics is not a form or system outside of sovereignty that directly challenges its primacy, but a way of being in relation to sovereign power; fugitive politics persists most vividly in Shakespeare's aesthetic archive that survives its enunciation, and there it becomes political philosophy. *Shakespeare's Fugitive Politics* contends that these dramatic moments in his plays, which archive the political when it is re-enacted and remembered, make Shakespeare pertinent to debates about the nature of democracy today: the viability of radical politics, the limits of liberalism and deliberative democracy, and the role of conflict in emerging democratic institutions.

CHAPTER 2

FRIENDSHIP, SOVEREIGNTY AND POLITICAL DISCORD IN *CORIOLANUS*

And what politics could one still found on this friendship, which exceeds the measure of man without becoming a theologeme? Will it still be politics?

Jacques Derrida,
'Politics of Friendship'

Politics doesn't always happen – it actually happens very little or rarely.

Jacques Rancière, *Disagreement:
Politics and Philosophy*

This book's extended foray into Shakespeare's fugitive politics continues with an uncomfortable admission. The figure that it most associates with a politics of dissensus is, in fact, one of Shakespeare's most reluctant politicians. Caius Martius, renamed Coriolanus after his punishing defeat of the Volscian army at Corioles, refuses politics, opting for war as his contribution to the Roman state. His unwillingness to participate in the republican body politic depicted famously in the belly metaphor in the play's first act signals Coriolanus's rejection of politics, if by politics we mean the process of coordinating differences into broad consensus – a value of the Roman republican tradition. If Roman politics requires representing factional desires as common interests, Coriolanus explicitly rejects this model of politics because he understands its threatening potential. A politics of representation built on common interests and coordination 'will in time', according to Coriolanus, '[w]in upon power and throw forth greater themes / For insurrection's arguing' (1.1.210–12). As a Roman leader content to police the plebeians rather than acknowledge that their world intrudes on the sensible world of Roman republican politics, Coriolanus's political aspirations in republican Rome seem suspect, to say the least.[1] His inability to perform the ritual of humility that would secure his position of political power and his forced departure from the city to seek a world elsewhere confirm the citizen's condemnation of Coriolanus as the declared 'chief enemy / to the people' (1.1.6–7). Aristotle would be disappointed; a political animal Coriolanus is not.

This chapter proposes to take seriously the citizen's condemnation of Coriolanus that dismisses him as the 'enemy to the people'. In privileging friendship over enmity as its foundation for a political community, the citizen endorses a politics predicated on consensus, fraternity and affiliation; enmity, in other words, is banished along with Coriolanus as a threat to the proper practice of politics in Rome. In *Coriolanus*, however, Shakespeare rewrites the early modern friendship theory at the core of the citizen's charge, turning its implicit emphasis on concord and amity into political liabilities. Shakespeare instead conceives the constitution of friendship as a political event that affirms antagonism and discord as the irreducible dimensions of early seventeenth-century alternative political thought. In this chapter, I argue that Shakespeare understands friendship's political potential beyond the dialectic of virtue espoused in classical models of sovereign friendship.[2] The chapter shows that *Coriolanus* represents a concept of friendship fraught with division and violence. In reconfiguring classical notions of friendship common during the early modern period, Shakespeare makes the case that sovereign absolutism is, in fact, nourished by friendship characterised by consensus and a concept of indivisible fraternity. More specifically, the chapter sets the groundwork for a critique of sovereignty explored in Chapters 3 and 4 by arguing that the play's representation of a counter-politics of friendship, one paradoxically characterised by dissensus, redistributes the force of sovereign absolutism by disrupting community in favour of the force of division and discord. According to this reading of Shakespeare's political philosophy, a form of political antagonism, explored in *Coriolanus* through the contours of personal and political friendships, is the basis for the political outside of the scope of early modern absolutist and republican models.

Early in the play, the rhetoric of friendship is established as the discourse that characterises Coriolanus's relationship with the Roman people. In act 2, scene 1, Menenius, Brutus and Sicinius discuss the people's affection for Coriolanus. The three Romans use the metaphor of the wolf and the lamb to clarify the citizens' love for the warrior. After Menenius claims that the people 'love not Martius' (3), they use animal imagery to clarify their point:

SICINIUS. Nature teaches beasts to know their friends.
MENENIUS. Pray you, who does the wolf love?
SICINIUS. The lamb.
MENENIUS. Ay, to devour him, as the hungry plebeians
    would the noble Martius.
BRUTUS. He's the lamb indeed, that baas like a bear.
MENENIUS. He's the bear indeed, that lives like a lamb.

(5–11)

In his effort to establish the play's sustained focus on the formation of community, Stanley Cavell has pointed out the grammatical ambiguities in the exchange that, according to his influential reading, make 'the paradox and reciprocity of hungering' the play's central concern.[3] Cavell notes that the pronoun 'who' in Menenius's question 'who does the wolf love?' is either the verb's subject or object. As Cavell points out, if the question asks for the object of the wolf's affection, the grammatically correct question would be 'whom does the wolf love?'. For Cavell, this grammatical quibble is important because Sicinius's answer, the lamb, does not help to clarify if the wolf loves the lamb or if the lamb loves the wolf. Cavell's reading of this moment reinforces the 'circle of cannibalism, of the eater eaten by what he or she eats' that structures the play.[4] Reflected in the patricians' exchange about the wolf and the lamb is the play's more general concern over incorporation; according to Cavell, 'Coriolanus cannot imagine, or cannot accept, that there is a way to partake of one another, incorporate one another, that is necessary to the formation rather than to the extinction of a community.'[5] The mutual incorporation foundational to Cavell's notion of community is precisely what I want to argue that the play militates against.[6] In *Coriolanus*, to know one's friend is at the same time to know one's enemy – or, more precisely, to know one's friend as, at the same time, an enemy. Mutual incorporation is also an act of rejection. Expressed in the patricians' exchange, then, is a concept of friendship that upsets the formation of community and exposes the limits of a politics of consensus – a type of mutual incorporation or, according to Michel de Montaigne's image of friendship, a 'being in common' that in Shakespeare's political philosophy erases necessary and constitutive antagonisms at the core of civic communities.[7]

Friends Fast Forsworn

'Oh, come, go in' (4.5.130) invites Aufidius in act 4, in an instance of hospitality that calls attention to the threshold that demarcates the guest and the host, the enemy and the friend. In *Of Hospitality*, Derrida explores the erosion of this threshold in moments of absolute hospitality, the kind that Aufidius appears to extend to his rival:

> 'Enter quickly,' quickly, in other words, without delay and without waiting [. . .] the stranger, here the awaited guest, is not only someone to whom you say 'come,' but 'enter,' enter without waiting, make a pause in our home without waiting, hurry up and come in, 'come inside,' 'come within me,' not only toward me, but within me: occupy me, take place in me, which means, by the same token, also take my place [. . .][8]

Hospitality in Derrida's account is depicted as an occupation, a surrogation that twines host and guest. At the threshold of the house, Coriolanus and Aufidius are transformed; the inviting host, as Derrida observes, 'becomes the hostage [. . .] The guest becomes the host's host.'[9] For Derrida, as for Shakespeare in this moment of hospitality and friendship, the threshold between guest and host structuring hospitality is obscured by the aporetic logic of substitution informed by a friendship that transforms enemies into friends.

In *The Politics of Friendship*, Derrida returns to the surrogatory logic of political friendship, speculating on the potential meaning of Montaigne's use of Aristotle's declaration: 'O my friends, there is no friend.'[10] For Derrida, this 'impossible declaration' (p. 1) seems irreconcilable, '[u]njoinable [. . .]' (p. 1). Derrida focuses on the declaration's capacity to include opposing elements within the same syntactical structure: 'In two times but at the same time, in the contretemps of the same sentence' (p. 1). Derrida suggests that Aristotle's declaration of friendship paradoxically 'states the death of friendship' (p. 27), which is, for Derrida, the 'locus of the problem – the political problem of friendship' (p. 27). In a politics of friendship, the friend and the enemy 'ceaselessly change places' (p. 72): 'Hence, every time, a concept bears the phantom of the other. The enemy the friend, the friend the enemy' (p. 72). The rhetoric of friendship in *Coriolanus*, which dramatises Aristotle's paradox, offers a critique of sovereignty that was actively redistributing the contours and consequences of absolutism to other, more putatively democratic political formations. I will argue that his depiction of friendship in the play, especially his depiction of the intimate hospitality in act 4, where the Roman warrior is described as 'more a friend than e'er an enemy' (4.4.150), challenges the culturally and politically dominant concept of political friendship informed by philosophers such as Aristotle and Cicero and outlined trenchantly by Laurie Shannon in *Sovereign Amity*.

Shannon argues that 'friends, flatterers, counselors, monarchs, tyrants and their minions, and the tales of consent and counsel they enact all join to embody a mythography of the political institution before liberalism'.[11] According to Shannon, Renaissance writers 'stress the making of a consensual social bond or body that is not inherently subordinating'.[12] Specifically, discourses of friendship in the sixteenth century 'invariably link the mirroring of selves with this making of (quasi-civic) bodies'.[13] This aspect of doubling common in the rhetoric of early modern friendship allegorises an 'instance of political formation, and it finds repeated valorization in the texts of Renaissance self-fashioning'.[14] In drawing our attention to the period's rediscovery of classical friendship theory, Shannon shows us too how early modern writers conceptualised the bonds of friendship as sovereign – that is, both maximally healthful and consensually hierarchical. In effect, sovereign amity, as Shannon points out, describes dual sovereigns consenting to a social form of parity. She writes,

'Instead of expressing dissent as such, friendship models con-
figure an image of political consent, offering a counterpoint
to prevailing types of polity. These political valences are
central to "sovereign" friendship's rhetorical, affective, and
political dispensations.'¹⁵ The intimacy of early modern sovereign amity, as Shannon shows, stresses parity and consent
within friendship as viable political forces. Shakespeare's
Roman play shows, however, that while there can be no form
of democracy without a community of friends – 'without the
calculation of majorities, without identifiable, stabilizable,
representable subjects all equal' (p. 22) as friends – these
democratic forms must also respect the 'irreducible singularity' (p. 22) that in *Coriolanus* is immanent in the fragile and
fleeting political economy of friendship.¹⁶

Entering Aufidius's house in act 4 after being banished from
his beloved Rome, Coriolanus wagers that he brings more
value to Aufidius alive than he brings to him dead. Antium,
Aufidius's city that Coriolanus once imagined as an apocalyptic site 'to oppose his hatred fully' (3.1.20), is now a 'goodly
city' (4.4.1), and the Roman warrior surprisingly announces
that his 'love's upon / This enemy town' (4.4.23–4). Indeed,
scenes 4 and 5 in act 4, in which Coriolanus and Aufidius forge
an alliance against Rome, are remarkable precisely because
of the shift away from the militaristic, antagonistic tone that
characterises much of the play. Upon entering his sworn enemy's house, Coriolanus's vocative exclamation announces this
shift: 'O world, thy slippery turns!' (4.4.12). The 'slippery
turns' that Coriolanus goes on to describe involve friendship,
specifically turning a sacred friend into an enemy and turning
an avowed enemy into a friend:

> [. . .] Friends now fast forsworn,
> Whose double bosoms seems to wear one heart,
> Whose hours, whose bed, whose meal and exercise
> Are still together; who twin, as 'twere, in love

Unseparable, shall within this hour,
On a dissension of a doit, break out
To bitterest enmity.   (4.4.12–18)

The hero's description of his former relationship with
Rome is rich with the rhetoric of friendship common in the
early modern period. The use of phrases such as 'double
bosoms', 'one heart', 'still together', 'twin' and 'unseparable' to describe the nature of the bond of friendship that
conjoins him to Rome seems to have been taken directly
from descriptions of *amicitia perfecta* from John Tiptoft,
Montaigne, Elyot and Nicholas Grimald, whose work
Shannon explores in *Sovereign Amity*. As Shannon shows,
as early as 1481 Tiptoft emphasised the similitude that
characterises ideal friendship, translating Cicero's famous
description of a friend as 'another [. . .] the same' and suggesting of friends that 'of those tweyne he shold make wel
nygh one'.[17] Half a century later, Elyot writes that ideal
'frendshippe' is 'a blessed and stable connexion of sondrie
willes, makinge of two persones one in hauinge and suf-
fringe [. . .] properly named of Philosophers the other I.
For that in them is but one mynde and one possession.'[18]
Employing similar tropes of friendship, Nicholas Grimald
makes amity the subject of a poem that appears in *Tottel's
Miscellany*. In 'Of Frendship', he writes, 'Behold thy frend,
and of thy felf the pattern fee: / One foull, a wonder fhall
it feem, in bodies twain to bee.'[19]

Other Renaissance humanists translate treatises into English that have friendship as their central theme. Nicholas
Udall's translation of Erasmus's *Apophthegmes* describes the
relationship between Alexander and Haphestion according to
the proverb '*amicus alter ipse* [. . .] two frendes are one soul
and one body'.[20] Shannon has pointed out that the error in
Udall's translation is intentional according to classical models
of friendship: 'The errors here, [. . .] substituting "one" body

for "two bodies", make no mistake: two equal corporeal bodies bound in friendship constitute a single corporate or juridical
body, a legal fiction creating an operative unity.'[21] Montaigne
makes a similar observation in his essay 'Of Friendship': 'In
the friendship I speak of, our souls blend and melt so entirely,
that there is no more sign of the seam which joins them. If I am
pressed to say why I loved him, I feel that I can only express
myself by answering, because it was he, because it was I.'[22] In
his essay, Montaigne contemplates the 'fusion of [. . .] wills' in
an ideal friendship and concludes, 'Everything actually being
in common between them [. . .] and their relationship being
that of one soul in two bodies, according to Aristotle's very
apt definition [. . .], they can neither lend nor give anything to
each other.'[23] Montaigne's ideal friendship has 'no other model
than itself, and can be compared only with itself',[24] a solipsism
that seems to confirm Aristotle's remark 'O my friends, there
is no friend'.[25]

For these early modern writers, the bonds of ideal friendship appear unbreakable and irreplaceable; for Coriolanus,
however, untwining his bond with Rome means also replacing
one friendship with another and counting on the hospitality
of his enemy:

> Unseparable, shall within this hour,
> On a dissension of a doit, break out
> To bitterest enmity. So, fellest foes,
> Whose passions and whose plots have broke their sleep
> To take the one the other, by some chance,
> Some trick not worth an egg, shall now grow dear friends
> And interjoin their issues. So with me.
> My birthplace hate I, and my love's upon
> This enemy town.　　　　　　　　　　　　　(4.4.16–24)

Coriolanus's rapid transfer of affection from Rome to
Antium – '[o]n a dissension of a doit' (4.4.17) and 'by
some chance' (4.4.20) – seems to counter the bonds of true

friendship, which are, according to Elyot, 'confederated' and 'issuinge [. . .] out of the one body, and entringe in to the other'.[26] Using Coriolanus as an exemplum for failed friendship, Cicero warns that 'alliances of wicked men not only should not be protected by a plea of friendship, but rather they should be visited with summary punishment of the severest kind, so that no one may think it permissible to follow even a friend when waging war against his country'.[27] The play, it seems, operates at the crossroads between classical friendship and the political.

Well before his alliance with his enemy, however, Coriolanus's relationship with Rome suggests that he seems at least to view a concept of true friendship as the core tenet of his political philosophy, more valuable than any doit – the worthless coin that Coriolanus says eventually pays for his break from his Roman fraternity. Before turning in detail to Coriolanus's break from Rome and the political alliance with his enemy, I want to establish, to the extent possible, what Roman republican politics might mean in early modern England, specifically a Machiavellian republicanism forged from conflict and dissensus that informs Coriolanus's friendship with Aufidius and gives shape to civic life in the play.

Hostages for Rome

In the 1590s in England there was no general history of the Roman republic available to Shakespeare in English,[28] and if *Titus Andronicus* is a measure, then it seems right to conclude that fidelity to Roman history was not one of Shakespeare's preoccupations in his early drama. T. J. B. Spencer's assessment that Shakespeare 'seems anxious, not to get it all right, but to get it all in' is an accurate description of how Shakespeare used Roman history in his early drama.[29] Fidelity, however, is only one way to view Shakespeare's relationship to Roman history and politics, and as scholarly debates about Shakespeare's commitment to republican politics make clear, perhaps the more pressing question is to what degree Shakespeare makes possible the articulation of an early modern political philosophy by using aspects of Roman political history. In *Shakespeare and Republicanism*, Andrew Hadfield makes the most forceful case to date that Shakespeare was interested in and meditates on republican political philosophy, arguing that theories of republicanism had become a political force in Shakespeare's England.[30] His work, along with important scholarship from Annabel Patterson, Patrick Cheney, James Kuzner and Graham Hammill, has redefined the terms by which literary critics make the case that early modern writing prior to 1640 intervenes in the development of republican political theory. Patterson's *Shakespeare and the Popular Voice* is premised on the argument that '[a]s the Elizabethan moment waned, and Shakespeare's social vision deepened, so did these ambivalences; and though optimism briefly revived at James' accession, it was quickly replaced by an intense political skepticism, then by a mature radicalism.'[31] For Patterson mature radicalism means the 'belief that Jacobean England desperately needed to borrow from the strengths, as well as learn from the difficulties, of republican political theory'.[32]

Writing not about Shakespeare's but about Christopher Marlowe's commitment to republican ideals, Patrick Cheney describes 'republican representation' in the playwright's works, as opposed to a coherent republican agenda. While not calling Marlowe a republican in any programmatic sense of the term, Cheney focuses on his literary form, calling it 'representational republicanism'.[33] Marlowe's work, for Cheney, 'constitutes a significant register and clear herald of republican representation, both in the later Elizabethan era and finally in the early seventeenth century'.[34] Graham Hammill engages the debate about republicanism's viability as a political philosophy in the late sixteenth and early seventeenth centuries by shifting the focus slightly from the political alliances of the authors to the intended audiences of their work. His nuanced account of republican potential in Spenser, I think, represents a turning point in debates about Shakespeare's republican politics. Hammill focuses attention on 'the ways [Spenser's] poetry mediates political thought'.[35] Resisting a concept of republicanism in terms of identity, Hammill develops the concept of mediation to mean the way 'engagement with republican thought' is reflected in a poet's 'textual and literary strategies by which he represents that thought'.[36] Mediation of theories of republicanism, for Hammill, allows poetry to enjoin 'a perspective, or multiple perspectives' from which those republican theories might be understood.[37]

James Kuzner's understanding of *Coriolanus*, which turns Shakespeare's republican intervention on its head, is enabled by Hammill's interpretation that finally liberates republicanism from a firm notion of political identity. Underscoring the non-systematic way that Shakespeare engages republican themes, Kuzner shows how Shakespeare 'rejects republicanism' in *Coriolanus* if republicanism means producing a concept of citizen with a bounded self – the notion that a subject's sense of integrity and invulnerability increases with the evolution of republicanism into a coherent political agenda.[38] Kuzner's argument establishes the critical value of the inchoate nature of republican themes in the playwright's drama, whether or not the playwright endorses those themes. He understands the lack of uniformity in Shakespeare's politics not as an indication of a failure in civic vision that it would take until the mid-century to rectify but as a sign that republican politics is, indeed, fragile and subject to its own limitations and challenges.[39] Kuzner's account of the politics of vulnerability presses the point most clearly that the forces constituting republicanism need not cohere with the mid-seventeenth-century monarchical collapse. Indeed, in exploring the mixture of conflicting political forces before the English Civil War consolidated them, Kuzner's *Open Subjects* advocates the important process of remapping the murky waters of early modern political theory, moving literary criticism beyond purely historicist accounts of programmatic republicanism.[40]

Despite the work of these scholars, which deeply contextualises Shakespeare's investment in both classical political theory and early modern networks of republican discourse, many critics remain unconvinced that Shakespeare's work articulates a viable form of republican politics. Contributors to *Shakespeare and Early Modern Political Thought* complicate or, in many cases, reject the notion that Shakespeare shares a deep and coherent republican ethos, showing him instead to be sceptical, indeed, as Warren Chernaik has suggested, even hostile, to this notion. For example, Eric Nelson's reading of what many critics view as a transition to viable republican government from *Titus Andronicus* to *Julius Caesar* concludes,

> This view casts Shakespeare as an altogether more conventional Renaissance figure, one who uses the dramatization of Roman history to defend a particular view of the *optimus reipublicae status* – namely, that virtue cannot survive in the absence of a republican government. Yet, [. . .] this may be too hasty. The titles have surely changed, but politics, Shakespeare seems to be saying, is politics.[41]

Far from an expression of apathy or a posture of indifference, Nelson's conclusion endorses a cynicism about Shakespeare's political investments that is productive, as the authors of the collection's introduction make clear: 'Cynicism [. . .] was a rational response to what was perceived to be a dangerous and corrupt political world. It should not be mistaken for political disengagement, but was instead a form of commitment to survival and self-interest.'[42] In Chernaik's assessment, the most that republicanism offers Shakespeare and his audience is 'temporary shelter from the storm', fleeting and limited in programmatic political advice or action.[43] Consonant with Nelson's view of Shakespeare's political philosophy, Chernaik concludes that Shakespeare seems to present republicanism as 'more of the same':[44] that is to say that like its counter, royal absolutism, republicanism as a political doctrine in Shakespeare's early modern drama has at its core a resistance to the idea that liberty and a free state are possible and barely disguise the truth that self-interest and survival are primary. For Chernaik, and for many of the scholars writing in *Shakespeare and Early Modern Political Thought*, Shakespeare is not a republican playwright but rather a political rhetorician who presents both sides of the political debate (*in utramque partem*).[45] These critics who resist identifying a political doctrine in Shakespeare's plays share a common belief that searching for the collective or coherent form of Shakespeare's 'constitutional loyalty' is motivated by the anachronistic desire to make sense of Shakespeare though our own contemporary political investments,[46] and for them Shakespeare's plays and poetry may invoke a doctrine of political philosophy but not endorse it in a doctrinal way. According to this view, Shakespeare's political aesthetic exploits this generic convention, making him 'even more elusive than many of his contemporaries'.[47]

The issue of the political dimension of Shakespeare's drama is even more problematic if we consider how the reputation of Machiavelli's civic factionalism affected Shakespeare's political vision. Although Machiavelli's *Il Principe* appeared in only a few English manuscript translations until Edward Dacres's first printed English version in 1640, Paul Rahe makes the case that Machiavelli's influence in early modern England was significant. Rahe points out that the relative functional system of local and state parliaments, in parishes, shires and boroughs, 'caused some of the English crown's subjects to think of themselves as citizens and even to conceive of England as a republic of sorts'.[48] The effect of an interest in Roman and Venetian politics, according to Rahe, was that 'Playwrights, such as William Shakespeare and Ben Jonson, seized upon this fashion as an opportunity for the exploration of republican themes [. . .] In England, a handful of statesmen even turned to the *Discourses* for enlightenment concerning their country's aptitude for imperial grandeur.'[49] John Roe goes so far as to claim that 'Shakespeare (an impressionable twenty-year-old in 1584, and on the verge of a theatre career) can hardly have failed to have access to Machiavelli, either directly or at a slight remove.'[50] However, intellectual interest in Machiavelli remained theoretical: 'it did not, at that time, eventuate in the public advocacy of a concrete program of reform, much less in a political movement aimed at the establishment of a republic on English soil'.[51]

In England, as Rahe points out, most understood that their king ruled by divine right and most understood their rights in relation to common law 'made rational by trial and error and sanctioned by time; some were inclined to think their monarchy as some sort of mixed regime, but republicans in the strict sense they were not'.[52] J. G. A. Pocock asserts that Machiavelli was not a 'critic or an analyst of kingship, or even of monarchy' and concludes that it would be a mistake to 'associate him with "republicanism" whose opposite was "monarchism"'.[53] Indeed, according to Victoria Kahn, a sense of Machiavelli's republicanism emerges from the reading habits and the rhetorical training of his Renaissance interlocutors, who used his arguments as evidence for and against tyranny or republicanism, 'depending on the historical situation and the needs of the moment'.[54] Machiavelli's English translator uses the term 'ambidexterity' to describe this aspect of his early modern appeal,[55] and Jean Bodin, commenting on the fragile balance between popular desires and aristocratic values that seems to characterise Machiavelli's political vision, writes, 'no man can judge what this wicked and inconstant man meanes'.[56]

Early modern interpretations of Machiavelli to endorse republicanism crystallised by mid-century in England, as James Harrington, Marchamont Nedham and John Milton, among others, made the case for liberty. Yet, even for Shakespeare in 1606, when he was writing *Coriolanus*, Machiavelli's political contribution was influential. In the *Discorses*, Machiavelli uses the example of Coriolanus to illustrate the productive nature of mixed republican rule. The tribunes were the legal means that the people used to vent their anger at Coriolanus's indifference to their condition. They created a buffer separating popular passion from political policy, reducing 'fear [. . .] factions in the cities, and factions cause their ruin' (1.7.132).[57] Machiavelli makes the case for restoring a republic, and one reading of his justification for a republican state is that popular reformation strengthens a democratic ethos, which counters tyranny and creates a balanced, mixed government. In the Roman model, Machiavelli saw a pattern useful for modern states: a popular resistance to aristocratic rule resulted in the creation of tribunes who gave a legal, political voice to the people, restoring civic virtue.[58] Machiavelli writes,

> when the people wanted to obtain law, they resorted to some of the extremes of which we have just spoken [. . .] so that the Senate was obliged to satisfy them in some measure [. . .] and if their fears are ill founded, resort is laid to public assemblies where the mere eloquence of a single and respectable man will make them sensible in their error.   (1.4.120)

Huffman summarises the beneficial function of the mixed republic described in this reading of Machiavelli: 'Far from being seditious, the tribunate protected both the state, by regulating the people's complaints, and the people, by providing legal means of expression of popular wishes.'[59] This image of a multitude venting its discord appropriately through the tribunate so as to ensure republican stability and concord minimises, I think, the importance that conflict plays in Machiavelli's political philosophy and that is his major contribution to Shakespeare's own theory of civic engagement.

Quentin Skinner identifies in Machiavelli's political writings a powerful argument about discord and tumult shaping a viable republic state. According to Skinner, Machiavelli's emphasis on disunion and conflict was a radical departure from an entire tradition of pre-humanist writers who stress concord as the foundational element of a healthy republic. In exploring discord, Machiavelli is refuting Cicero and Sallust and their uncritical reception in early modern Italian politics.[60] Echoing Skinner, Filippo Del Lucchese shows how, in reworking notions of the common good, 'the phenomenon of conflict invokes a "phantasm" that is threatening to the power and sovereignty of states. The leading philosophers of this period condemn conflict – be it religious, civil, or political – in an effort to exorcise its destabilizing effects. Machiavelli, on the contrary, assigns a positive value to political and social conflicts in his theory.'[61] Stressing the impact of dissensual events on a theory of radical politics, Miguel Vatter argues that Machiavelli presents for the first time in the history of political thought 'the concept of the productivity of social conflict for political development'.[62] Machiavelli's defence of discord, according to Claude Lefort, 'destroys the beautiful image of the state [. . .] [and] roots order in social conflict'.[63] What these recent approaches to Machiavelli's political writings offer is a way to measure Machiavelli's influence on Shakespeare without totalising the Machiavellian legacy in terms of the presence of a coherent republicanism in his plays.

In *Discourses*, dissensus is a central component to the development of a republican state. In book 1, chapter 2, Machiavelli writes,

> But let us come to Rome. Although she had no legislator like Lycurgus, who constituted her government, at her very origin, in a manner to secure her liberty for a length of time, yet the disunion which existed between the Senate and the people produced such extraordinary events, that chance did for her what the laws had failed to do.

Even as Machiavelli identifies the influence of a noble leader like Lycurgus in establishing a republican state, he identifies a contingent and productive 'disunion' resulting in 'extraordinary events' that supervened laws to give shape to republican politics. Machiavelli closes chapter two claiming that this process 'rendered the constitution perfect', perfection achieved by 'the disunion of the Senate and the people'.

In book 1, chapter 6, Machiavelli more forcefully associates conflict with political sovereignty. He describes the salubrious effect of discord in the formation of the Roman state:

> But if the republic had been more tranquil, it would necessarily have resulted that she would have been more feeble, and that she would have lost with her energy also the ability of achieving that high degree of greatness to which she attained; so that to have removed the cause of trouble from Rome would have been to deprive her of her power of expansion.

Moreover, Machiavelli maintains 'that those who blame the quarrels of the Senate and the people of Rome condemn that which was the very origin of liberty' (1.4). In linking the motivating force of Roman liberty to turmoil, Machiavelli stresses the 'good effect' that conflict produced: 'and all the laws that are favorable to liberty result from the opposition of [the nobles to the people]' (1.4). In claiming in the closing of chapter four that '[t]he demands of a free people are rarely pernicious to their liberty; they are generally inspired by oppressions, experienced or apprehended', Machiavelli acknowledges the value of the political that privileges conflict over consensus and compromise. Machiavelli's emphasis on conflict and antagonism as the condition for the political helps to reimagine the political dimension in *Coriolanus*'s depiction of the fraught friendship, especially the friendship between the two rival warriors.

Unsevered Friends

As the vehicle in *Coriolanus* for Shakespeare to explore the political effect of dissensus, the rhetoric of friendship appears in both public and private settings. The play imbricates friendship and politics in its first scene in which Menenius hears grievances from Rome's hungry citizens. First Citizen describes Caius Martius as 'chief enemy to the people' (1.1.6–7), and the friend-enemy distinction is reinforced when Menenius confronts the crowd. He calls the citizens 'my good friends, mine honest neighbors' (55). Four more times before Caius Martius arrives, Menenius addresses either the group of citizens or an individual citizen as 'friends' (58, 121, 132) or 'friend' (118). His rhetorical attempt to quell the anger of the citizens notwithstanding, his use of the rhetoric of friendship in his address to the hungry mob frames the scene and suggests its role in the political dynamics of the play. Martius's disdain for the citizens in this scene and throughout the play, I suggest, is an extension of his insistence on an alternative form of a politics of friendship foundational to the Roman state.

Martius's rejection of the citizens is motivated by their inability to embody true friendship. Their position as 'great toe' (1.1.146) of the Roman assembly describes the citizens' inferior position relative to other Roman statesmen and makes flattery and supplication their most effective political strategy. In the fable of the belly, Menenius compares the senators to 'the good belly' (139), nourishing the citizens, who are 'mutinous members' (140), nerves, veins and appendages of the body. The very structure of power in Rome explored in their language militates against a politics of friendship informed by similitude, confederation and union.[64] Friendship implies parity and symmetry, 'through rational desire and free choice rather than hierarchy, physicality, and self-loss or self-dilution'.[65] Indeed, Martius's rejection of the citizens in act 1, scene 1, along with his refusal of their desires throughout the play, is a rejection of Roman republicanism. Moreover, motivating his insults – he calls the citizens 'curs' (1.1.159), 'dissentious rogues' (155), 'scabs' (157) and 'fragments' (213) – is an implicit challenge to the political dependency that structures Roman politics in the play.

If, as I am suggesting, we view Coriolanus's rejection of the citizens, along with his refusal finally to participate in Roman political custom later in the play, as a commitment to a form of friendship emerging in the space of failed republicanism, the play offers an affirmative politics imagined in the portrayal of the intimate hospitality between Aufidius and Coriolanus in act 4. Yet, the alliance forged between the two bitter enemies destabilises friendship as a political force at the same time that it suggests its liberating potential.[66] More precisely, the intimacy of the new relationship between Coriolanus and Aufidius embodied in the scene of absolute hospitality in act 4 radically reconceptualises the logic of friendship common in the early modern period, suggesting that the play disrupts the communitarian space imagined in the classical rhetoric of friendship that sutures over the potentially productive and politically viable force of enmity immanent in the bonds of friendship structuring political relationships in the play.[67]

My focus on the constitutive condition of friendship's failure, informed by the absolute hospitality in the scene, as a sustainable force that shapes political sovereignty follows rich lines of inquiry offered most recently by Graham Hammill and Julia Reinhard Lupton. In a related reading of Marlowe's *The Jew of Malta*, Lupton emphasises the erosion of 'prepolitical fellowship' into a notion of community formed by uncivil politics,[68] and Hammill argues that Marlowe's depiction of betrayal becomes his 'response to [. . .] the sovereign bond'.[69] Hammill elaborates on the productive nature of betrayal reflected in early modern literature in terms of the formation of political alternatives to sovereign absolutism: 'instead of positing a public space based on national identity, [English writers] imagined a far more fractured and fragile sense of community based on temporary political affiliations, divided between friend and enemy, and threatened by the tyrannical inclinations of sovereign power – both real and imaginary'.[70] At the core of the warrior-friendship between Aufidius and Coriolanus in *Coriolanus* is conflict that precludes rapprochement and establishes rejected friendship as the critical reaction to Roman tyranny.[71]

The treatment of Martius after his victory at Corioles expresses the political power of the concept of friendship in the play. Brutus acknowledges Coriolanus's banishment in language that relies on the friend-enemy distinction: 'There is no more to be said, but he is banished / As enemy to the people and his country' (3.3.114–15). Rejoicing over his banishment, other witnesses to Coriolanus's punishment echo Brutus's language. An Aedile says, 'The people's enemy is gone, is gone' and the others on stage shout, 'Our enemy is banished! He is gone!' (3.3.133–4). Indeed, even before his banishment, the custom of showing his wounds to the citizens and wearing the gown of humility is depicted as a ritual of friendship. The Fourth Citizen, speaking for the common people, says to Coriolanus: 'You have been a scourge to [Rome's] enemies; you have been a rod to her friends. You have not loved the common people' (2.3.85–6). The Fifth Citizen follows, 'We hope to find you our friend, and therefore give you our voices heartily' (97–8). As Coriolanus asks the citizens for their voices to make him consul, the citizens express their response in terms of friendship. Seventh Citizen says, 'Therefore let him be consul. The gods give him joy, and make him good friend to the people!' (127–8). In an effort to save Coriolanus's consulship, Volumnia compares honour and policy to 'unsevered friends' (3.2.42) that in war 'grow together' (43) and encourages her son to maintain the friendship between honour and policy in peace, where 'each of them by th' other lose / That they combine not there' (44–5). And in language that foreshadows Coriolanus's alliance with Aufidius in act 4, she says, 'I know thou hadst rather / Follow thine enemy in a fiery gulf / Than flatter him in a bower' (90–2).

The language of comity that structures the scene between Coriolanus and the citizens, as he struggles to ask for their voices, establishes friendship as a force in support of absolutism even as the politics of friendship seem to enfranchise citizens, giving them a voice in the republic.[72] In an acknowledgement of the paradox of their enfranchisement, Third Citizen says, 'We have power in ourselves to do it, but it is a power that we have no power to do. For if he show us his wounds and tell us his deeds, we are to put our tongues into those wounds and speak for them. So, if he tell us his noble deeds, we must also tell him our noble acceptance of them' (2.3.4–9). The emptiness of the ritual, I suggest, hints also at the emptiness of a politics of friendship that sustains Roman absolutism. The Third Citizen identifies a type of friendship predicated on telling and speaking – vividly imagined as putting a tongue in Coriolanus's wounds. In the play's extended association of the coming political community and the rhetoric of friendship throughout acts 2 and 3, the citizens' voices depict a form of communicative sociability necessary to sustain political friendship and by extension civic enfranchisement, a drive to expand the economy of friendship to include more friends in the *communitas*. Coriolanus's rejection of this mode of friendship suggests his refusal to sustain a concept of community that obscures the rejection at friendship's core with the glib discourse of inclusion, unanimity and agreement.

Framed by the epithet 'enemy' from Brutus and the Aedile, Coriolanus's rejection of Rome punctuates the rejection in friendship, dramatically imagining the naked force of antipathy shared between friends.[73] At the end of act 3, Coriolanus banishes Rome:

> You common cry of curs, whose breath I hate
> As reek o' th' rotten fens, whose loves I prize
> As the dead carcasses of unburied men
> That do corrupt my air: I banish you [. . .]   (3.3.117–20)

Coming after Roman tribunes banish him – 'It shall be so, / It shall be so. Let him away. He's banished, / And it shall be so' (3.3.102–4) – Coriolanus's decree reversing the force of banishment and exiling the city complicates the logic of rejection at stake in the play. Kuzner associates this moment of rejection with the trope of the gay outlaw or the sodomite, whose very vulnerability inaugurates and sustains his tenuous but potent political viability.[74] Coriolanus's 'vagabond exile' (3.3.86), in which he turns his back on the city in search of 'a world elsewhere' (132), is precisely the moment that the reject assumes a force preventing him from becoming a static figure vitiated of a politically agonistic potential.

Rejecting Roman friendship is only Coriolanus's first step in recalibrating friendship's political potential. Coriolanus enters exile 'alone, / Like to a lonely dragon that his fen / Makes feared and talked of more than seen' (4.1.29–31). He proclaims the isolation of his reject status, boasting to his mother Volumnia that he '[w]ill exceed the common' (32) and defy capture. Given his dramatic exit as an outcast who transforms rejection into a form of heroism, it is curious that by the end of act 4 the Roman reject seeks an alliance with Aufidius. In turning away from Roman friendship to Aufidius, however, not only is Coriolanus a figure who separates himself from classical notions of friendship that have been co-opted by the absolutist state, but he also exposes friendship's fugitive political force to its own contingent limitations.[75]

Coriolanus's language as he enters Aufidius's house in act 4 emphasises conventional, early modern tropes of friendship and recalls the perversion that characterises absolute hospitality. The divisions that previously separated the two rival warriors are sutured over: 'double bosoms' (4.4.13) are now 'one heart' (13), 'still together' (15), 'twin' (15) and '[u]nseparable' (16). He imagines a future in which foes 'grow dear friends / And interjoin their issues' (21–2). The next scene in Aufidius's house reinforces this suture, as the stage directions announce that '*Music plays*' (4.5) and the servingman's repeated request for 'Wine, wine, wine!' (1) creates a sense of plenitude at Aufidius's 'hearth' (26). The companionship and plenitude suggested in the scene, however, prove equivocal, as the servingmen refuse to welcome Coriolanus into the 'goodly house' (4). Framing the scene of friendship between rivals, then, is a division that persists beneath the images of plenitude and fellowship established in the opening lines of the scene. Coriolanus acknowledges this lingering division as he enters: 'The feast smells well, but I / Appear not like a guest' (5–6). The caesura in the line appearing after Coriolanus's description of the pleasant smell of food and the conjunction 'but' are formal reminders of the division that will subtend the two enemies' eventual union.

The servingmen's reaction to their guest, too, illustrates the tension between division and comity that informs the scene. Using the language of friendship in their address to Coriolanus, both servingmen express the ambivalence that, I am suggesting, is at the core of friendship in the scene. The First Servingman says, 'What would you have, friend? Whence are you? Here's no place for you. Pray, go to the door' (4.5.7–9); followed by the Second Servingman, 'Whence are you, sir? Has the port his eyes in his head, that he gives entrance to such companions? Pray, get you out' (12–14). Both servants describe Coriolanus in terms common in the rhetoric of friendship in the period, yet both reactions suggest that there is an aspect of Coriolanus that is not knowable: 'Whence are you?' The question posed by both servingmen lingers as the play's acknowledgement that an unutterable truth – what Derrida calls the 'nothing sayable'[76] – divides friendship and prevents it from being appropriated by sovereign absolutism in service of the state. Even as the ambiance of the scene – its music, its food and its wine – intimates unity, hospitality and friendship, Coriolanus introjects division, insulting the servingmen by ordering them to '[f]ollow your function, go, and batten on cold bits' (31–2), and saying to another, 'Thou prat'st, and prat'st. Serve with thy trencher. Hence!' (47–8).

The scene's ambivalence toward friendship and hospitality in the moments before the portrayal of the alliance between Aufidius and Coriolanus helps to shape how we are

to understand their strategic union. Coriolanus asks for an
alliance based on revenge; in doing so, he intensifies his position as a reject – turning his reactive rejection of friendship
from the Roman state into an active rejection.[77] Coriolanus's
decision to surrender to Aufidius, eventually offering his
throat to his enemy as a gesture of his abjection, implies his
renewed commitment to his rejection of the type of friendship offered by the state. Coriolanus tells Aufidius:

> [. . .] But if so be
> Thou dar'st not this, and that to prove more fortunes
> Th' art tired, then, in a word, I also am
> Longer to live most weary, and present
> My throat to thee and to thy ancient malice;
> Which not to cut would show thee but a fool,
> Since I have ever followed thee with hate,
> Drawn tuns of blood out of thy country's breast,
> And cannot live but to thy shame unless
> It be to do thee service.   (4.5.91–100)

In asking Aufidius to 'make [his own] misery serve [Aufid-
ius's] turn' (87), Coriolanus reminds us (and himself) that
he is a reject in friendship, and he redirects the force of
rejection against himself – a gesture intended to prevent any
rapprochement with Rome.[78]

Aufidius's passionate reaction to his rival's offer reconfigures the proposed strategic alliance into a bond of friendship.
He accepts Coriolanus into his home with the language of
intimate hospitality:

> [. . .] But come in.
> Let me commend the first to those that shall
> Say yea to thy desires. A thousand welcomes!
> And more a friend than e'er an enemy;
> Yet, Martius, that was much. Your hand. Most welcome.
>   (4.5.142–6)

The surplus value of friendship in Aufidius's greeting – '[a] thousand welcomes' and 'more a friend than e'er an enemy' – risks obscuring its recognition of the disavowed truth: that is, immanent in friendship is its self-negating counter. This ambivalence at the core of friendship helps to explain the remarkable interplay of eroticism and violence that characterises Aufidius's extended response to Coriolanus:

> [. . .] Let me twine
> Mine arms about that body, whereagainst
> My grainèd ash an hundred times hath broke,
> And scarred the moon with splinters. Here I clip
> The anvil of my sword, and do contest
> As hotly and as nobly with thy love
> As ever in ambitious strength I did
> Contend against thy valor. Know thou first,
> I loved the maid I married; never man
> Sighed truer breath; but that I see thee here,
> Thou noble thing, more dances my rapt heart
> Than when I first my wedded mistress saw
> Bestride my threshold [. . .]
> Thou hast beat me out
> Twelve several times, and I have nightly since
> Dreamt of encounters 'twixt thyself and me.
> We have been down together in my sleep,
> Unbuckling helms, fisting each other's throat,
> And waked half dead with nothing.   (4.5.104–25)

Aufidius's desire to 'twine' his arms around Coriolanus's body is a reminder of his quest to defeat his Roman enemy, yet it is also a description of an embrace of unrequited love that previously had 'scarred the moon'. After acknowledging that his 'rapt heart' prefers Coriolanus to his 'wedded mistress', Aufidius extends both the violent and the erotic imagery of their new bond by describing how in his dreams their two bodies become one: 'We have been down together in my sleep / Unbuckling helms, fisting each other's throat, / And waked half dead with nothing' (123–5). In Aufidius's rhetoric of friendship, their martial exploits morph into erotic play, and the two rivals merge into one indivisible body. The play's imagery highlights the migration from difference to similitude, and emphasises the suturing power of the rhetoric that sustains an economy of friendship in early modern political philosophy. The violence embedded in the migration, however, captured in the active logic of the participles '[u]nbuckling' and 'fisting', lets us glimpse the 'motility of division' – an ineradicable antagonism – that structures a politics of friendship in the play.[79]

Described as a 'strange alteration!' (4.5.147), the new bond of friendship suggests union and similitude between enemies, but the servingmen reveal an aspect of the bond that exceeds indivisibility. The Second Servingman says of Coriolanus: 'I knew by his face that there was something in him. He had, sir, a kind of face, methought – I cannot tell how to term it' (153–5), and the First Servingman seems to agree: 'He had so, looking as it were – Would I were hanged, but I thought there was more in him than I could think' (156–8). The play points to the surplus that always exceeds friendship's claims of consensus and union, a silent surplus that conceals the truth about political friendship: that is, friendship is predicated on irreducible division and enmity. Again, the play allows a servingman to express most cogently the play's insight about friendship's immanent division: 'But the bottom of the news is, our general is cut i' th' middle and but one half of what he was yesterday; for the other has half [. . .]' (197–9). The servingmen anatomise and divide the alliance that in Aufidius's rhetoric was characterised by rapturous plenitude and erotic wholeness.

Though initially presented in terms that erotically imagine the unification of two bodies into one soul, Aufidius's
understanding of the politics of friendship relies on the
recognition that friendship's irreducible division is sutured
over by his own erotic rhetoric. The play hints at the covert
nature of enmity – disguised, even as its presence is visceral in the imagery of the erotic act of fisting each other's
throats – in the servingmen's discussion of the ambivalence
of Roman friendship in the face of Coriolanus's return.
The servingman responds to a discussion of the violence
in store for the Roman people when Coriolanus returns to
'mow all down before him' (4.5.201): 'Do't? he will do't!
for, look you, sir, he has as many friends as enemies; which
friends, sir, as it were, durst not, look you, sir, show themselves, as we term it, his friends whilst he's in directitude'
(205–8). Elaborating on his meaning, the servingman says,
'But when they shall see, sir, his crest up again, and the
man in blood, they will out of their burrows like conies
after rain, and revel all with him' (210–12). The servants'
discussion of covert, strategic friendship hints at its opposite – the immanent, yet unspeakable enmity that divides
sovereign amity and fractures a concept of community
predicated on it.

Let Me Have War, Say I

Aufidius's form of friendship – embodying the political ideology of dissensus and not those attributes most associated with
early modern friendship theory such as consensus, agreement,
unity or accord – is the productive force that drives the polity.
His actions after his allegiance with Coriolanus suggest that
he accepts, indeed even demands as a necessity, the incommensurability of competing political claims. Shakespeare's
description of the citizens in act 4, responding to the news of

Coriolanus's return, reflects the play's interest in interrogating a fugitive form of political dissent. The play no longer employs the logic of Menenius's belly metaphor to describe the citizens' relationship to the Roman state that integrates them into a seamless, functional political system. Indeed, by the end of act 4, Menenius twice calls the citizens 'clusters'.[80] Describing the citizens' responsibility in banishing Coriolanus, Menenius says, 'We loved him, but, like beasts / And cowardly nobles, gave way unto your clusters, / Who did hoot him out o' th' city' (4.6.121–3). The second use of the word occurs a few lines later, as a troop of citizens enter the scene. Menenius responds to the citizens' arrival: 'Here come the clusters. / And is Aufidius with him?' (128–9). According to the *Oxford English Dictionary*, the word 'clusters' denotes a number of persons, animals or things gathered or situated close together. In 1576, Abraham Fleming used the word in a translation of Hippocrates to describe citizens who gather in a cluster, as in an assemblage, swarm or crowd. As these are the only uses of this word in his entire body of work, Shakespeare makes a distinction between how division operates early in act 1 and how the play understands its force by acts 4 and 5. The rhetoric of friendship that shapes the belly metaphor in act 1 – 'good friend' (1.1.118), 'incorporate friends' (121), 'my good friends' (132) – is replaced by the concept of the cluster. As an assemblage, the cluster of citizens, I suggest, is an affiliation of differences, unintegrated by the belly metaphor into absolute sovereign power. Indeed, Menenius's second use of the word – 'Here come the clusters. / And is Aufidius with him?' – implies its capacity to include division as a primary force. The statement and question in the passage align three of the play's antagonistic forces: common citizens ('clusters'), Aufidius, and Coriolanus ('him'). In doing so, Shakespeare imagines a politics that privileges division over incorporation and antagonism over similitude. In short, he imagines fugitive politics.

Although the play ties Coriolanus's fate to Aufidius's jealousy at being overshadowed or 'dark'ned' (4.7.5) by the Roman warrior's exploits and reputation, his betrayal of Coriolanus is also a reaction to the threat of incorporation implied in Volumnia's seduction of her son back into Roman society and shows just how precarious and fleeting fugitive politics can be. Volumnia embodies the threat of rapprochement that defuses a politics of friendship predicated on division. In her plea to her son to spare Rome, the power of Volumnia's appeal is that it erases all antagonism and division:

> If it were so that our request did tend
> To save the Romans, thereby to destroy
> The Volsces whom you serve, you might condemn us
> As poisonous of your honor. No, our suit
> Is that you reconcile them while the Volsces
> May say 'This mercy we have showed', the Romans,
> 'This we received', and each in either side
> Give the all-hail to thee and cry, 'Be blest
> For making up this peace!'   (5.3.132–40)

Volumnia's peace accord imagines a form of consensus with the power to contaminate and cure the divisive desires that compel vying factions. Her extended appeal in act 5 is a form of political sociability that Coriolanus has already rejected from the commoners in act 1. Volumnia's final words in the play, 'And then I'll speak little' (5.3.182), contrast with her hyper-gregariousness and sociability immediately before her silence, and the stage directions after her long plea reinforce this contrast, as Coriolanus *'holds her by the hand, silent'* (5.3. s.d.). By silencing Volumnia at the moment of her victory, where she ensures accord, unity and peace for Rome, the play indicates, I think, the problem of consensus. That is to say, Volumnia's silence even in her 'happy victory to Rome' (186) has jeopardised her future political viability.

Coriolanus's reaction to the new concord reinforces this
point. He says to his mother:

> But we will drink together; and you shall bear
> A better witness back than words, which we,
> On like conditions, will have counter-sealed.
> Come, enter with us. Ladies, you deserve
> To have a temple built you. All the swords
> In Italy, and her confederate arms,
> Could not have made this peace.   (5.3.203–9)

Coriolanus's words return us to a concept of sovereign amity
associated with conventional friendship. His reaction stresses
harmony with words such as 'together', 'like conditions',
'counter-sealed' and 'confederate arms'. Rapprochement is
complete; division repaired. Aufidius's aside at this moment,
however, threatens the new concord: 'I am glad thou hast set
mercy and thy honor / At difference in thee. Out of that I'll
work / Myself a former fortune' (200–2). His refusal to be
reconciled to a Roman peace – an insistence on the force of
irreducible division – aligns him with the reject that enables
a politics of dissensus critical in reshaping Roman tyranny.

With the collapse of the friend-enemy distinction in act 5,
Shakespeare's play tries to imagine the logical end to an early
modern politics of friendship by reconfiguring traditional early
modern models. Entering the final scene, Coriolanus claims,
'We have made peace / With no less honor to the Antiates /
Than shame to th' Romans' (5.6.78–80). He brings with him
the seal of the Roman senate that '[t]ogether' (82) with and
'[s]ubscribed by' (81) the tribunes represents what '[w]e have
compounded on' (83). The language of consensus structures
the scene but is quickly displaced by Aufidius's insistence on
division, calling Coriolanus a 'traitor' (84, 86). Coriolanus
himself implores the Volsces to '[c]ut me to pieces' (110), insist-
ing yet again on the irreducible division that forms the core of
friendship and a polity structured on the logic and language
of classical friendship theory. Coriolanus's demand that they

cut him to pieces becomes the demand of the people as well as of the conspirators: 'Tear him to pieces!' (119), the people shout, followed by the conspirators, who shout, 'Kill, kill, kill, kill, kill him!' (129). Division remains, but its political force is unpredictable and simply reworks a political community that can absorb and suture the divide. Aufidius says to the lords present at Coriolanus's murder: 'My lords, when you shall know [. . .] / [. . .] the great danger / Which this man's life did owe you, you'll rejoice / That he is thus cut off' (5.6.134–7). After the murder, Aufidius says that his 'rage is gone' (145) and that he is 'struck with sorrow' (146) at the event. His reaction captures the ambivalence of a politics of friendship necessarily fuelled by enmity as much as amity, and difference as much as similitude. Aufidius's melancholic reaction is a reminder that the possibility of the death of a friend inhabits friendship itself as the irreducible division that creates desire and proves unsustainable as both an absolutist politics nurtured by conventional notions of sovereign amity and the dissident politics of fugitive friendships.[81]

To conclude this chapter on Shakespeare's representation of the potential of a radical politics of friendship in *Coriolanus* that recognises as a civic virtue the 'dissension of a doit' (4.4.17), I want to return to the servingmen in act 4. Responding to the hospitality between Aufidius and Coriolanus, the servingmen in act 4 offer us arguably the most radical insight into the play's political philosophy. After the compact between Aufidius and Coriolanus, the Third Servingman brings news of the impending war against Rome. His fellow servant asks, 'But when goes this forward?' (4.5.222). The servingmen's exchange is as follows:

THIRD SERVINGMAN. Tomorrow, today, presently. You
　　shall have the drum struck up this afternoon [. . .]
SECOND SERVINGMAN. Why, then we shall have a stir-
　　ring world again. This peace is nothing, but to rust iron,
　　increase tailors, and breed ballad-makers.

> FIRST SERVINGMAN. Let me have war, say I; it exceeds
> peace as far as day does night; it's spritely, waking,
> audible, and full of vent. Peace is a very apoplexy, leth-
> argy; mulled, deaf, sleepy, insensible; a getter of more
> bastard children than war's a destroyer of men.
> SECOND SERVINGMAN. 'Tis so: and as war, in some
> sort, may be said to be a ravisher, so it cannot be denied
> but peace is a great maker of cuckolds.
> FIRST SERVINGMAN. Ay, and it makes men hate one
> another.
> THIRD SERVINGMAN. Reason; because they then less need
> one another.   (214–29)

On one level, this exchange articulates a concept of perpetual war that my reading of friendship and hospitality in the
play risks ignoring. Indeed, to argue as this chapter has done
that Coriolanus's disdain for others, shaped by and articulated through the rhetoric of friendship, is in fact the play's
expression of a counter-politics to an absolutism obscured
by the logic of sovereign amity is to seem to excuse the play's
state-sanctioned aggression and conflict as forms of Sorelian
violence that are politically justified and regenerative. The
play calls this militant force 'a perpetual spoil' (2.2.117), and
until Coriolanus's Rome had satisfied its imperial desire for
'[b]oth field and city' (118), the war machine 'never stood /
To ease his breast with panting' (118–19).

The political philosophy of the servingmen, however,
paints a different picture of perpetual conflict, one abstracted
from the material effects of Coriolanus's particular rage.
Conflict is naturalised and nourished in their description, 'a
parcel of their feast' and as immediate as the wiping of their
lips. Conflict holds the promise to produce 'a stirring of the
world again' – an energy contrasted with what peace brings,
'nothing but to rust iron'. The 'lethargy' of peace makes more
bastard children than 'war's a destroyer of men'. In the final
irony of the exchange, a servingman says that peace 'makes

men hate one another' because, another claims, 'they then less
need one another'. Even as Coriolanus and Aufidius are necessarily rejects in a politics of friendship that has the two rivals
'hate alike' (1.8.2), the irreducible division in their friendship
gives the play's politics its force, a force registered even in
the most intimate scenes of hospitality between social and
political outcasts preparing dinner for nobility. Embedded in
Coriolanus's need for Aufidius and in Aufidius's reciprocal
desire is the force of rejection that ironically makes friendship
and the political asymmetrical:[82] always appearing elsewhere,
and, according to the philosophical servingman, 'a strange
alteration', divided, fugitive, arriving '[t]omorrow, today,
presently', like the fragile form of community that briefly, if
only imaginatively, emerges from it.

The servingmen's mock encomium of war during this
scene of friendship dramatises the antagonistic force of politics immanent in the scene of absolute hospitality between
Aufidius and Coriolanus. To the servingmen, friendship
produces 'apoplexy' (4.5.223) and 'lethargy' (223), and a
world that is 'mulled, deaf, sleepy, insensible' (223–4). In
Schmittian terms, the friendship dramatised in the scene
worries the servingmen because it threatens to result in a
'completely pacified globe'.[83] In the confederation between
Aufidius and Coriolanus, the servingmen witness simultaneously the birth of a new war machine – an assemblage with
the potential to destroy Rome – and of an unconditional
friendship that guarantees a disturbing consensus.[84] The
Third Servingman describes the strange effect of the union:
'our general is cut i' th' middle and but one half of what
he was yesterday' (4.5.198–9). The rivals' new friendship
is a 'strange alteration' not because the two warriors make
awkward bedfellows. It is strange because their new confederation ironically suggests the possibility of a depoliticised
world – a Roman republic without politics. In their reaction
to the events that transpire in front of them, the servingmen

echo Schmitt: 'A world in which the possibility of war is utterly eliminated [. . .] would be a world without the distinction of friend and enemy and hence without politics.'[85] For the servingmen, the end of the political embodied in the warriors' strange alliance makes the turn to the absolute hostility of war – 'a stirring world' (218–19) – necessary to recover a form of civic life.

CHAPTER 3

TOUCHING SOVEREIGNTY IN *HENRY V*

I shall be heal'd, if that my King but touch,
The evil is not yours: my sorrow sings,
Mine is the evill, but the cure, the Kings.
Robert Herrick, 'To the King, to cure the
Evill', Hesperides, 1648

I touch you to touch you again. To touch is not to know.
Erin Manning, Politics of Touch

Henry V is a play that explores the contours of political sovereignty. To argue this, however, is to risk trying to make exceptional what by now has become something of a critical commonplace.[1] Reflecting on royal power in act 4, Henry himself expresses a fundamental limit of sovereignty to Michael Williams, memorably asserting, 'every subject's duty is the King's, but every subject's soul is his own' (4.1.181–2). Indeed, that *Henry V* is the final play in a dramatic cycle about the education of the future king remains a critically compelling way of reading and teaching it. Henry's reformation from 'sweet wag' (1.2.52) of the taverns in 1 *Henry IV* to King Henry at Agincourt in *Henry V* appears to ennoble absolute sovereignty, making it both benign and seductive to the English nation. Benign sovereignty is best illustrated at the end of act 4 after the Battle of Agincourt, when Henry learns that 'the number of our English dead' (4.8.96) included 'Edward the Duke of York, the Earl of Suffolk, / Sir Richard Keighley, Davy Gam Esquire; / None else of name, and of all other men / But five-and-twenty' (97–100). Exeter's response to the news, ''Tis wonderful' (107), reinforces the benign nature of Henry's kingship. The play registers absolutism's seductive force famously in act 5, when Henry woos Catherine in both French and English: 'Now fie upon my false French! By mine honour, in true English, I love thee, Kate' (5.2.206–9).

The play, however, actually begins its seduction early in act 1, as the new king navigates the paradox of absolute sovereign power. In the prelude to war with France, Henry appeals to Canterbury and Ely to justify the invasion. Henry asks, 'May I with right and conscience make this claim?' (1.1.96). Echoing Carl Schmitt's definition of the sovereign as 'he who decides on the exception',[2] Henry contemplates a decision that only he, as sovereign, can make; as a question posed to his bishops, however, Henry's inquiry gives shape to the borderline condition of absolute sovereignty – that it is both inside and outside the juridical order.[3] Henry's question about the legitimacy of his claim on France fuses legal justification for war with concerns about his conscience and illustrates the tension between 'how decisions should be made' and 'who should decide'.[4] In other words, the play's inaugural moment depicting the sovereign exception also confuses this concept with procedural logic and historical precedent that mitigates absolutism's unconditional power.

The ambivalence registered in the king's question hints at the play's more sustained critique of absolutism evident in Henry's royal wager that his heroic actions validate his absolute power. Henry's question to Canterbury and Ely about his claim on France is, at its core, a question about the right to interfere and the right to dominate.[5] At a geopolitical level, the play's investment in establishing the grounds for war with

France touches on what is at the heart of republican political theory – that political liberty is non-domination.[6] In this chapter I make the case that Henry's execution of sovereign authority throughout the play is, paradoxically, an act that provides the foundation for a form of dissensus and antagonism central to what Jacques Lezra calls radical republican politics.[7] More specifically, the play's depiction of Henry's precarious authority that we witness in his martial exploits in France, in his courtship of Kate, and in his domestic consolidation of power entangles sovereign absolutism simultaneously with its counter – political dissent.

In staging Henry's consolidation of power through the conquest of France, the play engages in a bit of sleight of hand, and what we take as royal absolutism in the formation of nation-state hegemony is, as the Chorus describes, 'imaginary puissance' (1.1.25) – imaginary not because the play is critical of the crown's illusory power or of the sovereign exception. On the contrary, Henry's royal absolutism is 'imaginary' because its efficient execution – in its antagonistic expression and in its arbitrary deployment – is precisely the precondition of politics that unsettles sovereign absolutism. Shakespeare's depiction of the war on France becomes one way for the play to engage pressing political questions about absolutism's indivisible authority unique to England at the end of the sixteenth century. Henry seduces his audiences on stage and off because, in executing the sovereign exception, he makes room for political dissent, and the play recognises this paradox in its depiction of the act of touch.

The play's depiction of tactility, specifically its deployment of the trope of touching, bridges theo-political readings of *Henry V* with an understanding of the play as a response to immediate events. To touch is to lay one's hands upon – to exercise the sense of feeling upon another, to bring into mutual contact – and it also means, according to the *Oxford English Dictionary*, 'to write of, treat of, mention, tell, relate;

now always, to mention briefly, casually, or in passing; to refer to, allude to'. In *Feeling Pleasures: The Sense of Touch in Renaissance England*, Joseph Moshenska suggests that touch assumed a 'unique and distinctive prominence' during the early modern period because tactility 'attracted such wildly contrasting interpretations and valuations'.[8] Shakespeare is a long way from the modern world described by Charles Taylor as withdrawn from 'promiscuous intimacy',[9] yet in the cultural and religious shift away from 'an affectively charged, enchanted, and immediately accessible world' that was one important outcome of the Reformation, the significance of touch, as Moshenska argues, was perceived to have waned.[10] In accounts of tactility in early modernity, according to Moshenska, 'Touch seems always to be located somewhere else, in an earlier epoch of solidity and enchantment that has receded beyond reach.'[11] Henry's sovereignty is located in a royal, ameliorative touch described by the Chorus as 'a little touch of Harry in the night' (4.0.47), yet his sovereignty is also characterised by deliberative decisionism. Canterbury uses the trope of touch to describe Henry's consideration of English policy regarding France. 'He seems indifferent', Canterbury says to Exeter, to 'causes now in hand / [. . .] / As touching France' (1.1.72, 77–9). One touch embodies a political theology that increasingly cannot ensure sovereignty's galvanising presence in early modernity and the other form of touch tropes tactility, transforming it into an indication of deliberation, counsel and consent.

We Are No Tyrant, But a Christian King

Before turning to the play's interrogation of sovereign power through the rhetoric of touch, I want to establish its relationship to varied and at times contradictory political currents taking shape in early modern England during the late sixteenth and early seventeenth centuries. Even as *Henry V* is part of a sequence of plays that dramatise English history, its representation of sovereignty illustrates how antagonistic politics is a politics of potentiality, not dependent on narratives that link it to the republican events surrounding the execution of Charles I in 1649. Fugitive politics in the play, in other words, is not a culmination of events that proceed according to the logic of historical progress but is instead the potent expression of desire within and in relation to the sovereign demand. The argument of this chapter that touch in *Henry V* animates dissensual politics may strike some as counter-intuitive, especially given recent critical attention to the remnants of theo-political sovereignty in an increasingly secularised early modern England.[12] It is true that *Henry V* is more normally associated with sacred kingship and the sovereign exception than with a politics of dissent. Henry's order to execute the French prisoners of war in act 4 and his decree in act 3 to execute all Englishmen who steal from the defeated French provide ample evidence of the persistence of what Schmitt calls sovereignty's 'absolute decision'.[13] Henry's legend in early modernity, however, was associated with popular dissent as well as with royal absolutism.

Markku Peltonen points out that the mythology of the historical Henry V served as a touchstone for a form of government more akin to republicanism than absolutism.[14] In the mid-seventeenth century during the height of English political republicanism, one of its chief propagandists Algernon Sidney links Henry V's rule to the historical reign of Elizabeth. For Sidney, Henry was a 'wise and valiant prince, who scorned to encroach upon the liberties of his subjects, and abhorred the detestable arts by which they had been impair'd';[15] Henry's conquest of France was achieved only 'by the bravery of a free and well-satisfied people'.[16] Sidney's republican account of Henry's reign continues, 'He desired not only that his people should be free during his time, but that his successors should not be able by oblique and fraudulent ways to enslave them.'[17]

Sidney's characterisation of Henry's reign seems designed in the end to tell us more about Elizabeth I than Henry; linking the two sovereigns, Sidney writes,

> She did not go about to mangle acts of parliament, and to pick out what might serve her turn, but frequently passed forty or fifty in a session, without reading one of them. She knew that she did not reign for herself, but for her people; that what was good for them, was either good for her, or that her good ought not to come into competition with that of the whole nation; and that she was by oath obliged to pass such laws as were presented to her on their behalf. This not only shews that there is no such thing as a legislative power placed in kings by the laws of God and nature, but that nations have it in themselves. It was not by law nor by right, but by usurpation, fraud and perjury that some kings took upon them to pick what they pleased out of the publick acts. Henry the fifth did not grant us the right of making our own laws; but with his approbation we abolished a detestable abuse that might have proved fatal to us. And if we examine our history we shall find, that every good and generous prince has sought to establish our liberties, as much as the most base and wicked to infringe them.[18]

For Peltonen, Sidney's political account of the reigns of Henry and Elizabeth suggests that political theorists instrumental to the formation of English republicanism in the mid-seventeenth century recognised that the period between 1570 and 1590 enlisted classical 'republican concepts and values', even as many critics argue that those republican concepts had been superseded by 'the values of neo-medieval chivalric culture'.[19] Huw Griffiths identifies these same political concepts, necessarily muted but responsive to the turbulent political and cultural events of the 1590s, in *Henry V*. He acknowledges that the play 'may seem like a move away from the more radical interrogations of kingship that are a feature of the history plays from earlier in the 1590s [. . .] *Henry V* may play more of a role in the 1590s' search for alternative forms of government than might, at first, be thought.'[20] Griffiths concludes that the play manifests an 'occluded republicanism, a product of the difficult and paranoid political circumstances of the 1590s'.[21] Griffiths's evocative phrase 'occluded republicanism' registers the same discomfort with the available terminology to describe the form of political life in early modern England as Andrew Hadfield's sense of the 'inchoate and unformed nature' of republicanism in the period.[22]

Critical investment in identifying articulations of republican political impulses in the century before 1649 is in large part a response to J. G. A. Pocock's claim that before the regicide, there was an absence of an identifiable civic consciousness in England.[23] In famously characterising Elizabethan politics as a 'monarchical republic', Patrick Collinson challenges this thesis, countering the notion that Shakespeare wrote in a period without popular conscious political intentions. In Collinson's account, he argues that 'Pocock underestimated [. . .] quasi-republican modes of political reflection and action within the intellectual and active reach of existing modes of consciousness and established constitutional parameters',[24] concluding that 'citizens were concealed within subjects'.[25] Peltonen has extended Collinson's conclusion significantly in tracing the intersection of classical humanist and republican arguments in early modern England, decentring its political community to cities and towns outside of London proper. For Peltonen, the marginal location of this intersection underscores its 'controversial nature': 'It was less dangerous to employ [. . .] [republican arguments] in such obscure places as Tewkesbury or Ireland; as soon as they were brought to the centre, they were marginalized by the use of translations of foreign treatises to convey the message.'[26] Peltonen establishes a link between English participation in substantial reform programmes in Ireland, described by Nicholas Canny as 'clearly-defined radical programme[s] of reform which would involve the erection of a completely new commonwealth upon firm foundations', and the alternative political approaches informed by Machiavelli's humanist work in communities outside London. Accounts of Irish political reformation reported in Richard Beacon's *Solon his follie: or a politique discourse, touching the reformation of common-weales conquered, declined or corrupted* (1594) were, according to Peltonen, perhaps the first to offer a 'thorough and positive use of Machiavelli's republicanism in the *Discorsi*'.[27]

Outsourced, occluded, inchoate or unformed, the impression of an identifiable republicanism in Elizabethan England remains qualified for critics who seek to establish an emergent form of dissent that would take shape as the dominant political discourse of republicanism by the mid-seventeenth century, when Algernon Sidney was beginning to write *Discourses Concerning Government*. Indeed, part of the problem in locating a proto-republican moment in Elizabethan England emerges from the critical emphasis on a Marxist concept of historical progress – that is, emergent republicanism must be a precursor to the events of 1649, which establish English republicanism as the dominant political philosophy. In *On Revolution*, Arendt links this critical tendency to the way we come to understand the structure of revolution:

> It is a strange and sad story that remains to be told and remembered. It is not the story of revolution on whose thread the historian might string the history of the nineteenth century in Europe, whose origins could be traced back to the Middle Ages, whose progress had been irresistible [. . .] and which Marx, generalizing the experiences of several generations, called 'the locomotion of all history'. I do not doubt that revolution was the hidden *leitmotif* of the century preceding ours, although I doubt [. . .] [the] conviction that revolution had been the result of an irresistible force rather than the outcome of specific deeds and

events. What seems to be beyond doubt and belief is that
no historian will ever be able to tell the tale of our country
without stringing it 'on the thread of revolutions' [. . .][28]

Arendt identifies the intellectual tendency of the nineteenth
century illustrated in the most influential work of Marx and
Darwin to view 'everything as being only a stage of some
further development'.[29]

Arendt's critical assessment of the locomotion of history,
relevant to discussions of republican politics in and after
Shakespeare, helps reframe an interpretation of *Henry V* as
a play about the scandalised remnants of sovereignty that
potentially decouple past and present.[30] Her rebuke of history's perceived movement enables a reading of the political in
history as 'eventful' – fugitive encounters not bound by a law
of historical motion.[31] Arendt identifies the law of historical
motion with terror, the 'essence of totalitarian domination',[32]
which makes possible the 'force of nature or of history to
race freely through mankind, unhindered by spontaneous
human action'.[33]

In a rereading of Arendt's understanding of terror that
makes it necessary to and constitutive of radical republicanism, Jacques Lezra explores the two principle components of
the law of movement – the refusal to accept things as they
are and the insistence that they inaugurate a future development. In *Wild Materialism*, he writes that in today's political
setting, a proper relationship between the law of movement
and terror 'entails decoupling Arendt's two propositions
and fashioning a sort of thought between refusal and provi-
dentialism, on the edge of or in the fissure between the two
terms'.[34] In his link between terror and radical republicanism, Lezra upends the historical argument about the chrono-
logical development of European modernity by revealing the
'residues of an incomplete secularization, and an incomplete
desacralization of the sovereign's body' haunting European

modernity.[35] What is unique about Lezra's stirring account of European modernity is that it is also 'punctual'.[36] With a logic that unravels Arendt's account of the incorporation of contingency into the agentive forces of progress and nature, *Wild Materialism* 'moves between the period of early modernity, the late Enlightenment, and the struggles of European decolonialization in the mid-twentieth century'.[37] It is the contention of this chapter that *Henry V* engages in a form of punctual politics – contingent, eventful and even radical. In staging permutations of the royal touch, *Henry V* demonstrates how efforts to reconsolidate power through touch may activate responses that soften sovereignty's hard condition.

In staging Henry's sovereignty as punctual and eventful, the play qualifies Alain Badiou's definition of an authentic, and therefore radical, event. In *Being and Event*, Badiou's discussion of the event hinges on the distinction between an event that carries with it the potential for 'radical transformational action' and an event which undoes itself to the point of 'being no more than the forever infinite numbering of the gestures, things and words that co-existed with it'.[38] In an argument about the punctuality of *Henry V*, Badiou might recognise the terms that tend to guide allegorical accounts of the play's early modern topicality: the emerging cosmopolitanism of the taverns, English expansionism, the emergence of national identity, the explosion of English exceptionalism, and so forth. Badiou might claim that there is no event in this customary account of history; indeed, his work suggests that this type of allegorical reading practice has the effect of colluding with, and being limited by, a form of topicality. Literary criticism that reads for historical homology or allegorical connection engages a historical event to be sure, but it also alienates the event from its own transformational potential. Put otherwise, historical topicality translates events at the threshold of their abolition.[39] For Badiou, a revolutionary event emerges when it signals itself both as the 'infinite multiple of the sequence of facts' that give it shape and scope and as 'an immanent résumé and one-mark of its own multiple',⁴⁰ or, as Slavoj Žižek observes, 'a contingency (contingent encounter or occurrence) which converts into necessity, i.e., it gives rise to a universal principle demanding fidelity [. . .] [A] contingent upheaval (revolt) is an Event when it gives rise to a commitment of the collective subject to a new universal emancipatory project, and thereby sets in motion the patient work of restructuring society.'⁴¹ According to Badiou, fidelity to an event is the necessary condition that gives rise to an event's authenticity and potentiality and is the groundwork for future political formations that might transform the civic landscape.

In *Lyric Apocalypse*, Ryan Netzley argues that Badiou's account 'remains tethered to the logic of retrospective rupture, the arresting interpellation of a crisis demanding careful and singular fidelity of the true revolutionary'.⁴² Returning us to the concept of historical progress with which this chapter began in relation to the education of a prince, Netzley points out that Badiou's 'auto-generated immanent breaks that amount to events' repeat the 'internally generated anti-thesis' that fuels the locomotion of progress in Marxist accounts of history. Netzley concludes that 'models of events like Badiou's effectively prevent change by turning events into unreachable, transcendent impossibilities'.⁴³ To claim that Shakespeare's eventful politics appears elsewhere – in 1649, 1688, 1776 or 1789 – deferred by fidelity through time, is, as Netzley's work on apocalypticism in Marvell and Milton demonstrates, a 'wagered maintenance of a singular event that occurs elsewhere. [. . .] [R]evealed presence is not gambling on a hopeful future but a confident and hopeful rendering of an immanent occurrence.'⁴⁴ Shakespeare transforms what Netzley might describe as a singular occurrence in *Henry V* with the event of touch – a haptic force that gives political presence to immanence.

In *Politics of Touch*, Erin Manning explores how touch, in combination with other senses, redefines the sovereign body, making the body 'processual – a body-in-movement, relational, and in excess of itself'.[45] In Manning's application of touch to questions of bodily stability and its political affect, she proposes that the act of touch 'enables the creation of worlds' that deterritorialise the body, 'national body-politics, stable genders, political consensus'.[46] According to Manning, a politics of touch has the potential to reallocate the organisation of time that 'casts an opposition between the temporal and the atemporal, the eternal and the transitory, the finite and the infinite'.[47] Juxtaposing the duration of the politics of touch to what Michael Shapiro calls 'national time', the act of touch produces 'time to express, to reach toward, to pace space' and what results is a political dimension that 'opens the way for a thinking of a democracy-to-come'.[48] Eric Santner's argument in *The Royal Remains* that the flesh of the modern sovereign migrates to encompass social formations bears on Manning's understanding of the politics of touch. Santner writes,

> When the sovereign thing, whether phallus, father, or king, can no longer discharge the duties of its office, it discharges the remains of its flesh it has heretofore pretended or appeared to embody. The *arcana imperii*, the secret of the master/sovereign, becomes a kind of chronic, spectral secretion of the social body at large, one registered as a surplus of immanence that oscillates between the sublime and the abject and calls forth the apparatuses of biopolitical administration.[49]

Manning's impression of the deterritorialising force of touch shares Santner's sense of the 'surplus of immanence' embodied in the migrating, oscillating flesh of the sovereign that Henry's touch – a biopolitical wager to reinforce power – seeks to manage. That act of touch, for Manning, however, redefines the 'now' from a temporal measure that remains in the present and turns it into a 'now' that must be 'negotiated, again and again'.[50] Echoing Badiou but with Netzley's scepticism of a revelatory future that gives meaning to a past event, Manning describes the act of touch as 'a trace, always deferred, always leading toward another moment, another imprint, another touch'.[51] Touch 'does not then transfer into a knowable commodity, but into another possibility of reaching out: I touch you to touch you again. To touch is not to know.'[52] The politics of touch that Manning explores is not solely a politics of consensus, incorporation or consolidation now or in the future. In other words, touch is not proto-republican politics. In *Henry V*, the trope of touch – its rhetorical and performative dimensions – is the borderline event or interruption that inaugurates the political at the same time that it functions to consolidate the demands of absolutism, exposing sovereignty's immanent divisibility as the foundation for a form of fugitive politics.[53]

Bid Thy Ceremony Give Thee Cure!

Returning to the rhetoric of touch in *Henry V*, the Chorus in act 4 describes the calming effect of Henry's presence on the eve of the Battle of Agincourt in language that turns royal touch into something cute, diminishing its connection to the sacred:

> A largess universal, like the sun,
> His liberal eye doth give to every one,
> Thawing cold fear, that mean and gentle all
> Behold, as may unworthiness define,
> A little touch of Harry in the night.   (4.0.43–7)

Touch here takes a back seat to the king's vision, his 'liberal eye', which democratises sovereign power, giving its 'largess universal' to 'everyone', and comforting the soldiers' fear on the eve of battle. A 'little touch' is in stark contrast to a 'largess universal, like the sun' and a 'liberal eye'. Yet, Harry's 'little touch' is the king's major preoccupation after his encounter with Bates, Williams and Court later in the scene. After his disguised encounter with the soldiers about the responsibilities of sovereign and subject, Henry's extended soliloquy about ceremony and the burdens unique to kingship identifies the royal touch as one of the necessary aspects of sovereignty that makes it spectacular and, therefore, powerful. For Henry, however, the royal touch that he inherited has been transformed into the act of self-touching – an auto-tactility that he hopes might repair sovereignty's fractured condition. Henry describes his troubled royal condition and the act of self-touching in what is perhaps his most intimate disclosure in the play:

> [. . .] O, be sick, great greatness,
> And bid thy ceremony give thee cure!
> Think'st thou the fiery fever will go out
> With titles blown from adulation?
> Will it give place to flexure and low bending?
> Canst thou, when thou command'st the beggar's knee,
> Command the health of it? No, thou proud dream,
> That play'st so subtly with a king's repose.
> I am a king that find thee, and I know
> 'Tis not the balm, the sceptre and the ball,
> The sword, the mace, the crown imperial,
> The intertissued robe of gold and pearl,
> The farcèd title running fore the king,
> The throne he sits on, nor the tide of pomp
> That beats upon the high shore of this world,
> No, not all these, thrice-gorgeous ceremony,
> Not all these, laid in bed majestical,
> Can sleep so soundly as the wretched slave [. . .]   (228–45)

Henry compares sovereignty defined by 'flattery' and 'place, degree, and form' to a 'poisoned' body with 'fiery fever'. In his account of the royal condition, ceremony offers the only palliative to the king's disease. Yet, the efficacy of the ceremony imagined in 'the balm, the sceptre and the ball' to remediate the king's illness is inadequate to cure the royal condition. Henry asks himself, 'Think'st thou the fiery fever will go out / With titles blown from adulation?' (230–1) and 'Will it give place to flexure and low bending?' (232). His self-reflection is at its core an interrogation into the power of sovereign majesty to make the body whole. Henry's questions uncouple the king's charismatic body from its temporal one and imagine royal ceremony in the futile process to cure itself: 'Canst thou, when thou command'st the beggar's knee,' asks Henry, 'Command the health of it?' (233–4). Enfolding the effect of the king's touch into itself, the ritual appears inadequate to cure the disease affecting its body. Henry's self-examination recognises the limits of the royal touch by acknowledging sovereignty's exceptionalism – 'I am a king that find thee' (236) – and immediately dividing sovereignty by qualifying the power of its touch: 'I know / 'Tis not the balm, the sceptre and the ball [. . .]' (236–7). As part of the 'thrice-gorgeous ceremony' (243), the balm that Henry exposes as empty alludes to the ritual of the king's touch that can cure a subject's 'fiery fever'. Shakespeare's use of the word 'balm' gestures to multiple meanings simultaneously: the *Oxford English Dictionary* defines 'balm' as a fragrant oil used for anointing royalty, and a healing, soothing or softly restorative agency or influence. Again, sovereignty's ritual efficacy is folded back into an image of the king's body. Either as oil that anoints royalty or as the balm that, in the logic of Henry's lament, touches the body itself, it fails its ritual function.

The complicated image of the king's self-reflexive, healing touch draws on the ceremony of the king's touch still practised during Elizabeth's reign to cure the disease known as the King's Evil. In *Macbeth*, Shakespeare makes clear that he is familiar with the ceremony, referring to it as 'a most miraculous work' and a 'strange virtue' (*Macbeth*, 4.3.149, 157). In an exchange among the Doctor, Malcolm and Macduff in front of King Edward the Confessor's castle, they address the power of the king's touch:

> MALCOLM. Well, more anon. [*To the* DOCTOR] Comes
>   the King forth, I pray you?
> DOCTOR. Ay, sir. There are a crew of wretched souls
> That stay his cure. Their malady convinces
> The great assay of art, but at his touch –
> Such sanctity hath heaven given his hand –
> They presently amend.
> MALCOLM. I thank you, doctor. *Exit* [DOCTOR]
> MACDUFF. What's the disease he means?
> MALCOLM. 'Tis called the Evil.
> A most miraculous work in this good king,
> Which often since my here-remain in England,
> I have seen him do. How he solicits heaven
> Himself best knows; but strangely-visited people,
> All swoll'n and ulcerous, pitiful to the eye,
> The mere despair of surgery, he cures,
> Hanging a golden stamp about their necks,
> Put on with holy prayers; and 'tis spoken,
> To the succeeding royalty he leaves
> The healing benediction. With this strange virtue,
> He hath a heavenly gift of prophecy,
> And sundry blessings hang about his throne
> That speak him full of grace.   (4.3.141–60)

In the exchange Shakespeare describes the ceremony in some detail. After exhausting all other treatments ('convinces / The great essay of art' (142–3)), the afflicted subjects petition the king for his touch. The sovereign touches the afflicted body, and through his hands God's healing grace is delivered. Malcolm's familiarity with the ritual event – 'often [. . .] seen him do' (148–9) – may suggest the relative frequency and popularity of the ceremony during Elizabeth's reign.[54]

The King's Evil was, specifically, a tubercular infection of the lymph nodes in the neck, and both French and English monarchs treated the malady in the years between about 1250 and 1789 (1712 in England).[55] In the English court, the ritual of touching probably emerged in imitation of the French practice, with some uniquely English modification, between 1259 and 1272. Frank Barlow credits the court of Henry III and the rituals that surrounded the translation of the body of Edward I to a rebuilt Westminster Abbey as the moment that 'may well have made the cure of the royal disease a strand in the rites', confirming for Henry the 'cult of English sacramental kingship'.[56] The last English monarch to practise the royal touch was Queen Anne, who on 30 March 1712 touched Samuel Johnson as the last of 300 subjects suffering from scrofula.[57] Carole Levin argues that the sixteenth and seventeenth centuries in England appear to be when the ceremony was most popular, suggesting that its frequency grew during this period because of the crown's need for legitimacy during and after the break from Rome.[58] In addition, Levin points out that the ceremony's increased frequency and theatricality during the Elizabethan period helped to secure the queen as female ruler of the nation. She writes that the ceremony was part of the spectacle that made sovereignty 'so awe inspiring and powerful it could even encompass a female ruler – inconceivable for a fifteenth century woman'.[59] According to Levin, touching for the King's Evil was one 'manifestation of the sacred aspect of monarchy Elizabeth represented to a people suffering from the dislocations of so many changes in church and state'.[60] Deborah Willis notes that Shakespeare's depiction of what she describes as 'sacred magic' that reinforces monarchical authority 'has its own kind of precariousness'.[61] Because of the religious implications of the healing ritual in Protestant England, the ceremony had the effect of making the nature and efficacy of a monarch's cures 'more ambiguous', diluting the popular impression that the sovereign possessed a 'unique sacred power'.[62] Willis concludes that the monarchs depicted on stage in plays such as *Pericles* and *Macbeth* lack the 'innate sacredness' reserved for royal children and wives. Instead, those monarchs experience conversion that puts them in proximity to the sacred, indicating 'their submission to a divine will', not an identification with it.[63] The royal touch in Shakespeare 'contributes to a discourse in which the monarch's legitimacy derives from his submission to a sacredness most visible in persons less powerful than himself'.[64]

Late in Elizabeth's reign, the ceremonial practice was documented by William Clowes, Elizabeth's surgeon. In *A right frutefull treatise for the artificiall cure of struma* (1602), Clowes describes how successful Elizabeth's touch was in curing scrofula. Supporting this observation, Robert Laneham recounts a ceremony in a letter describing the queen's progress at Kenilworth in 1575 in which there were 'nyne cured of the penyfull and daugnerous diseaz, called the king's evill'.[65] Records indicate that Elizabeth would actually touch the diseased bodies, placing her hands on the tumours around the neck.[66] Richard Tooker describes this particular aspect of the ritual:

> her most serene Majesty lays her hands on each side of them that are sick and diseased with the evil, on the jaws, of the throat, or the affected part, and touches the sore places with her bare hands, and forthwith heals them: and after their sores have been touched by her most healing hands the sick persons retire for a while, till the rest of the ceremony is finished.[67]

Tooker's description includes the image of Elizabeth in prayer 'meekly kneeling upon her knees' and 'prostrate on her knees, body and soul wrapt in prayer [. . .] her exquisite hands, whiter than the whitest snow, boldly and without disgust pressing their sores and ulcers and handling them to health, not merely touching them with her finger-tips'.[68] Clowes's prayer for Elizabeth near the end of her reign indicates the degree to which the healing touch was associated with her charisma as sovereign. He asks God to 'blesse, keepe and defend her Sacred person, from the malice of all her knowne and unknown enemies, so that shee may raigne over us [. . .] even unto the ende of the world, still to cure and heale many thousands moe, then ever she hath yet done'.[69]

Henry's sceptical description of ceremony in act 4 offers a critical response to Tooker's encomiastic account. Tooker's moving image of Elizabeth 'kneeling' and 'prostrate on her knees' in the healing ceremony is in contrast to the royal touch in Henry's soliloquy, summoned to 'give thee cure' (229) from the 'fiery fever' (230). Tooker's record of the process of the royal touch captures the belief in transactional piety of a prostrate queen in the ritual, and it emphasises the tactility of the ceremony's gross materiality. Tooker records that Elizabeth's 'healing' hands touch 'jaws', 'the throat', 'the sore places', while Henry forcefully questions the transactional nature of the royal touch. He refers to the diseased condition of sovereignty – 'be sick, great greatness' (228) – and to the physical act of the sovereign bowing, prostrate in the healing ceremony intended to remedy what in this scene is the King's Evil. In his frustration with ceremony that he equates with fever, or a literalised form of the King's Evil plaguing ceremonial sovereignty, Henry asks if the disease '[w]ill [. . .] give place' to ritual (232). In asking the question 'Canst thou, when thou command'st the beggar's knee, / Command the health of it?' (233–4), Henry imagines that sacred sovereignty compels supplication, but he, more critically, imagines sovereignty itself, like Elizabeth in Tooker's account of the healing ceremony, prostrate on a 'beggar's knee', in supplication and awaiting a self-administered royal touch that promises to heal the king's malady.[70] 'I am the king that find thee' (236), says the king to his sick self, exposing the emptiness of the royal touch on the sovereign who suffers from sickness. In seeking to administer the royal touch on his abject body, Henry embodies both the sovereign exception and bare life simultaneously.

The topic of Henry's contemplation shifts in the long soliloquy, however. The description of a king measuring sovereignty's diseased condition against itself gives way to the more familiar comparison of the figure of sacred kingship, 'subject to the breath / Of every fool' (211–12), to 'the wretched slave' (245), who sleeps soundly, with 'vacant mind' (246). The shift late in the soliloquy, however, only serves to repair the impression of divided sovereignty that Henry contemplates in relation to the trope of sovereign touch. Moshenska describes the status of touch in fifteenth-century England as 'distinctive precisely because it persistently operated in this borderland'[71] – a liminal space between efficacy in the act of touch and the 'indecision among reformers about the validity of devotional contact'.[72] In his soliloquy in act 4, Henry seems to anticipate and enact this logic. For Henry, the promise of the royal touch imagined in this moment – an act of self-touching that might 'cure' and 'command' the health of the sick king – fails as a limit event because of the radical divisibility, without suture, inherent in the fractured figure of a sick king's hard condition poised between bare life and the sovereign exception.

O, Hard Condition

Shakespeare explicitly explores sovereign divisibility in relation to Henry as early as 1 *Henry IV*. In act 3, scene 2, in the encounter with his father, who accuses the young prince of 'vile participation' (87) in the taverns, Harry's response reveals the desire to suture the division that defines him as sovereign: 'I shall hereafter, my thrice gracious lord, / be more myself' (91–2). Outside of the royal court, Harry's divided sovereignty appears during the play extempore in the taverns. Harry, playing his father, banishes Falstaff from the prince's company:

> FALSTAFF. No, my good lord, banish Peto, banish Bar-
>   dolph, banish Poins: but for sweet Jack Falstaff, kind
>   Jack Falstaff, true Jack Falstaff, valiant Jack Falstaff, and
>   therefore more valiant, being, as he is, old Jack Falstaff,
> Banish not him thy Harry's company,
> Banish not him thy Harry's company,
> Banish plump Jack, and banish all the world.
> PRINCE HARRY. I do; I will.   (2.5.432–8)

Harry's theatrical declaration, 'I do', becomes the sovereign perfor-mative, 'I will', in this scene. We need not use Schmitt's definition of sovereignty to understand that at this moment Hal's acting *as if* a sovereign gives way to his enunciating the sovereign exception. In what appears as a shift from theatrical to actual power, Harry proj-ects the fiction of sovereign indivisibility. Perfectly balanced in form and structure, Harry's different decrees suggest a self-possessed, coherent sovereign who can reconcile present impossibilities with future certainties: the theatrical fantasy ('I do') gives way to the sovereign decision ('I will') to banish Falstaff, effectively letting him live or die. Read otherwise, however, the balanced line 'I do; I will' captures the aporetic logic of sovereign indivisibility. Harry's staged banishment lacks any force in the present that would make it a singular sovereign act within the staged play of the tavern.

On one level, Falstaff's grumbling to '[p]lay out the play!' (444) in response to Bardolph's interruption to announce the sheriff's arrival points to a desire for fidelity to the act that might make banishment eventful in Badiou's sense. In other words, banishment as an event appears dependent on its temporality, its appearance in time as a consequential action. Yet, on another level, the singularity suggested in the event of Falstaff's staged banishment and the fidelity desired in the request to '[p]lay out the play' collapses with the sheriff's knock at the door. With what appear to be asymmetrical performatives, Harry fails to balance the present banishment of Falstaff – 'I do' – with the promise of banishment in the future – 'I will'. This asymmetry is what gives poignancy to the scene in the context of Falstaff's fate at the end of 2 *Henry IV* and *Henry V*. Just as the staged event collapses in on itself with the sheriff's interruption to reveal the divisible nature of sovereignty, Harry's future-oriented decree fails to deliver its promise. In the final scene of 2 *Henry IV*, Falstaff's desire to play out the play seems to materialise. The newly crowned king refuses Falstaff, banishing him from London. 'I know thee not, old man[,]' says King Henry. 'I banish thee, on pain of death' (5.5.45, 61). The play immediately challenges the singularity of this sovereign decision, however, as Falstaff reassures his friends that he 'shall be sent for in private by him' (74). Like the fate of Hal's theatrical banishment of Falstaff, the decree at the end of 2 *Henry IV* is also empty due to its own theatricality. The epilogue promises Falstaff's return: 'If you be not too much cloyed with fat meat, our humble author will continue the story, with Sir John in it' (23–5). As in the play extempore in the tavern, the logic of performance dictates that sovereign singularity become sovereign divisibility.

With its contemplation of the royal balm or cure during Henry's soliloquy in act 4, the play seems to want the act of touch to suture the sovereign division characteristic of his royal power. The trope of touching and of its failure as an ameliorative ritual, however, underscores the play's more critical depiction of the essential role of sovereign division in formulating a politics of dissent that I describe as fugitive. Henry's promise to his father to be more himself in 1 *Henry IV* is a commitment to indivisibility that King Henry's exegesis on ceremony and the royal touch deconstructs. In *Wild Materialism*, Lezra explores the condition of sovereign divisibility, what he describes as 'wounded sovereignty'.[73] In demonstrating the 'motility of division' inherent in a sovereign's putatively indivisible status as the one who decides the exception,[74] Lezra contends that the 'early modern sphere of cultural production' provides traces of what Derrida calls the 'aporetic of divisible sovereignty'.[75] Derrida's logic, according to Lezra, helps to unpack Richmond's enigmatic phrase in *Richard III* that appears to bring an end to the War of the Roses and stages unequivocally the birth of England's Tudor Myth: 'All this divided York and Lancaster, / Divided, in their dire division. / O now let *Richmond* and *Elizabeth*, / The true succeeders of each royal House, / By God's fair ordinance conjoin together' (5.8.27–31). Lezra's powerful counter-reading of Richmond's decree concludes that 'Richmond's form of sovereignty replaces Richard's but cannot be divided from it without retaining the very notion of an unregulated division, an unsmoothing of the face of providence.'[76] In Lezra's account of the interpretive crux, the act of dividing or separating the Tudor dynasty from Richard's iniquity contaminates the sovereign desire for separation with the fact of divisiveness:

> Richmond's words work not only as Shakespeare's description of a state of affairs, one might say, but as a sort of fantasy or as a vehicle for forgetting. We must be 'divided' from the 'dire division' represented by the civil war – and this dividing must be both an example of the new order and yet 'divided' from the 'dire division' *direly*: absolutely, unambiguously, unbridgeably.[77]

The transitive force of division, its contagious motility, makes the pure sovereignty of Schmitt's influential treatise impossible. During what Lezra describes as 'the incipient decoupling of the claims of sovereignty from the onto-theology its performance requires',[78] the distribution of absolutism through division enables the logic of sovereignty at the moment of its early modern secularisation to define the parameters of the incipient moments of productive terror that fuels radical republicanism.

In *Henry V*, the productivity of division is what enables the king's invasion of France. Canterbury's fable of the beehive in act 1 provides the military strategy for war with France and seems a long way from a concept of dire divisibility that Lezra locates in the increasingly secular sovereign. For Canterbury, the sacred force of division generates comity:

> Therefore doth heaven divide
> The state of man in divers functions,
> Setting endeavour in continual motion;
> To which is fixed, as an aim or butt,
> Obedience: for so work the honey-bees,
> Creatures that by a rule in nature teach
> The act of order to a peopled kingdom.   (183–9)

Canterbury argues that the sovereign exception is sacred, necessary to fuel the 'continual motion' (185) that constitutes a functioning kingdom. He anchors the motion to the concept of obedience and clarifies the form and function of the *civitas* in the comparison with a beehive.[79] According to Canterbury's advice to the king, the beehive's officers are like magistrates, merchants, soldiers, masons, civil citizens, a poor mechanic and justice, all of whom report to the king. Concluding that 'many things, having full reference / To one consent, may work contrariously' (205–6), Canterbury emphasises a cascading litany of division that informs consent. What begins as heaven's prerogative in the first part of the passage migrates to the king, whom Canterbury implores, 'Divide your happy England into four' (214). As a strategy for war, division seems necessary, but the logic of sovereignty imagined in Canterbury's simile for the commonwealth comes close to embodying the form of theopolitical sovereignty offered in Schmitt's historical reading of Bodin. For Canterbury, the secularity of the industrious hive is ultimately enforced and structured by heaven. The pertinent passage from *Political Theology* that illuminates Canterbury's desire reads:

> All significant concepts of the modern theory of the state are secularized theological concepts not only because of their historical development – in which they were transferred from theology to the theory of the state, whereby, for example, the omnipotent God became the omnipotent lawgiver – but also because of their systematic structure [. . .].[80]

Exeter, whose brief description of government often goes uncommented in critical responses to the play's theory of commonwealth, suggests this exact shift immediately before Canterbury's use of the fable of the beehive. He tells Henry,

> For government, though high and low and lower,
> Put into parts, doth keep in one consent,
> Congreeing in a full and natural close,
> Like music.   (180–3)

Cristopher Hollingsworth reads Exeter's and Canterbury's comments to mean that the commonwealth coheres because it is God's will. He describes the beehive as 'a heaven-approved gird, as a system of correspondences [. . .] [in which] men and bees naturally participate in a Divine order and according to their place in the chain of being'.[81] This reading of a community built on consensus, however, undervalues productive political division. The freedom to engage in a dissensual politics is a radical force of equality not registered in the harmony of the beehive. Indeed, its logic rests on a divided, particularised universal, 'distorted in its very definition by the police logic of roles and parts'.[82]

In his interpretation of 'dire division' in *Richard III*, Lezra offers a counter-reading of the persistence of division that helps to explain Exeter's music analogy as a sign of discord, not harmony. He points to the archaic reference to musical division in *Richard III*: 'the execution of a melodic transition between longer notes achieved by dividing each of them into shorter notes'.[83] In musical theory, more divisions in a musical line indicate virtuosity and better approximate the undivided sound of nonpercussive instruments such as the human voice. The appearance of musical indivisibility demands, it seems, division, and if Exeter's music analogy is to make sense in terms of this demand, so too does the political process of 'one consent, / Congreeing in a full and natural close' of the beehive. Joseph Campana reminds us that the etymology of 'entoma' and 'insect' denotes divisibility, 'something segmented or cut into pieces, referring to the segmented insect carapace'.[84] Campana's speculations on the political implications of early modern depictions of insects, including bees, cohere with Lezra's on sovereignty's division: 'Since Jean Bodin, an inviolable quality of sovereignty is its indivisibility, yet does the insect kingdom indicate a more mobile, divisible sovereignty, one that must also carefully consider hive collectivity?'[85] The hive's 'continual motion' (185) and the collective consent arrived at through the contrary labour of the bees capture the impression of a fragmented and mobile sovereignty occluded in Canterbury's application of the simile emphasising consent.

In Canterbury's consensual model of civic structure, division in the end serves comity; Canterbury's simile partitions sovereignty, and in the act of dividing it, the division reconstitutes a 'happy England' (214). This 'act of order' (189), as Canterbury describes it, glimpses, however, the politics of the fugitive. What Canterbury claims to be the fixed and obedient 'state of man' (184) is more akin to a 'dire division', a 'pharisaical emblem of divisible sovereignty: ranks folding into and across ranks, attributes conditioning subjects [. . .]'.[86] A divisible sovereignty of this sort is fugitive, incomplete, always in the process of consolidating itself, of becoming more itself, yet always a form of sovereignty just out of reach, untouchable, diseased like Henry's own sovereign body, and antagonistic in its divisibility as a precondition for political life.[87]

You Have Witchcraft in Your Lips

Henry's demand for sovereign indivisibility in *Henry V* – his journey to be more himself, his desire for his touch to cure his 'fiery fever', his eliminating the logical space between 'I do' and 'I will' – contrasts with Catherine's expression of fugitive politics. As Henry's 'capital demand' (5.2.96) during the peace negotiations between England and France, her powerful, though limited, presence in the play ushers in a politics of sensation that illustrates how touch can be an affective form of political antagonism. According to Jacques Rancière, the paradox of 'the part of no part' in his political philosophy constitutes politics as an antagonism emerging from a basic contingency in social forces designed to appear ordered and natural. A 'part of no part' signals the antagonism between the structured body politic, in which every part has a function, and the part in excess of the structure that disrupts bodily coherence by contradicting the principle of universality. Rancière elaborates, 'Politics exists through the fact of a magnitude that escapes ordinary measurement, this part of those who have no part that is nothing and everything.'[88] The surplus condition of parts that form the structural integrity of the body, and at the same time exceed the structure, is the aspect, according to Rancière, that resists an 'allocated subordinate space'.[89] Slavoj Žižek explains this concept fundamental to Rancière's definition of politics:

> Politics proper thus always involves a kind of short circuit between the Universal and the Particular: the paradox of a *singulier universel*, a singular which appears as the stand

in for the Universal, destabilizing the 'natural' functional order of relations in the social body. This identification of the non-part with the Whole, or the part of society with no properly defined place within it (or resisting the allocated subordinated place within it) with the Universal, is the elementary gesture of politicization [. . .][90]

In both Žižek and Rancière, the political consequence of the 'part of no part' is the radical contingency deterritorialising the body politic even as it rhizomatically produces new temporary alliances. This body politic divides a functioning society into distinct parts, only to make the hierarchy of divided elements appear natural and in service to the whole, like Canterbury's beehive. The cohesive body politic formed via division and exclusion is the political formation that Canterbury describes but that Catherine's body – and her touch – by contrast fractures.

In act 3, the play stages Catherine's divided body in what appears to be a prelude to its inevitable reconstitution. In Catherine's language lesson, the body part that she and Alice begin with is the hand. Kate asks, '*Il faut que j'apprenne a parler. Comment appelez-vous la main en anglais?* [I must learn to speak it (English). What do you call *la main* in English?]' (3.5.4–5). Alice responds, '*La main? Elle est appelée* de hand [*La main?* It is called "de hand"]' (6). Beginning the lesson with the part of the body that touches, Catherine acknowledges that her future in relation to the English king is linked to tactility. The bodily elements of Catherine's language lesson – the hand, the fingers, the nails, the arm, the elbow, the chin and the foot – anatomise her body, dividing it into constituent parts, which, like Canterbury's fable of the beehive, have 'full reference / To one consent' (205–6). The act of consent is Henry's primary concern in act 5 as he tries to seduce Catherine into marrying him. Burgundy comments that Catherine's innocence makes the king's offer of love hard to 'consign to' (5.2.274), and he responds to Henry's request that Burgundy 'teach [Catherine] to consent wink-ing' (278–9), saying, 'I will wink on her to consent' (280).

On one level, Catherine's consent is simply for show since her future is 'comprised / Within the fore-rank of our articles' (5.2.96–7), according to Henry's comment to the French queen. Her consent is all the more per-functory given Charles's response to Henry associating Catherine with a walled French city (297–9). Henry's vio-lent threat in act 3, scene 4 to the city governor that he 'will not leave the half-achieved Harfleur / Till her ashes she lie buried' (8–9) lingers in this final exchange that links Catherine's body and her consent to a walled city that 'war hath never entered'. On another, more critical level, however, her consent becomes a 'part of no part' – that radically contingent element that remains outside of sovereignty even as it universalises sovereignty's absolut-ism. The exchange between Henry and Charles illustrates the problem of Catherine's consent in relation to the king's sovereign power:

> KING. Shall Kate be my wife?
> KING OF FRANCE. So please you.
> KING. I am content, so the maiden cities you talk of may
> wait on her: so the maid that stood in the way for my wish
> shall show me the way to my will.   (295–9)

At this moment of consent achieved through the voice of a sovereign surrogate, Catherine's silence – her refusal to give consent – is an expression of the logic of sover-eignty's divisibility. The gap separating Henry's wish from his will is what Henry describes in act 4 as a sovereign's

'hard condition' (4.1.209). Henry begins his contemplation of ceremony regretting that his private wishes, his
'infinite heartsease' (213), must surrender to 'general' and
'idol' ceremony (216, 217) because of the obligations of
sovereignty. The balm of the king's touch, according to
Henry, proves worthless in suturing this division. In act
5, Burgundy also describes Catherine as suffering a 'hard
condition' (5.2.274) separating her desire from her will.
According to Burgundy, Catherine's modesty prevents her
from embracing the erotics of desire imagined as Cupid, a
'naked blind boy' (271). Although difficult for Catherine
to 'consign' (274) to the naked allure of Cupid's love, Burgundy implies that she can be taught the proper meaning of
consent through the act of touch. He tells Henry:

> I will wink on her to consent, my lord, if you will teach
> her to know my meaning. For maids, well summered and
> warm, are like flies at Bartholomew-tide: blind, though they
> have eyes. And then endure handling, which would not
> abide looking on.   (280–4)

Burgundy's misogynist simile compares maids well-prepared
for love to flies saturated with warmth and food. Only then
will the satiated flies tolerate 'handling'. Burgundy's suggestion is that the event of consent is wrapped up with touch,
something that Henry understands.

Henry's faith in the act of consent, even if achieved
through a surrogate, conceals what Peter DeGabriele points
out in his study of consent in the eighteenth-century novel is
a 'profound belief in a literal or authentic form of consent
(literally a feeling-together) that would immediately guarantee the propriety of touch'.[91] For Henry, by contrast, proper
touch guarantees consent and sutures the division in sovereignty that the act of consent reveals. Henry's touch in the
scene is his kiss. Although stage directions announcing the

kiss are not part of early editions of the play, Henry memorably announces the kiss this way:

> We are the makes of manners, Kate, and the liberty that follows our places stops the mouth of all find-faults, as I will do yours, for upholding the nice fashion of your country in denying me a kiss. Therefore, patiently and yielding. [*He kisses her*] You have witchcraft in your lips, Kate. There is more eloquence in a sugar touch of them than in the tongues of the French Council, and they should sooner persuade Harry of England than a general petition of monarchs.   (250–8)

The kiss has a particularly powerful effect described as 'witchcraft' by the playful king. Kate's voice is embodied in the touch of her lips; the 'sugar touch' of her lips offers more eloquence than the 'tongues' of the royal court. Catherine's rhetorical fluency is embodied in the king's metaphor, only to be subsumed by sovereign desire and the act of consent – legitimated by treaty, endorsed by Burgundy, and surrogated by her father – that follows the touch. Following the royal kiss, the play grapples with how to make sense of the materiality of Catherine's body. To Henry, she becomes inscrutable, and he is incapable of conjuring up 'the spirit of love in her' (266); to Burgundy, she is like a fly, 'blind, though they have their eyes' (283–4); and to her father, she is a French city 'girdled with maiden walls that war hath never entered' (293–4). Indeed, Charles's comment to Henry that he sees a French city and the French maid 'perspectively', transforming one into the other, reveals the surplus materiality and the insensible force of the female body in proximity to sovereignty's consolidating power.[92]

Catherine's insensible body is the location of dissensual politics in this final scene ostensibly about the consolidation of sovereign power enabled through her body.[93] After kissing

Catherine, Henry tells Burgundy that as he has 'neither the voice nor the heart of flattery about me, I cannot so conjure up the spirit of love in her that will appear in his true likeness' (265–6). The king looks for evidence of Catherine's consent. He wants to perceive in her body 'the spirit of love' in 'his true likeness'. Yet, Catherine's body withholds this type of perceptible evidence, refusing the sensation that would confirm the consolidating force of Henry's sovereign touch. The witchcraft that Henry attributes to the event of touch is the play's acknowledgement of political dissensus. While not a disagreement between established groups in any traditional sense, the witchcraft is, instead, 'the production, within a determined, sensible world, of a given that is heterogeneous to it'.[94] Henry juxtaposes the sensation generated by his touch to the sensible, ordered world of 'the tongues of the French Council' and the 'general petition of monarchs' (5.2.256, 258–9).

This comparison returns the play to its opening moments and to the English king's question to his council: 'May I with right and conscience make this claim?' (1.2.96). The sensible world characterised by law, precedent and reason informs the sovereign decision, yet the same historical and juridical claim that produces Catherine as the English's 'capital demand' (5.2.96) assaults the logic of sovereignty – 'may Harry with right and conscience claim Catherine?'. Catherine's sugar touch reduces the assumed efficacy of legal articles that consolidate sovereign power. Westmorland says, 'The King hath granted every article: / His daughter first, and so in sequel all, / According to their firm proposed natures' (5.2.302–4). Yet, the play leaves us with a surrogation of consent, outsourced in the end to her father's voice: 'Take her, fair son [. . .]' (317).[95] Henry and Catherine's surrogates are invested in transforming the effects of exclusion – an unrepresentable barrier, or a fugitive, sutured by touch to sovereignty that magically executes politics that Rancière would describe as 'strictly identical to the law of consensus'.[96] The repetition of the request for consent in the scene underscores the precarious condition of sovereignty – a hard condition that, despite Henry's best efforts, the event of touch throughout the play fails to suture.[97]

The politics of sensation produced in the act of touching Catherine's body emerges as a rupture in the normative allocation of bodies. Henry simply cannot figure out what to do with her. According to Rancière, during a political event, 'the order of distribution of bodies into functions corresponding to their "nature" and places corresponding to their functions is undermined, thrown back on its contingency'.[98] The radical contingency in relation to sovereign hegemony in this scene is fugitive. Politics emerges for a moment, antagonistically exposing the processes of power, not its singular execution, and the play's fugitive politics at this moment transforms the horizon of expectation for what we might term 'resistance'.

In forming a theory of resistance in response to Derrida's work on the crisis of sovereignty, Peggy Kamuf speculates about resistance 'beyond the level of the subject or subjects, beyond performative effectivity in the world'.[99] Ewa Ziarek thinks about resistance in similar ways, shifting the political ethos from 'the liberation of repressed identities to an invention of new modes of life, eroticism, and social relations'.[100] The historical genealogy of a docile female body that informs Catherine's stage presence in the play's final act makes it difficult to suggest, as this chapter has tried to do, that a form of resistance to sovereignty's fantasy of indivisibility energises the scene. When read in light of the touch that unsettles Henry's quest for consent, Catherine's language lesson illustrates the volatility of bodies and the idea, *pace* Butler, that 'embodiment is the materialization of power'.[101] We glimpse Catherine's new form of life, perhaps, in the winks and metaphors that work hard to corral the power of sensibility exposed in her touch, but it is her touch that gestures toward sovereignty's 'dire division'. In the final moments of *Henry V*, Shakespeare doubles down on divided sovereignty, as the quest for 'dear conjunction' (5.2.321) between England and France is conjured, like magic. This magic does not serve a new politics of consensus; instead, it disavows what Henry knows too well – that his royal touch is powerless to make sensible the fugitive condition of a dissensual politics immanent at the core of his, and her, hard condition.

CHAPTER 4

SOVEREIGNTY'S SCRIBBLED FORM IN *KING JOHN*

What government has to do must be identical with what the state should be [. . .] To govern according to the principle of *raison d'État* is to arrange things so that the state becomes sturdy and permanent, so that it becomes wealthy, and so that it becomes strong in the face of everything that may destroy it.

Michel Foucault, *The Birth of Biopolitics*

In a word, bureaucracy can itself function as the key locus of a *radical movement*.

Eric Santner, *The Royal Remains*

It seems to me that something akin to this alluring confusion also characterizes modern bureaucracies. Is it possible that maligned structures are also powerfully attractive to us, that bureaucratic entanglements are also sometimes occasions for enchantment? When enchanted, one is intensively engaged, and dealing with a bureaucracy might very well require high levels of attentiveness.

Jane Bennett, *The Enchantment of Modern Life*

In Chapter 3, we saw how touch in *Henry V* is an acknowledgement of sovereignty's fractured condition; the royal touch fails to suture the divisibility at the core of sovereign power in the play. Catherine's 'sugar touch' (5.2.255) can be read as a usurpation and inversion of the efficacy of royal touch – reducing the majesty of absolute power and exposing its tactical responses to agitating subjects that escape the forceful logic of the sovereign exception. Shakespeare's less popular and rarely performed play *King John* (1596) is also concerned with divided sovereignty, and, as if anticipating the diminutive tactility of a 'little touch of Harry in the night' (4.0.47), the play also expresses its concern about sovereign force through the metaphor of touch. John's legitimacy on the English throne is jeopardised because of the claims of the young Prince Arthur, John's oldest brother's son. In a response to the French king Philip's willingness to forego Arthur's rightful claim in order to ally with John, Constance, Arthur's mother and surrogate for her son's claim to power, says, 'You have beguiled me with a counterfeit / Resembling majesty, which, being touched and tried, / Proves valueless' (3.1.25–7). Calling the royal union a trick that only appears majestic, Constance's rejection of Philip and John's alliance evokes tactility – 'being touched and tried' – as one way to determine kingship's legitimacy.

King John literalises Constance's metaphoric critique of the indivisible bond that characterises sovereignty in its depiction of a foreign policy predicated on the strategic alliance between England and France animated by a sovereign touch that consolidates the geopolitical friendship. The play describes this type of foreign policy as 'the conjunction of our inward souls / Married in league, coupled and linked together' (3.1.153–4), confirmed with a 'deep-sworn faith, peace, amity, true love' (158) between kingdoms 'and our royal selves' (158). Amity between rival kings guarantees sovereignty's survival in the play, yet, as our discussion of the friendship between Coriolanus and Aufidius in Chapter 2 demonstrates, the desire for friendship to produce consensus and accord only disavows the fugitive condition of politics that I am arguing Shakespeare depicts on the London stage.

More than any other of Shakespeare's history plays, *King John* explicitly describes sovereignty in language that reveals its divisible, fragile absolutism. In the play's opening exchange, Shakespeare initiates a critique of sovereign power that is the play's central focus. In Châtillon's message to King John and his mother, Queen Eleanor, in act 1, the French embassy challenges the lawful majesty of English sovereignty. He describes John's crown as 'borrowed majesty', a phrase that puzzles the queen: 'A strange beginning,' she says, '"borrowed majesty"' (1.1.4, 5). King John's legitimacy as the rightful English king is the play's historical focus, and challenges to his royal authority from France and Rome comprise the play's dramatic tension. The play, however, consistently returns to the image of a fraudulent or divided sovereignty and in the process makes the status of kingship, irrespective of the legitimate claims of any nation-state, its philosophical obsession. Indeed, the contested crown is at different moments in the play described as a 'scribbled form' (5.6.32), a 'bawd' (2.1.583; 2.2.259, 260), 'usurped authority' (3.1.86), 'perjured' (3.1.33), and 'dangerous majesty' (4.2.214); its divisibility is characterised in the mirror image of the crown 'resembling majesty' (3.1.26) or as 'double majesties' (2.1.481). In a play that literalises sovereign excess with its multiple kings conjoined by a precarious, even enchanting friendship that only temporarily sutures division and discord, sovereign power is divided and distributed to subjects in new and imaginative ways.[1]

With the character of the Bastard as its critical focus, this chapter on *King John* revisits the force of divisible sovereignty through the concept of bureaucracy. The Weberian account of bureaucracy, describing it as an iron cage and a necessary evil, would seem to call into question Eric Santner's claim in this chapter's epigraph about its radical potential. According to Weber, a bureaucracy is like a machine with 'non-mechanical modes of production': 'Precision, speed, unambiguity, knowledge of the files, continuity, discretion, unity, self-subordination, reduction of friction and of material and personal costs – these are raised to the optimum level in the bureaucratic administration.'[2] The effect of the bureaucratic machine, according to Weber, is alienation, dehumanisation and an eradication of anything that resembles an agentive political form of life. Indeed, absolute royal power is attenuated but no less potent in this bureaucratic frame, and its persistence in a Weberian bureaucracy would seem to prevent what Jane Bennett describes as other potentially 'magical or charismatic modes of authority'.[3]

As a corrective to accounts of bureaucracy that totalise its negative effects, I argue that a play like *King John* explores the effects of an attenuated, bureaucratic sovereignty that gives rise to a political subject confined by its iron cage but also energised and mobilised by its structure.[4] Reflected in the autonomy of the wilful Bastard and informed by the legal and cultural status of bastardy in Elizabethan England, bureaucracy in the play is an ambivalent structural foil to absolute sovereignty, tenuously positioned relative to the absolute state to expand the parameters of sovereign authority even as it defines a new political dispensation with potential to denude the threat of the sovereign exception. Edward Gieskes's account of the growth of professions in Elizabethan England emphasises this point. He shows how social transition in early modernity – the shift from medieval notions of sovereignty to modern configurations of state power – gives rise to the 'transformation of authority of traditional elites and the growth of new groups, like the professions, with claims to at least part of that authority'.[5] The eroding efficacy of touch in *Henry V* that expresses the vicissitudes of theo-politics of sovereign power is radically redistributed in *King John* along the lines that Gieskes suggests. Depicting foreign policy through the illegitimacy of the rhetoric of royal friendship, the play demonstrates how geopolitics based on comity between friends is insufficient to account for the collateral effects of sovereign power that early modern bureaucracy, in the character of the Bastard, begins to manage.

Despite its modern connotations associating it with totalitarianism and imposing complexity, the word 'bureaucracy' has a medieval origin. It derives from the medieval French *burel*, which were the cloths that covered the tables on which administrators worked.[6] Early modern bureaucracy built upon efforts in the fifteenth century to relocate official state business away from the king's household or court and into what some historians consider an independent administrative service. According to G. R. Elton's influential thesis, the shift from household government to an increasingly depersonalised administration represents the central development in Tudor government.[7] A. L. Brown's substantial study of governance in late medieval England confirms the claim that there was a shift in administrative work from the king's household to Westminster offices. He describes the nature of the new bureaucrat: 'The "civil servants" who worked there, still mostly clerics but increasingly career laymen, knew all about "proper channels" and authorizations, due caution, precise accuracy of statement and all the trappings of a literate, professional administration.'[8] Since Brown, other scholars point to the appearance of professionalised and independent administrators trained for work outside of the royal household. A class of 'centralizing agents', or 'ministeriales', emerged; these agents functioned simultaneously in patrimonial (feudal) and bureaucratic officialdom.[9]

This new system of state organisation at Westminster away from the king's court created an enormous archive of state documents. By the mid-fourteenth century, West-minster offices were justifiably described as bureaucratic.[10] Thirty to forty thousand letters were being issued each year by the offices in the king's name on the authority of nameless officials, not by the king or his Council. With the proliferation of written letters, the day-to-day workings of the state became 'parchment-bound'.[11] Copies of loose documents were kept in files and on parchment rolls some-times in duplicate and triplicate.[12] No longer considered as the products of a single authorial figure,[13] these docu-ments point to a bureaucracy operating in a 'semi-auton-omous cultural space' characterised by the 'diffusion of state power into forms incomprehensible to the outsider'.[14] The agents became mercenary, resembling the 'accidental agents' in Hannah Arendt's influential account of bureau-cracy.[15] In his study of the development of early modern bureaucracy, Gieskes makes the case 'demand for trained administrators in the Queen's government led to the growth of an administrative profession'.[16] Characterising his new association with sovereign power as being a 'bastard to the time' (1.1.207), the Bastard in *King John* identifies himself as this new type of agent to the Crown. The identity of this 'accidental agent' is productively unnatural in that, like the Bastard, he is able to act politically not out of a filial loy-alty to power identified by knightly clothes and a coat of arms – 'Exterior form, outward accoutrement' (211) – but from 'inward motion' (212). As an accidental agent with an inward motion that determines his actions, the Bastard commodifies his will, the 'sway of motion' (2.1.579) that he comes to worship by act 2 after the political alliance between England and France.

The Bastard embodies what Brown describes as 'a profes-sional world of skilled men who understood the traditional, technical work of their offices and of government as a whole, who hired out their professional services, who schemed for rewards and promotion'.[17] Extending Brown's historical account of this new class of skilled men, Gieskes identifies a reallocation of the educational capital of the Tudor trained civil servants to a 'bureaucratic capital' that the Bastard embodies, securing his power in government. This community was in its early stage of development, 'its boundaries still in the process of definition' and its relationship to sovereignty still very much in question.[18]

In relation to sovereign power in *King John*, the Bastard illustrates that there was much more to the 'agency of the state than the monarchical will'.[19] Bureaucratic formulations in early modern political systems included state administration, functional officials and a hierarchical organisation of departmental responsibilities.[20] Elton notes that the Tudors knew how to ensure efficient government by controlling a network of obligation and patronage. Richard Stewart's study of the English Ordinance Office between 1585 and 1625 argues that constant war preparations forced the English bureaucracy during Elizabeth's reign to advance significantly from its original condition, which had remained fairly unchanged for nearly two centuries before 1585.[21] Spain's threat to England's security and the improvement of arms and munitions during the sixteenth century forced the government to organise well in advance of any military engagement, and the logistical planning and implementation created a new, more sophisticated bureaucratic framework than ever before experienced. Another location in Tudor state building where bureaucratic formations were evident is the development of vagrancy laws during the sixteenth century. Linda Woodbridge identifies several examples of English policy-making that result in bureaucratic structures, including 'the mechanics of the Reformation' and the Crown's 'suppression of local saints' cults'.[22] She concludes that bureaucratic formations constituted by the Tudor Poor Laws 'forged the modern, federal state'.[23]

The development of bureaucratic networks meant that, on one level, sovereignty's power and reach had potentially expanded, but, on another level, the personal power of the sovereign ironically had been diminished.[24] As the early modern bureaucratic apparatus expanded, individuals like Shakespeare's Bastard, who exercises his office and in the process lays claim to a form of life derived from the legacy of theo-politics that both empowers and constrains him, increasingly come to navigate within the limits and possibilities of fractured sovereignty temporarily sutured, in the case of *King John*, by geopolitical friendship.[25]

Both Are Alike; And Both Alike We Like

The rhetoric of friendship is the discourse of foreign policy in *King John*. Until act 2, scene 1, when the Bastard presents friendship between England and France as a strategy to gain entrance into the city of Angiers, the play depicts rival sovereigns contesting legitimate kingship. The language of legitimacy makes sovereign divisibility the play's primary concern, yet it deflects its own critique of kingship by staging the battle for proper English sovereignty as a foreign policy dispute with France. Châtillon's dismissal of John's legitimacy as 'borrowed majesty' (1.1.4), a product of a sword that 'sways usurpingly' (13) over England properly ruled by 'young Arthur's hand' (14), establishes the precise nature of the conflict destined to end in 'fierce and bloody war' (17) if John fails to surrender the throne. John's response to Philip's French emissary makes the battle for legitimate sovereignty seem inevitable: 'Here we have war for war, and blood for blood, / Controlment for controlment: so answer France' (19–20). With rival claims to the throne so clearly defining the diplomatic landscape, the geopolitical posturing taking shape in the play's earliest moments overshadows its more pressing critique of the general condition of sovereignty echoed in the Citizen's equivocating defence of Angiers. The Citizen responds to demands from France and England to choose the legitimate sovereign or risk annihilation:

> KING JOHN. Whose party for the townsmen yet admit?
> KING PHILIP. Speak, citizens, for England: who's your king?
> CITIZEN. The King of England, when we know the King.
> KING PHILIP. Know him in us, that here hold up his right.
> KING JOHN. In us, that are our own great deputy
> And bear possession of our person here,
> Lord of our presence, Angiers, and of you.
> CITIZEN. A greater power than we denies all this,
> And, till it be undoubted, we do lock
> Our former scruple in our strong-barred gates,
> Kinged of our fear, until our fears resolved
> Be by some certain king, purged and deposed.   (2.1.361–72)

The Citizen's riddling response – 'King of England, when we know the King' (363) – adds a temporal dimension to kingship, deferring the emergence of legitimate sovereignty in the play. Postponing with 'strong-barred gates' (370) the arrival of a 'certain king' (372), the Citizen's refusal to confirm sovereignty's indivisibility and to solve the 'undetermined differences of kings' (355) is evidence of what Jacques Lezra calls the motility of division immanent in sovereignty itself, compounding and clarifying the effect of this divisibility with the historical crisis of royal legitimacy.[26] The battle between England and France at Angiers over legitimate sovereignty externalises the division at the core of kingship, and friendship is the play's response to suture the wound.

The Bastard introduces friendship in the play as prudent political strategy in act 2. He asks John and Philip to '[b]e friends awhile and both conjointly bend / Your sharpest deeds of malice' on Angiers (379–80). According to the Bastard's advice, once the two forces joined by sovereign amity conquer Angiers, with its citizens described as 'naked as the vulgar air' (387), the kings can 'dissever' their 'united strengths / And part your mingled colors once again' (388–9). The Bastard's 'wild counsel' (395) is informed by the same politics of friendship that I argue in Chapter 2 explains the relationship between Coriolanus and Aufidius, described as a 'strange alteration' (4.5.147) by the servingman. The Bastard's 'wild counsel' proposes a union between enemies that redefines political friendship, making it a political tactic that exceeds friendship's claims of consensus in its very application as a policy which houses its own necessary dissolution. Páraic Finnerty argues that the rhetoric of friendship in *King John* offers 'rectifying alternatives to the play's ever-shifting expedient political alliances'.[27] According to Finnerty, the play's insistent disruption of the bonds of friendship 'divides England, opening it up to the threat of foreign invasion'.[28] Finnerty's argument assumes an indivisible sovereignty somehow made even more indivisible by the supplement that friendship with France provides. Friendship in the play, however, appears to shore up sovereignty's wounded majesty while marking the fundamental fracture in sovereignty's 'mad composition' (2.1.562).

Producing a new form of sovereignty described by the Bastard as a 'mad composition', friendship serves as the prosthesis that sutures divisibility. In using the term 'prosthesis' in this context, I draw on the early modern use of the word as a rhetorical trope. Thomas Wilson's *Arte of Rhetorique* (1553) uses the word 'prosthesis' to describe a linguistic composition in which a new word is formed with the addition of a syllable:

Of addition. As thus: he did all to berattle hum. Prosthesis. Wherein appereth that a sillable is added to this worde (rattle.)[29]

In his innovative account of the first appearance of 'prosthesis' in English, David Wills notes the ornamental quality of
the word in the margins of the text – an ornamentality that
captures the supplementary quality of the rhetorical device.[30]
Wills's conclusion about the effect of amputated and artificial
body parts in early modern medical discourse emphasises an
emergent discourse challenging the sovereignty of the natural
body while working to create the impression of wholeness
or integrity. Records of amputations and prostheses 'make
explicit the very break that constitutes the human body;
the mechanistic rupture that is its relation to and dependence upon the inanimate, the artificial. [. . .] [Prosthesis]
represents the monstrosity of interfering with the integrity
of the human body, the act of unveiling the unnatural within
the natural.'[31] Put otherwise, in a manner consistent with the
trope of the prosthetic paradox, friendship in *King John* sup-
plies the deficiency in the logic of sovereign power – that
is, it both makes absolute power singular *and* exposes its
divisibility.[32] Through the act of friendship, the body of the
sovereign in Shakespeare's play is made to appear whole,
and the precarious balance between the king's two bodies –
literalised by the play's geopolitical alliance between England
and France – appears intact.

Friendship, however, initially enters the play with a different purpose. The Bastard's policy of dissensus, which uses
friendship within an antagonistic, not prosthetic, model of
politics, is at first embraced by King John, who says, 'I like it
well. France, shall we knit our powers / And lay this Angers
even to the ground; / Then after fight who shall be king of
it?' (2.1.398–400). Here, friendship is not a suture for the
division at the core of the play's 'double majesties' (481); it
only redistributes the antagonism that indicates divisibility.
The play amplifies the paradox of friendship, however, at
the precise moment that the Bastard plots to reallocate its

ameliorative impulse to generate further violence. Describing the military logic of their union that will result in England's enemies inadvertently firing at each other, the Bastard says, 'O prudent discipline! From north to south / Austria and France shoot in each other's mouth. / I'll stir them to it' (414–16). The Citizen of Angiers, however, immediately proposes peace by 'fair-faced league' (418) that will win the city without violence. In language that naturalises this union, which the Bastard's proposal presents as contingent and temporary, the Citizen recommends marriage between Lady Blanche and Louis the Dauphin. He describes the perfectly balanced equation of their inevitable union:

> He is the half part of a blessed man,
> Left to be finished by such as she;
> And she a fair divided excellence,
> Whose fullness of perfection lies in him.
> O, two such silver currents, when they join,
> Do glorify the banks that bound them in;
> And two such shores to two such streams made one,
> Two such controlling bounds shall you be, kings,
> To these two princes, if you marry them.   (438–46)

Echoing the logic of the beehive metaphor in *Henry V*, explored in Chapter 3, that attempts to produce an image of union from difference and particularity, the couple's 'divided excellence' gives way to 'fullness of perfection', a union of different currents with a singular force, bound and magnified by the banks of one river. As if understanding the fragile condition of a politics of friendship, the Citizen's rhetoric of love usurps the Bastard's rhetoric of friendship, confounding political policy. The condition of sovereign amity is altered as friendship shifts from enemies who 'knit' (398) their powers 'conjointly' (379) to a 'knot' (471) between lovers that 'congeal[s]' (480) the division between the two kings. Claiming that he is 'bethumped with words' (467),[33] the Bastard understands the consequences of this shift in the rhetoric of friendship: politics vanishes once the antagonism fundamental to its condition disappears.[34] For him, the structure of power that enables politics has changed irrevocably at this point. He is left as an observer of the play's action – a fugitive without political consequence – until Pandolf, the pope's legate from Rome, enters to dismantle the political consensus achieved by a friendship that appears natural, even sacred.[35] The play gives shape and form to the surplus of irreducible division in the figure of the Cardinal, who eventually severs the alliance.

As an interloper in the friendship between John and Philip, Pandolf literally seeks to break the tactile bond of friendship – to undo the prosthetic relationship between sovereigns. The hand that unites John and Philip – England and France – and that makes sovereignty complete emerges as the scene's central image; the force of the royal touch examined in Chapter 3 is doubled in an act that unifies sovereign power.[36] That is, an ailing English king is cured by the royal touch of a French king ironically made whole by that same sovereign touch. Recognising the power of their tactile alliance, Pandolf orders Philip: 'Let go the hand of that arch-heretic, / And raise the power of France upon his head, / Unless he do submit himself to Rome' (3.1.118–20); Philip responds to Pandolf's order to end the friendship with England in language that draws attention to its tactile force:

This royal hand and mine are newly knit,
And the conjunction of our inward souls
Married in league, coupled and linked together
With all religious strength of sacred vows;
The latest breath that gave the sound of words
Was deep-sworn faith, peace, amity, true love,
Between our kingdoms and our royal selves   (3.1.152–8)

He describes their hands in religious terms – 'purged of blood' (165) and 'joined in love' (166) – and asks how their bond of friendship might ever be severed, 'palm from palm' (170). Described as a 'royal bargain of peace' (161), their royal touch ensures the continuing friendship that is the pre-condition for a politics of accord imagined as a unified, indivisible sovereignty of which I argue the play is critical. Once Philip releases John's hand, the politics of friendship that sutures royal division proves inadequate. Philip says, 'England, I will fall from thee' (246), announcing the return of a fugitive politics – a majesty banished from itself, 'both alike' (2.1.338) yet wounded by the 'undetermined differences of kings' (2.1.355).

The scandal of the friendship between John and Philip can be seen in how it begins to secularise the royal touch that affirms their alliance. The return of a politics of discord, then, is also the reassertion of political theology in the play that had begun to define sovereign relations outside of a theo-political framework. Called a 'royal bargain' (3.1.161), Philip's relationship with Rome is countered by John's disdain for the pope. John expresses this disdain upon meeting Pandolf:

> What earthly name to interrogatories
> Can task the free breath of a sacred king?
> Thou canst not, Cardinal, devise a name
> So slight, unworthy, and as ridiculous
> To charge me to an answer, as the Pope.	(3.1.73–7)

Part of the challenge in reading *King John* is in pinpointing the play's politics in the sea of shifting relationships and agendas.[37] The pope's 'usurped authority' claimed by John (3.1.86) is also John's usurped authority at issue throughout the play, and the distinction between the sacred and the profane seems to collapse. Refusing to linger long in a

world usurped of its theo-politics, the play seems to respond
to this disenchantment through a form of the sacrament.
In response to Pandolf's threat to excommunicate him if he
does not break his bond with John, Philip refers to the Holy
Eucharist:

> Play fast and loose with faith? so jest with heaven,
> Make such unconstant children of ourselves,
> As now again to snatch our palm from palm,
> Unswear faith sworn, and on the marriage-bed
> Of smiling peace to march a bloody host,
> And make a riot on the gentle brow
> Of true sincerity? O, holy sir,
> My reverend father, let it not be so!
> Out of your grace, devise, ordain, impose
> Some gentle order; and then we shall be blest
> To do your pleasure and continue friends.   (168–78)

He describes the union forged by sovereign friendship as a
'marriage-bed / Of smiling peace' (71–2) desecrated by the
march of a 'bloody host' (72). Pandolf's order disrupts peace,
according to Philip, like an invading army or 'bloody host',
which is generally how the bloody host is understood. The
host is also, however, a consecrated wafer offered in the sacrament of the Eucharist. The appearance of the bloody host
at this moment, as Rome disrupts the new royal alliance that
pushes theological difference to the background in favour of
a politics of friendship, reasserts the political theology that
characterises early modern English sovereignty.

Despite Philip's description of his relationship to John in
terms of a sacramental marriage – 'conjunction of our inward
souls' (153), '[m]arried in league' (154), and linked together
with the 'religious strength of sacred vows' (155) – the violated marriage bed profaned by the bloody host is already
a bawdy one, according to Constance, who claims before

Pandolf arrives that Fortune has 'tread down fair respect of sovereignty' (2.2.58), making France 'the bawd' (59) to English majesty. The Bastard uses the same word to help make sense of the new alliance in act 2: 'this commodity / This bawd, this broker, this all-changing word' (2.1.582–3).[38] The royal touch that embodies their alliance is depicted in the Bastard's language as corrupt like relics or sacramentals, cult objects that often escape the control and purview of the church and enter popular circulation as love charms. Indeed, Pandolf intends to trade in this type of holy economic market, promising to bless the hand that rebels against the alliance between France and England: 'meritorious shall that hand be called / Canonized and worshipped as a saint, / That takes away by any secret course / Thy hateful life' (3.1.102–5). A promise to turn the hand of a royal assassin into a sacred commodity, 'worshipped as a saint' (103), Pandolf's threat situates kingship far removed from the force of the exception that defines its singular force.

The Cardinal clearly imagines a form of sovereignty circumscribed by the theo-juridical boundaries that justify its authority. 'There's law and warranty, Lady,' the Cardinal says to Constance, 'for my curse' (3.1.110). At this point, the play seems sceptical of a political theology defined by any relationship with Rome, and the bawdy politics that define the Bastard's new relationship to the crown seem to inform Pandolf's brokered relationship to sovereign power. The Bastard's vow to worship the brokered 'gain' of commodity is refused in John's condemnation of the 'juggling witchcraft with revenue' that seduces the 'kings of Christendom' (3.1.95, 98). In both, however, a new form of sovereignty emerges seemingly divested of its sacred theological force. The political theology that gives ritual potency to the sovereign exception transforms instead into political *oikonomia* – a form of sovereignty that is 'capable only of economy, not politics'[39] and, as Giorgio Agamben suggests in *The Kingdom and the Glory*, that is ultimately bureaucratic.

The shift from a theory of theo-political sovereignty to bureaucracy is in part a response to Giorgio Agamben's link between political theology, economy and governmentality. As an addendum to Schmitt's well-known assertion that '[a]ll significant concepts of the modern theory of the state are secularized concepts',[40] Agamben proposes a supplement. His elaboration on Schmitt's secularisation thesis imports the concept of political theology from the figure of the sovereign to the economy, implying that 'from the beginning theology conceives divine life and the history of humanity as an *oikonomia*, that is, that theology is itself "economic" and did not simply become so at a later time through secularization'.[41] For Agamben, the significance of economic theology is that it reveals 'that history is ultimately not a political but an "administrative" and "governmental" problem'.[42] He describes the double structure of power emerging from its theological origins. On one level, power is characterised by its governmentality, its authority and execution; on another level it is characterised by its sovereignty, the way it unifies force and act. Agamben summarises the conflict between these two forms of state power:

> the first is still dominated by the old model of territorial sovereignty, which reduces the double articulation of the governmental machine to a purely formal moment; the second is closer to the new economico-providential paradigm, in which the two elements maintain their identity, in spite of their correlation, and the contingency of the acts of government corresponds to the freedom of the sovereign decision [. . .] Insofar as it structurally exceeds ordered power [*potenza ordinata*], absolute power [*potenza assoluta*] is – not only in God, but in every agent [. . .] – that which allows one to act legitimately 'beyond the law and against it'.[43]

Working to disambiguate administrative power from sovereign, theo-political absolutism, much of Agamben's thinking about governmentality and absolutism comes from Michel Foucault's 1977–78 seminar *Security, Territory, Population*. Foucault identifies governmentality in terms of the legal, penal, and security systems that take shape in response to the modern state of population. Governmentality for Foucault functions according to 'logics' that illustrate that the '"how" of power is as important as "who" has power'.[44] Governmentality manages and distributes populations, according to Foucault, through various institutional contexts for instrumental purposes, but always exercises its force indirectly. Agency in Foucault's theory of governmentality is an impersonal force; as Jonathan Sterne points out, 'governmentality itself *acts*'.[45]

Foucault's governmental model of institutional power leads critics such as Tony Bennett to posit bureaucratic techniques of power as viable tools for political action.[46] This reading links Foucault's governmentality with bureaucracy in its efficiency and function, and although it views the political effects of bureaucracy differently, it is consistent with Max Weber's influential argument that bureaucratic logic abstracts function from outcome, objectively discharged according to '*calculable rules*'.[47] As in Schmitt's equation, the rise in governmentality in Foucault's formulation corresponds to the decline in the theo-political power of the sovereign. In an amplification of Schmitt's secularisation thesis, Foucault writes, 'While I have been speaking about population a word has constantly recurred [. . .] and this is the word "government". The more I have spoken about population, the more I have stopped saying "sovereign".'[48] Foucault locates a shift in the sixteenth century corresponding to scientific discovery as the moment in which the theo-political sovereign ceases to govern in a pastoral sense – as in a government of souls – in favour of political power 'in a sovereign manner through principles'.[49] Agamben traces the division much deeper. For him, the division is immanent at the origin of the Trinitarian *oikonomia*, which, according to Agamben, 'introduces a fracture between being and praxis in the deity himself'.[50] Agamben explains in detail the consequences of this fracture:

> The government of the world occurs neither by means of the tyrannical imposition of an external general will, nor by accident, but through the knowing anticipation of the collateral effects that arise from the very nature of things and remain absolutely contingent in their singularity. Thus, what appeared to be a marginal phenomenon or a secondary effect becomes the very paradigm of the act of government.[51]

The materiality of power's collateral effects and of the sovereign exception that generates those effects implies divided sovereignty. The potential for a Weberian outcome of bureaucratic state power is very much a constant possibility and is articulated most influentially in Arendt's treatise on totalitarianism. Arendt describes a bureaucratic state in Weberian terms: 'government by decree [. . .] becomes the direct source of all legislation', remaining anonymous and therefore seeming 'to flow from some over-all ruling power that needs no justification'.[52] However, the Bastard's wilful autonomy in *King John* in relation to the play's sovereign geopolitical friendship suggests that bureaucratic formations also produce a divided sovereignty.

Where Lezra associated this form of divisible sovereignty with radical republicanism, Agamben links it to the force of democracy – calling the 'providential-economical paradigm' a 'paradigm of democratic power': 'just as the theological-political is the paradigm of absolutism [. . .] The economic-governmental vocation of contemporary democracies is not something that has happened accidentally, but is a constitutive part of the theological legacy of which they are the depositaries.'[53] With the status of sovereignty so uncertain in the play, the Bastard emerges as a character touched by yet simultaneously beyond the reach of the sovereign exception, and his survival hints at the emergence of a bureaucratic form of power that ignores the pressures of politics defined by a 'deep-sworn faith, peace, amity, [and] true love' (3.1.162) between kingdoms and sovereigns. He represents a new and dynamic site of the dispersal of sovereign power, capable of operating in the paradoxical space within a perpetual state of exception in which the Bastard is power's accidental agent but complicit in sovereignty's radical transformation from the potency of the exception to the efficacy of administration and execution.

Mad World! Mad Kings! Mad Composition!

In a play where the central concern is the exercise of legitimate power – power between families, between individuals, between nations, between the crown and its subjects – the first appearance of Philip the Bastard in act 1 engages nearly all the claimants who vie for legitimacy during the course of *King John*. With his first words, the Bastard identifies himself to the king as 'Your faithful subject I, a gentleman' (1.1.30). His position as 'faithful subject' to the king normalises his relationship to sovereignty, and his claim to be 'a gentleman' places him in a struggle for aristocratic legitimacy with Robert Faulconbridge, who wants to deny him the royal patrimony that they both seek. The Bastard's first appearance comes immediately after King John all but declares war on France, weaving England's claims for legitimate action against its rival nation with the Bastard's own assertion of 'strong possession' (39). The scene of the Bastard's introduction suggests that legitimation can normalise relationships and justify action, but late in act

1 the Bastard recognises the tenuous status of legitimacy: 'Legitimation, name, and all is gone' (248). Only after he realises that he is King Richard Coeur-de-lion's illegitimate son does he begin to recognise the 'privilege' (261) that comes with bastardy. Originating from the loss of the very legitimacy that all parties seem to covet early in the play, the force of that 'privilege' is animated by a bureaucratic form of power that redistributes sovereignty, accentuating its fractured condition. With its representation of a king who becomes nothing more than a 'scribbled form, drawn with a pen' (5.7.32), *King John* deconstructs the sovereign exception in its depiction of the powerful claims of an emerging bureaucratic network of authority exemplified by the Bastard's 'madcap' (1.1.84) relationship to his past, his crown and his country.

There is something disingenuous about the Bastard's supplicating posture at the end of *King John* that appears to incorporate him unequivocally into the state: 'To whom, with all submission, on my knee, / I do bequeath my faithful services / And true subjection everlastingly' (5.7.103–5). The Bastard's contrary self-assertion early in the play, 'I am I, howe'er I was begot' (1.1.175), still resonates in the end, and its echo, I submit, is a sign of the play's ambivalence over sovereign absolutism that creates such unease in critics who want to claim that the Bastard has been rein-scribed by sovereign power at the end of act 5.[54] The Bastard's claim of self-identity, which effaces kinship and other familial bonds, echoes another famous Shakespearean 'bastard', Richard III. With its mirroring structure, Richard's claim, 'Richard loves Richard; that is, I am I' (5.3.185), creates the image of a hermetically sealed monarch who exists in a royal echo chamber. Richard's solipsistic self-assertion resembles the Bastard's statement to his queen: 'I am I, howe'er I was begot'. That Richard's self-assertion marks the king's earthly end while the Bastard's proclamation indicates a nascent moment in his new relationship with sovereignty is the critical difference between them. This difference points to a bureaucratic body politic in *King John* of which bastardy and illegitimacy are critical, a priori conditions for growth. From his earliest moments on the stage, the Bastard gives us glimpses of a skilled bureaucrat. Far from being reinscribed by orthodoxy at the play's end, the Bastard in fact usurps an increasingly diffused sovereign power creating a new political dispensation based on potent bureaucratic efficiency emerging during the time of *King John*'s composition.[55]

Shakespeare explores other articulations of sovereign power in his plays before *King John*. Looking again at *Richard III*, for example, a play written perhaps two years before *King John*, a peculiar short scene serves as a salient introduction to the way *King John* reallocates sovereign power to new bureaucratic forms. Near the end of the third act of *Richard III*, a Scrivener with 'a paper in his hand' (3.6. s.d.) enters the stage; his role in scribing 'in a set hand' (2) the legal indictment of Hastings comprises the entirety of the scene. The Scrivener's scene, with its emphasis on writing, documenting, and delimiting functions of other characters, gives the audience of the early modern drama a glimpse at the bureaucratic process:

> Here is the indictment of the good Lord Hastings;
> Which in a set hand fairly is engrossed,
> That it may be today read o'er in Paul's:
> And mark how well the sequel hangs together.
> Eleven hours I have spent to write it over,
> For yesternight by Catesby was it sent me.
> The precedent was full as long a doing;
> And yet within these five hours Hastings lived,
> Untainted, uncontaminated, free, at liberty.   (1–9)

For the Scrivener, Hastings's death is not the product of Richard's passion or despotism, but of the double time of transcribing the sequel of the death warrant sent to him by Catesby – a sequel that will be 'fairly [. . .] engrossed', sufficiently accurate and ornate so as to be publicly presented as an order of execution. Curiously, the source of the death warrant is absent in the Scrivener's soliloquy, and the language that describes Catesby's delivery of the indictment suggests an effect of the written order that dislocates it from agency, responsibility and specificity. The Scrivener describes the process by which he acquired the document in notably passive terms – 'For yesternight by Catesby was it sent me' (7) – and though the Scrivener's words near the end of his short scene appear a rhetorical lament about the nature of the social unrest during Richard's consolidation of power, his question 'Who is so gross / That cannot see this palpable device?' (10–11) quite literally suggests a dislocation of singular authority or, at least, the possibility that authority in the play does not emanate solely from Richard. In other words, when the Scrivener points to the 'palpable device', he describes a warrant that is itself a technology of execution – a 'device' with the performative authority to condemn a subject to death; the order is 'palpable' in that its effects are immediate and clear. The 'palpable device' here is interchangeable with royal authority, yet ironically it derives its potency from royal absence. As a reproduceable document, it demonstrates a proliferation of the king's power at the same time that it registers the absence of the royal body.

It is worth speculating that the Scrivener's scene articulates concerns about authority, kingship and power that would resonate in the minds of Shakespeare's audience. Marjorie Garber writes of the tension produced in the scene and in the historical record that it translates: 'Like the disparity between the "truth" of Shakespeare's play and the historical figure it encodes, the "palpable device" of the long-prepared indictment and the apparent history of Hastings's demise opens the question of authority.'[56] Describing the transformation of power during the emergence of a modern state, Jacqueline Rose suggests that subject formation is intimately linked to the fantasy of royal authority and to the reality of new forms of political power: 'Once real authority is no longer invested in the prince and his trappings, it loses its face and disembodies itself [. . .] The modern state enacts its authority as ghostly, fantasmatic authority.'[57] In language that might inform how we understand the Scrivener's scene, Arendt describes the emergence of a bureaucratic administrator who 'considers the law to be powerless because it is by definition separated from its application'; instead, the administrator responds to decrees that only exist at all when they are applied – decrees 'need no justification except applicability'.[58] The Scrivener's scene, with its emphasis on the fantasy and effacement of royal authority, takes as its subject the changes in absolute sovereignty that Rose and Arendt associate with the advent of a bureaucratic state.

In *King John*, the fate of Arthur, the young prince, speaks directly to the issues raised by the Scrivener's scene. Hubert, one of John's followers, is expected to carry out the king's most heinous decree – to burn out both of Arthur's eyes with hot irons. The 'palpable device' reappears as a writ ordering the torture. Arthur encounters royal authority as a written document. As Arthur reads the king's command, Hubert asks him, 'Can you not read it? Is it not fair writ?' (4.1.37). Shakespeare again makes a point to show disembodied sovereignty, and Hubert, like *Richard III*'s Scrivener, is resistant to and abstracted from the king's power. In an interesting historical analogue, Hubert's rejection of the royal order to kill Arthur seems to be a direct counterpoint to the Cecilian bureaucracy's efforts to execute Mary Queen of Scots when Elizabeth wished the opposite. And Hubert's question about the legibility of the king's order is suggestive of concerns about the warrant that sanctioned Mary's eventual execution in 1587. Drawing on Elizabeth's own rhetorical ambiguity in speeches to Parliament during the months before Mary's death, Lowell Gallagher describes the legal document ordering her execution as a 'warrant warrantless' that achieves for Elizabeth a level of unaccountability in relation to the events surrounding Mary's death.[59] The famous events surrounding the execution provide examples of bureaucracy growing more and more abstracted from royal authority. *King John* adopts as its central concern those anxieties about the face of authority: more fully than the Scrivener, the Bastard – with both his 'wild counsel' (2.1.95) and 'true subjection' (5.7.105) – embodies the range of possibility in a new bureaucratic relationship between the subject and sovereign.

A Madcap Hath Heaven Lent Us Here

Philip the Bastard's proclamation of identity in the first act of *King John* seems a logical, but futile, self-defence in a political space which demarcates identity with legal codes and cultural tradition. Perhaps such a sanguine proclamation – 'I am I, howe'er I was begot' – is utterable at all only because the Bastard has just been knighted, and assertions of self are always made easier when the cultural apparatus acknowledges one's fashioned identity. To be sure, it is easier for the Bastard to claim pride in his natural issue once its peripheral bloodline has been changed to Plantagenet lineage. However, the debate over the Bastard's origins

suggests the complexities involved in grafting a fixed identity on to an otherwise labile figure in the play and within
early modern culture more generally.

In scene 3 of the same act, John sends the Bastard to
collect money for the war effort. John exhorts the Bastard
to '[u]se our commission in [. . .] utmost force' to 'shake the
bags / Of hoarding abbots' (3.3.11, 7–8). During the next
scene, the audience learns that the Bastard '[i]s now in England ransacking the Church, / Offending charity' (3.4.171–2).
This pattern, which highlights the Bastard's complete inhab-
iting of new identity, continues in act 4. John tells the Bastard
to search for Lord Bigot and Lord Salisbury, and he immediately and successfully seeks them out (4.3.22). And in perhaps his most significant moment of bureaucratic efficiency,
the Bastard responds to the king's order at the opening of
act 5 to confront Pandolf. By the end of act 3, it is clear that
the Bastard has redefined his relationship to his king. Unlike
his earlier appearances that show him as both politically and
socially inept, when the Bastard hears King John declare war
on the French, he performs with alacrity and efficiency the
responsibilities of his office. A pattern emerges in which royal
decrees are immediately followed by reports of the Bastard's
successful response. In theatrical time, it takes only a scene
for the Bastard to emerge bloody, having executed the king's
command to 'go draw our puissance together' (3.1.340). He
enters the next scene holding Austria's head, suggesting both
a consolidation of forces and a renewed commitment to war.
The audience also learns in his report to the king that he has
rescued John's mother from certain danger. Having antici-
pated the request to attend to the royal mother, the Bastard is
able to report that he 'rescued her; / Her Highness is in safety,
fear you not' (3.2.7–8).

The Bastard literally echoes his king's position, becoming
a mouthpiece for kingship: 'Now hear our English King / For
thus his royalty doth speak in me' (5.2.128–9). This claim of

support for the crown comes during a time when the king's health has taken a turn for the worse. In the next scene we learn that the king is dying: 'This fever, that hath troubled me so long, / Lies heavy on me: O! my heart is sick' (5.3.3–4). Because John is dying and his control of the state is dissolving even as the Bastard speaks forcefully for it, the Bastard seems to articulate a relationship with authority not dependent specifically on the presence of John's body. In fact, his passionate defence of English sovereignty in act 5 locates sacred kingship within a bureaucratic body, not the king's. The bureaucratic body that includes and enables theo-political sovereignty is what sustains the Bastard, and the network of bureaucratic sovereignty is the authority to which he gives consent. This network of kingship established in the play and embodied in the Bastard's actions reveals a fundamental reconceptualisation of how a subject relates to sovereign power and authority.[60] On one level, the Bastard's responsive actions sound like the kind of office executed by subordinate agents who carry full sovereign authority, a form of delegated authority rather than a sign of a diffuse and therefore potentially diminished absolutism. On another level, however, his status as a bastard in the play, with its dramatic, legal and cultural signification, complicates this reading that locates him only within the claims of absolutism.

Efforts in *King John* to legitimise the Bastard by locating him in the patrilineal social system create the bureaucratic space from which he develops a new relationship with absolute power. The new relationship has considerable dramatic appeal for playwrights in the period. By the end of the sixteenth and the beginning of the seventeenth century, the figure of the bastard was a presence in as many as fifty-seven plays.[61] Medieval notions of bastardy carried relatively little social stigma; by the end of the twelfth century, the bastard was officially defined as *filius nullius*, a term that functioned primarily to distinguish between those offspring who were entitled to inherit and those who were not.[62] As Michael Neill points out, the *filius nullius* was not the son of nobody, but more accurately the heir of nobody. This relatively benign categorisation remained into the later Middle Ages, even as the church became more censorious. By the sixteenth century, however, a Puritan ethos emerged as the prevalent moral code, and illegitimacy began to incur 'a significant degree of publicly articulated moral opprobrium'.[63] Puritan reformers concerned with moral behaviour, and parish administrators intent on controlling the population of unwanted infants during periods of economic instability, reacted to an apparent rise in the rate of illegitimacy that began during the middle of the sixteenth century and continued up until 1620.

The codes regulating illegitimacy are one method by which domestic and political authority attempted to diffuse the potential threat that a fatherless child represented. Illegitimacy, the absence of a father, was an implicit challenge to gender and class distinctions; a bastard does not fit into the social order. He has no clear identity, no name, and as such he 'presents a threat to the hermetic household for [he] is a free-floating agent held in check by no clear anterior model of paternal authority'.[64] While examinations of the legal codes governing illegitimacy demonstrate one method by which the state simultaneously names otherness as a threat and controls the threat through the act of naming, the network of juridical codes and their appearance in *King John* suggest a more fluid relationship with the crown. As he supports different forms of authority in the play, the Bastard's negotiation of the tensions between a sovereignty defined by the claims of political theology and one shaped by bureaucratic practice highlights his labile and precarious identity.

In the opening act of the play, legal codes fail to contain the threat that the Bastard poses to sovereign power, and John's offer to rename the Bastard for his biological father seems an inadequate response to the potential subversion produced by the madcap's unnatural birth. The reallocation of sovereign force initiated by the bastard's shifting identity, combined with his survival in the play, signals the emergence of a bureaucratic authority that separates law from its application. Because this new relationship occurs, quite literally, on the body of the Bastard, he is written as the embodiment of this new relationship. Even though Robert makes the evidence of bastardy clear with his claim of non-access between his father and mother, and even though the law prohibiting inheritance to illegitimates is unequivocal, John ignores Robert's assertion that non-access precluded the Bastard's natural issue:

> Sirrah, your brother is legitimate,
> Your father's wife did after wedlock bear him;
> And if she did play false, the fault was hers;
> [. . .]
> In sooth, good friend, your father might have kept
> This calf, bred from his cow, from all the world;
> In sooth he might: then, if he were my brother's,
> My brother might not claim him; nor your father,
> Being none of his, refuse him: this concludes,
> My mother's son did get your father's heir,
> Your father's heir must have your father's land.
>
> (1.1.116–29)

As Alison Findlay suggests in her comments on the play, 'The illegitimate body and the word of law confront and contradict each other.'⁶⁵ Physical evidence and word are disjointed. The Bastard's material presence confronts the invisible, negative force of the law, and from the confrontation the Bastard emerges as 'Lord of thy presence' (1.1.137). His issue, then, is a sovereign decree, a form of the sovereign exception. John legitimises the Bastard outside of the laws that demarcate identity, and such a separation distances the Bastard from the legal networks that he will enforce later on. The Bastard establishes his material presence, not a juridical claim, as his primary access to identity:

> [. . .] if my brother had my shape
> And I had his, Sir Robert's his, like him,
> And if my legs were two such riding-rods,
> My arms such eel-skins stuffed, my face so thin,
> That in mine ear I durst not stick a rose,
> [. . .]
> And, to his shape, were heir to all this land,
> Would I might never stir from this place,
> I'd give it every foot to have this face.   (1.1.138–46)

Once the Bastard establishes his identity outside of the legal codes which name other men, both noble and common, his relationship with theo-political absolutism in the play is altered, giving presence to a new form of bureaucratic sovereignty. In articulating his new position to his mother, 'Legitimation, name, and all is gone' (1.1.248), the Bastard notes how events have transpired to write him outside of a contained system of laws and into a bureaucratic system that separates the agent of order from the laws that he enforces. With the bastard's identity fashioned outside of traditional legal codes, the events that transpire in the play become neither fully subversive nor completely statist, as critics tend to assume. Indeed, the Bastard's actions are those of a man who is neither the agent of rebellion nor the product of the sovereign exception, though he resembles both of those functions at various times throughout the play. More specifically, the Bastard operates as an administrator of decrees, working under the illusion of constant action, and superior to those people who are tangled in legal niceties and arguments over the legitimisation of both his character and the crown.[66]

The Bastard's bureaucratic development begins soon after he receives his new name. His relationship with John during the battle scene at Angiers suggests the confused nature of his bureaucratic role as theo-political sovereignty gives shape to theo-bureaucracy. The Bastard's confident recommendation to the feuding monarchs that their 'royal presences be ruled by [him]' (2.1.377) and his arrogant rhetorical questions that follow his battle strategy insinuate his self-perception in relation to the other impractical actors in the theatre of war. He asks the rival kings: 'How like you this wild counsel, mighty states? / Smacks it not something of the policy?' (2.1.395–6). He further separates his position from that of the other players by challenging the royal character and insulting the citizens under siege: 'And if thou hast the mettle of a king, / Being wronged as we are by this peevish town' (2.1.401–2). In this incarnation, the Bastard appears as a type of henchman, a strategist willing to affect the extermination of large numbers of the French. The Bastard's military strategy – 'From north to south – / Austria and France shoot in each other's mouth' (2.1.413–14) – has an effect that resembles the Elizabethan and Cecilian military strategy of the sixteenth century. Clearly the military complex that began to develop in the mid-sixteenth century formed the basis for the colonial military machine later in the century, and those pressed into service were often the 'straggling vagrants, loytering fellowes, and lewd livers (so they be fit for service)'.[67] Indeed, as Breight demonstrates, to blame bureaucratic disorganisation for the abuses done to draftees during the war is applying anachronistic analysis to the conditions extant during the Shakespearean war years. In fact, it is the alacrity with which such undesirables were shipped off to war, never to return, that bears witness to an organisational network in operation to secure and control provinces and parishes at home. The apparently disconnected acts of exterminating the enemy and eliminating fellow citizens are implicated in the bureaucratic strategies of violence that link them.

King John offers a domestic scene in act 4 that reinforces the connection between bureaucratic strategies of violence and the control enabled by those strategies. The treatment of Peter of Pomfret most vividly suggests the banality of violence that often emerges in the bureaucratic hierarchy. The Bastard describes Peter as a prophet from the streets of Pomfret. Holinshed describes him as a hermit 'about York'. His vagrant position secures his fate in a bureaucratic system predicated on efficiency and function. John's sudden and merciless order to imprison Peter and to 'let him be hanged' (4.2.157) indicates the violent end for those who have no function in the networks of obligation that exist in the hierarchical structures of power in the play. As Philip and John determine Pomfret's fate, the Bastard is the instigator of violence, yet he is clearly separated from its precipitation. Likewise, his position as putative policy-maker at Angiers seems to distance him from those who are affected by the policy that he inspires. The separation of those who rule from those who are ruled is central to the Bastard's bureaucratic function. His impulse, however, to inspire policy in the scene at Angiers, along with his role in Peter Pomfret's imprisonment and ultimate execution, suggests a bureaucratic subject emerging in the wake of the reallocation of sovereignty's authority.

Though many historians argue about the exact form that the nascent English bureaucracy took during the late sixteenth century, Wallace MacCaffrey has identified a tension in Elizabethan bureaucratic formations that I think is central to the Bastard's performance in the play. He writes, 'The practice of the Elizabethan administration mingles confusedly the notion of a professional, paid public service with that of personal service to the monarch.'[68] If we return to the Bastard's attempt to create policy at Angiers, we see that his relationship with the king is still deeply entrenched in old forms of service. As if confirming the royalty of his newly noble blood, his contribution to his king's war efforts seems more the recommendations of a second royal voice, not a functionary to the state who is separated from both the king who decrees and the law that emanates from his ordinance. That is to say, the Bastard's attempt at policy-making, his role-playing of royal presence, suggests a character not yet completely aware of the bureaucrat's function. Imploring John to invade the city, he figuratively usurps kingly authority by calling on the 'royal presences' to 'be ruled by' him (2.1.377). His reaction to the Citizen's alternative plan indicates his dissatisfaction with the results of his policy-making: 'Zounds, I was never so bethumped with words, / Since I first called my brother's father dad' (2.1.466–7). Ironically, he associates the bastardy of his former social status with his failed attempts to rule the king and determine policy.

For the Bastard, his illegitimacy – his rejected status as a ruler of kings – results from his attempt to exert influence based on inheritance and noble blood. His appeal to his ancestor King Richard I (Coeur-de-lion) is evident in his reaction to Austria, 'O tremble, for you hear the lion roar!' (2.1.294), before he tries to convince the king to invade. The legitimacy promised by the recognition of his royal blood proves illusory – inadequate as a way to participate in and benefit from state power. Armed with this recognition, Philip, in effect, creates himself anew, re-bastardising himself in relation to the king. He ceases to contribute to the events on stage; rather, he observes action, his only utterance being the aside and a lengthy soliloquy on the nature of commodity. His resignation of his previously proactive relationship with his king, his silence toward the royals after they reject his policy proposal, and the extended soliloquy itself demonstrate the Bastard's potentially labile position relative to the authority that governs him.

In addition to the silence that suggests the Bastard's bureaucratic subjectivity, his insistence that 'Since kings break faith upon commodity, / Gain be my lord, for I will worship thee' (2.1.598–9) seems an assertion that clearly delineates the Bastard's function within the structures of authority that operate in emerging bureaucratic politics. Read retrospectively through his final oath to the new king, the Bastard's speech can be viewed as an endorsement of royal power and a perpetuation of Tudor doctrine. Conversely, critical commentary has pointed out the tensions inherent in the speech as evidence of the hypocrisy and bad faith that contaminate the monarch as well as many of his supporters. Each reading, however, returns to an affirmation of an 'absolutist ethic'.[69] The latter simply gets there 'from a more hostile political stance'.[70]

It is true that the political theology of absolute sovereignty is infused with a bureaucratic ethos expressed in the Bastard's self-expression of autonomy. His clearly demarcated role after his decision to worship his lord seems nothing more than a functionary's position, and from act 3 until the play's end the Bastard's action is rational, administrative service. In fact, the speech on commodity seems an important act of consent in a system that delicately balanced coercion and legitimacy. The Bastard's statement on commodity indicates that he recognises the threat of coercion extant in the political system in which he participates. He has been rendered powerless after his failed attempt at policy-making at Angiers, and his act of consent (given first to John and then to Henry in the play's last act) becomes a bureaucratic commodity that guarantees survival by ensuring a function in the prevailing social system.[71] The Bastard's mimicry of voices in act 3 indicates the nature of his bureaucratic reliance on the royal voice even as it disperses the voice through a repetition of its centralised authority; more importantly, it indicates the nature of his consensual relationship with sovereignty. His words are not his own until John gives him his official responsibility, which inaugurates his bureaucratic sovereignty.

The Bastard's first words in the act repeat Constance's aspersion toward Austria. The variations of 'And hang a calf's skin on those recreant limbs' (3.1.55, 57, 59, 125, 146, 224) are all that he speaks until John provides the bureaucrat with a decree. John promises that France will regret its violation of the oath established earlier in the play: 'France, thou shalt rue this hour within this hour' (3.1.249). The Bastard responds in words that echo the king's promise: 'Old Time the clock-setter, that bald sexton / Time, / Is it as he will? Well then, France shall rue' (3.1.323–5). Compared to the mimicry of Constance's earlier language in the scene that reveals the Bastard's lack of identity, the echo of his king's promise provides him with a clear purpose. He speaks without mimicry only after he has been assigned a function, in this case to do violence to the French, and the Bastard's exit immediately after John's direct command to mobilise the troops is a visible sign that the Bastard has found a bureaucratic role.

That he announces his intention to 'stay behind / To do the office for thee of revenge' (5.7.70–1) after King John dies further demonstrates how his functional role is not dependent on the health of the royal body; defined by loyalty to an absent body, revenge becomes the Bastard's way of articulating his new relationship to the crown. The king's own dying words emphasise this new conception of royal power. Echoing the Scrivener in *Richard III* with his reproduceable 'palpable device' that enacts authority, John describes his royal body as a 'scribbled form' (5.7.32) – a 'parchment' (33) that, as his own account of his painful death makes clear, is subject to dissolution as well as duplication. The king is dead: long live the bureaucrat.

In Undetermined Differences of Kings

The king's description of his bodily dissolution in the final act – 'that all my bowels crumble up to dust' (5.7.31) – reveals a censorial force exerted on his body, described as a 'scribbled form' (32) that is about to 'shrink up' (34). John's body is deformed, his heart is 'cracked and burnt' (52), and his material presence is 'but a clod, / And module of confounded royalty' (57–8). His physical deformity is also the deformation of a text, 'a parchment' (33) altered by fire, and a symbolic sign of the claims of bureaucracy that reshape sovereign authority. With John's death, Shakespeare provides evidence that the nature of kingship is particularly dependent on the complicity of bureaucratic agency, specifically the redistribution of sovereign power into the written records that now generate authority. As early modern royal government was increasingly becoming a 'written government' and more and more a government 'by officials under the king',[72] the play's final depiction of the king's fate is particularly noteworthy. John describes the end of his kingship: 'I am a scribbled form drawn with a pen / Upon a parchment, and against this fire / Do I shrink up' (5.7.32–4). By depicting the king himself as bureaucratic and paper-based, the play asserts both political theology and political economy, and this scene helps to explain the Bastard's willing support for Prince Henry, a scene that critics read as the moment of sovereign entrenchment.[73] In the system of social and political order in the play, the king initiates and is subject to the same bureaucratic elements that circumscribe the Bastard's actions. For the Bastard, specifically because he is illegitimate before the sovereign encounter, sovereignty is not specific, delineating or decisive. In short, it is not Schmittian, and this is what makes his illegitimate body the perfect commodity in a new bureaucracy that manages the collateral effects of the sovereign decision.

The new bureaucratic sovereignty of Elizabethan England reconfigured the relationship between the subject and
the crown. Jean-Christophe Agnew has advanced our understanding of early modern identity by connecting it to a newly
fluid market characterised by the 'expanded circulation of
commodities' that 'commute specific obligations, utilities,
and meanings into general, fungible equivalents'.[74] His conclusion bears on the claims of identity of both King John
and the Bastard in the play: 'By deliberately effacing the
line between the self's iconic representation in art and ritual
and its instrumental presentation in ordinary life, Renaissance theater formally reproduced the same symbolic confusion that a boundless market had already introduced into
the visual codes and exchange relations of a waning feudal
order.'[75] Unlike the nobles in the play whose 'authenticity' is
guaranteed by inheritance, the Bastard becomes more and
more visible as an actor – an accidental agent with a contingent relationship to the state, detached from a singular identity to which other characters and the audience might have
expected him to commit.[76]

The illegitimacy of the Bastard both figuratively and literally places him outside of sovereignty's medieval theo-political power, making his rational bureaucratic function possible.
By not rebelling against sovereignty, the bureaucratic subject
manifests most vividly its loyalty to an impotent kingship – a
contingent loyalty that is instrumental to but not defined by
the sovereign exception. Impotent sovereignty is not powerless government. Indeed, sovereign impotence is a precondition of the birth of the machine of government in which
political theology defines one half of a divisible sovereignty
of kingdom and government. Impotent sovereignty, however, might benefit from a prosthesis, such as the friendship
between rival sovereigns, to supplement its wounded condition. Agamben notes that political *oikonomia* amplifies the
charisma of absolute kingship by diffusing the force of the

sovereign exception, leaving to other accidental agents the execution of the 'governmental *ratio*'.[77] Shakespeare's history play explores the parameters of this governmental ratio, and in the end shows us that the bureaucratic calculus is the epiphenomenon of a political theology at risk of dissolving.

In discussing the providential machine that he calls governmentality, Agamben observes that the 'providential-economical paradigm is, in this sense, the paradigm of democratic power, just as the theological-political is the paradigm of absolutism'.[78] If we return once again to Shakespeare's earlier play about a 'bastard' of a king – *Richard III* – we can begin to see how *King John*'s representation of political theology is part of a more general pattern interrogating the divisibility of sovereignty that gives shape to fugitive politics. Where Richard fails to understand the nature of the primitive, rational bureaucracy that he creates with his relationship to Buckingham's bureaucratic function, the Bastard – a bureaucrat with royal blood – is well aware that his fugitive survival and political efficacy are contingent on how he responds to the unintended contours of the sovereign decision, to its collateral effects that exceed ordered and absolute power: in other words, to that which allows him to act legitimately before, beyond and, even more critically, against the law.

A Will! A Wicked Will: A Woman's Will

As *Shakespeare's Fugitive Politics* considers the collateral effects of ordered and absolute power in a critique of theo-political sovereignty in Shakespeare, it is worth returning to Erin Manning's *Politics of Touch*, which shows us that a geopolitical alliance predicated on friendship and embodied by touch, as we see in *King John,* ignores the affective force at the core of the sovereign union. Manning writes that a politics of friendship 'proposes the challenge of creating a relation that cannot be symbolized through a coding in a fraternal nationalism. To create a pact is to explore the limits of what a body can do.'[79] At the same time that *King John* explores, along the lines proposed by Manning, the expanding contours of a *dividing* sovereignty – a 'burned', 'parchèd', 'confounded' and 'scribbled form' (5.7.39, 40, 58, 32) – the play also gives voice to sovereignty's new shape.

In a complete rejection of the alliance between France and England that reduces kingship's singular, coherent power by combining crowns, Constance, Arthur's mother, powerfully expresses a wilful and, according to her, a lawful resistance. After Cardinal Pandolf intervenes in their union, saying that there is 'law and warrant' for his curse of the new fraternal bond between John and Philip, Constance says,

> And for mine too: when law can do no right,
> Let it be lawful that law bar no wrong:
> Law cannot give my child his kingdom here,
> For he that holds his kingdom holds the law;
> Therefore, since law itself is perfect wrong,
> How can the law forbid my tongue to curse?   (3.1.111–16)

Constance applies a concept of law to her desire that encompasses and surpasses the local legal principles that govern the particularities of the scene of political friendship between John and Philip. She transforms the principles of political sovereignty that define regal power into principles that guarantee personal sovereignty – in this case, her right to curse the geopolitical alliance that alienates her son from the throne. Constance usurps sovereign law to activate what she perceives to be her own sovereign agency.

Constance's aggressive rhetoric of agency gives voice to what remains unspoken in the final moments of *Henry V* in which the new king claims Catherine, his capital demand. In my argument about sovereignty's divisibility in Chapter 3,

Catherine's sugar touch exposes Henry's fragile absolutism and her body articulates a vibrancy for which the sovereign decision fails to account. Each of these examples illustrates the limits of absolute sovereignty in its encounter with female desire, described by Constance as 'a will! a wicked will: / A woman's will; a cankered grandam's will!' (2.1.193–4). In describing Queen Eleanor's legal will that guarantees Eleanor's grandson the crown, Constance also expresses the menaced condition of female agency that often offers a trenchant, if unacknowledged, critique of indivisible sovereign power. Constance's lawful curse and Eleanor's cankered will are two forms of the same desire that parody the sovereign decision, transforming political theology into feminist politics that becomes the subject of the final chapter.

CHAPTER 5

BODY POLITICS AND THE NON-SOVEREIGN EXCEPTION IN *TITUS ANDRONICUS* AND *THE WINTER'S TALE*

What is needed are metaphors and models that implicate the subject in the object, that render mastery and exteriority undesirable.

Elizabeth Grosz, *Volatile Bodies*

Non-sovereign freedom is *plural* freedom.

Sharon R. Krause,
Freedom Beyond Sovereignty

In this final chapter exploring fugitive politics in Shakespeare, I want to extend the study's focus on the fractured power of the sovereign to include a discussion of divisible sovereignty at its most diffuse. *Titus Andronicus* and *The Winter's Tale* challenge the monitory function of the female docile body regulated by and reinforcing patriarchal desire. Indeed, these two plays hold much in common that commend them as dramatic set pieces bookending Shakespeare's dramatic career. If in 1594 with Lavinia in *Titus Andronicus* Shakespeare was interested in exploring the idea of the dangerous female body with a potency to kill, in 1611 he revisits this theme with Hermione in *The Winter's Tale*, exposing the affective claims

of the female body as a volatile object and staging the phenomenon of what Sharon Krause calls non-sovereign agency
that menaces the masculine fantasy of sovereign hegemony.

In staging the female body in both plays, Shakespeare
explores what Emily Watson describes as tragic overliving.
According to Watson, overliving involves

> the desire to be invisible and unseen; images of torture,
> heaviness, and the body as a burden; the loss of self-
> hood, order, meaning, and understanding; the presence
> of multiple, competing ways to understand time; the con-
> flict between human emotions and impersonal, historical
> responses to them; revenge as a possible solution to overliv-
> ing; regret at birth and desire for death; depictions of life
> as living death.[1]

The effects of tragic overliving in *Titus Andronicus* seem especially powerful with respect to Lavinia. She asks to be thrown
into a 'loathsome pit' (2.3.176), '[w]here never man's eye may
behold [her] body' (177); her tortured body is a spectacle for
others to interpret; Lucius, her uncle, calls her body an 'object'
that 'kills [him]' (3.1.64), and she loses any sense of self as
she becomes a property in Titus's culinary performance in act
5; Lavinia's fate precipitates the revenge narrative that brings
an end to her tragic overliving. Her willing participation in
Titus's plan for revenge that kills her suggests Lavinia's desire
for a death that is long overdue.

The Winter's Tale stages, by contrast, the political potential of overliving. In act 5 Polixenes and Paulina describe
Hermione's statue in language that captures the phenomenon
of overliving:

POLIXENES. Ay, and make it manifest where she has lived,
Or how stol'n from the dead.
PAULINA. That she is living,

Were it but told you, should be hooted at
Like an old tale: but it appears she lives,
Though yet she speak not. Mark a little while.

(5.3.113–18)

Polixenes sees Hermione's resurrection as one of two things: either a ruse – a staged deception hiding the truth that Hermione has been alive for the intervening sixteen years – or a mystery of living beyond the finality of death's grasp. Tragic overliving is to steal from death that which death irrevocably claims, to surpass the logic and time of the experience of death that would otherwise release Hermione from a painful earthly presence. Paulina's response to Polixenes' demand to know the truth of the events in front of him indicates the degree to which Hermione's body generates its own evidence beyond a narrative of events that Polixenes demands to know. Words fail to capture the vitality of her body at this pivotal moment in the play.[2] In one reading of this moment, Paulina's qualification of the body's vitality, 'it appears she lives', allows for the persistence of wonder, even confusion, that informs Polixenes' demand.

The syntax of Paulina's qualification has within it, however, an alternate reading, one that separates the visible body from Hermione herself. Paulina refers to the statue as a thing, a work of art, before the unveiling: 'Therefore I keep it / Lonely, apart. But here it is' (5.3.17–18), she says to Leontes before drawing the curtain to reveal the figure of Hermione. Leontes gives the statue an identity, referring to it in the third person feminine, gendering and transforming it into Hermione: 'Her natural posture / [. . .] / Thou art Hermione; or rather, thou art she / In thy not chiding, for she was tender / As infancy and grace' (23–7). In the dialogue that follows, Paulina, Leontes, Perdita and Polixenes refer to the statue alternately as a gendered body and a stone, inanimate object. By the time we arrive at Paulina's declaration of animation, the difference between the pronouns 'it', 'she' and 'her' in relation to Hermione's presence is utterly confused. Thus Paulina's qualification 'But it appears she lives' also imparts the division in the object's ontological status if the line reads 'But it appears, she lives'. This admittedly wilful reading of Paulina's key line captures the ambiguity of the scene's depiction of a prosthetic body – a fleshy body described by Leontes as 'too hot', surrogated and monumentalised by stone yet simultaneously still vibrant matter.

To appear is to seem, of course, but it also means to 'come forth into view, as from a state of concealment, or from a distance; to become visible' (*Oxford English Dictionary*). The statue appears *and* Hermione lives – subject and object merge. Both bodies act. In staging the phenomenon of overliving in *Titus Andronicus* and *The Winter's Tale*, Shakespeare travesties the concept of the king's two bodies central to early modern sovereignty, redistributing agency between subjects to objects and from intentions to effects. In its parody of sovereignty's charismatic survival beyond death, these plays, to different degrees, transform political theology into a feminist politics of overliving in which performing objects – Lavinia's body and Hermione's statue – evoke the phenomenon of non-sovereign agency that defines Shakespeare's fugitive politics.

Intersubjective Agency: Sharon Krause, Elizabeth Grosz and Ewa Ziarek

Before exploring Shakespeare's depiction of non-sovereign agency as an essential condition of fugitive politics in *Titus Andronicus* and *The Winter's Tale*, I want to clarify the terms 'intersubjective agency' and 'social uptake' that will become central to my reading of the two plays. In *Freedom Beyond Sovereignty: Reconstructing Liberal Individualism*, Sharon Krause argues that the 'corporeal and socially distributed aspects of human agency are linked because the bodily life of agency is itself an intersubjective affair'.[3] She insists that in political contexts, the efficacy of what we perceive as our desires and actions is contingent on how others interact with those desires and actions. She calls this interaction social uptake – 'that others understand your action in ways that are consonant with your understanding of it, and that they respond to the action in ways that sustain its meaning and impact'.[4] With social uptake as a central condition, Krause suggests that individual agency is 'socially distributed'.[5] This suggestion emerges from a particular reading of Thomas Hobbes, who, according to Samantha Frost, asks us to 'eschew the tendency to think of acts in terms of an agent whose energy and power are both self-originating and the single cause of an act'.[6] Drawing on Hobbes's account of active and passive power, Frost maintains that power is not 'a property of a body but rather a situation in which a body finds itself; power consists in a particular configuration of numerous causal factors in a given context'.[7] Krause affirms Frost's reading of Hobbes that finds 'neither the individuals nor the sovereign can act except with the existence or cooperation of others', describing this aspect of intersubjective agency in Hobbes as a 'profound interdependence' and the 'heteronomous character of action'.[8] A subject's agency requires for its realisation the 'passive power of a patient'.[9] Quoting Hobbes, Krause writes, 'The cause of something, as Hobbes puts it, includes "the power of the agent and patient together, which may be called entire or plenary power".'[10] Contending that plenary power is the central characteristic of human agency that includes the power of the actor and recipient together, her argument gives human agency 'material life' that is socially distributed in the sense that, citing Arendt, '"others become the agents of the individual's action"'.[11]

Krause's claim about the social distribution of agency is fundamental to the fugitive condition of politics in Shakespeare, and helps to link the claims of sovereignty located in sacred kingship to a notion of sovereignty associated with individual agency. As we've seen in previous chapters that explore a sovereign's claims on its subjects, the alliances that guarantee sovereign power are fragile, secured by a myth of sovereignty's indivisible power. Qualifying Krause's emphasis on an element of cooperation that she locates in Hobbes, I claim that fugitive politics emerges not necessarily in moments of rational consensus and consolidation but in moments that expose the fractured condition of power and the fragility of the often 'wounded attachments' formed between and among sovereign and subjects.[12] Wendy Brown coined the term 'wounded attachments' to describe the affective condition of identity politics in which a 'politicized identity's investments in itself and especially in its own history of suffering come into conflict with the need to give up these investments in the pursuit of an emancipatory democratic project'.[13] Brown explores how the emancipatory political demands of a particular identity group are consistently troubled, if not subverted, 'not only by the constraints of the political discourses in which its operations transpire but by its own wounded attachments'[14] – political alliances that 'breed a politics of recrimination and rancor, of culturally dispersed paralysis and suffering, a tendency to reproach power rather than aspire to it, to disdain freedom rather than practice it'.[15]

What links Brown's important work exploring the need for a new model of political dissent to Krause's recent scholarship on sovereignty is the way both reimagine the political subject. Krause and Brown both disassociate political identity from expressions of ontological fixity. Brown argues for a 'slight shift' in the political expression of identity that 'supplants the language of "I am" – with its defensive closure on identity, its insistence on the fixity of position, and its equation of social and moral positioning – with the language of reflexive wanting'.[16] She argues, instead, for a 'rehabilitation of the memory of desire' before the event of the subject's wounding 'and thus prior to the formation of identity as fixed position, as entrenched by history, and as having necessary moral entailments, even as they affirm "position" and "history" as that which makes the speaking subject intelligible and locatable'.[17] Brown understands 'I am' as a resolution of desire into 'fixed and sovereign identity'.[18] The partial dissolution of the sovereign subject proposed by Brown informs Krause's non-sovereign subject. What Brown calls the ongoing genealogy of desire includes the social uptake of a subject's wishes and intentions, transforming the sovereign subject into an intersubjective body in proximity to other bodies with no guarantee that desire, agency and action at all cohere.

Writing in the spirit of both Krause and Brown, Ewa Ziarek in *An Ethics of Dissensus* emphasises how a corporeal body's proximity to other bodies locates politics differently. Radical politics emerges in the transformation of the concept of resistance to hegemonic injustice into an 'aesthetics of existence' or an 'experimental praxis aiming to surpass the historical limits of bodies, discourses, and sexuality' from practices traditionally reduced to articulations of the self in private life.[19] Ziarek is no longer concerned with the autonomy of the subject but with the 'anarchic responsibility' that comes with 'the affirmation of irreducible alterity and the asymmetry of the Other'.[20] On one level, Ziarek's radical asymmetry of the agentive subject from the Other and the self seems incompatible with the notion of intersubjective agency and social uptake articulated in Krause. Her description of the ethics of a politics of dissent, however, puts these thinkers into productive alliance. Ethical respect for difference as it informs a politics of dissensus tempers a politics based solely on social antagonism, yet Ziarek's insistence on the 'necessary confrontation with the internal conflict, aggressivity, and the division of the subject' puts pressure on the belief shared by Jürgen Habermas and Seyla Benhabib that an 'idealized communicative rationality' is achievable and is the groundwork of politics,[21] redefining democratic politics to include ethical antagonistic encounters that impose an obligation to respond. Like politics that emerges only through disagreement in Rancière's formulation, ethics in Ziarek's argument is the political demand in an increasingly fragmented, global landscape, and the contemporary neo-liberal response to the ethical imperative of the dissensus has been a political failure.

Krause and Ziarek have in common a concept of intersubjective agency that attends with care to the problematic relationship between social inequality and freedom, an ethical relationship requiring constant vigilance especially if we view agency as a non-sovereign force.[22] The volatile body examined by Elizabeth Grosz, I contend, materialises the ethics of non-sovereign agency common to both Krause and Ziarek. In *Volatile Bodies*, Grosz explicitly connects non-sovereign agency to bodily proximity and corporeality. Echoing Ziarek, who argues that a politics of difference 'bears a necessary relation to embodiment',[23] Grosz takes issue with feminist theory that 'participates in the social devaluing of the body that goes hand in hand with the oppression of women'.[24] According to Grosz, the body is most often construed in terms of metaphor as an 'instrument, a tool, or a machine at the disposal of consciousness, a vessel occupied by an animating, willful subjectivity [. . .] a self-motivating automaton',[25] or the body, even in some feminist circles, is 'an object over which struggles between its "inhabitant" and others/exploiters may be possible. Whatever agency or will it has is the direct consequence of animating, psychical intentions.'[26] Grosz's conceptualisation of the body argues for its agentive vitality:

> Not being self-identical, the body must be seen as a series of processes of becoming, rather than as a fixed state of being. The body is both active and productive, although not originary: its specificity is a function of its degrees and modes of organization, which are in turn the results or consequences of its ability to be affected by other bodies [. . .] [and] human bodies have the wonderful ability, while striving for integration and cohesion, organic and psychic wholeness, to also provide for and indeed produce fragmentations, fracturings, dislocations that orient bodies and body parts toward other bodies and body parts.[27]

The orientation of Grosz's volatile bodies toward other bodies captures the mechanics of intersubjective agency central to Krause's reconfiguration of individual freedom beyond the fantasy of sovereignty. Bodies matter, for sure, but so do their proximity and linkages to other bodies. Linking bodies and body parts – both 'human and nonhuman, animate and inanimate'[28] – in what Krause might describe as an intersubjective constellation, Grosz writes in *Volatile Bodies*:

> the body is regarded as neither the locus for a consciousness nor an organically determined entity; it is understood more in terms of what it can do, the things it can perform, the linkages it establishes, the transformations and becomings it undergoes, and the mechanic connections it forms with other bodies, what it can link with, how it can proliferate its capacities – a rare, affirmative understanding of the body.[29]

Providing a framework for Grosz's volatile, productive, political bodies, Eric Santner's compelling work on the transformation of sovereignty in modernity is equally interested in the effects of corporeality in democracy. Quoting Claude Lefort, he writes that a concept of the '"flesh of the world" [. . .] serves as the very "stuff" that binds subjects to that space of representation that is the "body politic"'.[30] As Sara Melzer and Kathryn Norberg have demonstrated, within the context of the advent of French democracy, the diffusion of sovereign authority inaugurated a moment when '[s]uddenly every body bore political weight'.[31] Santner describes this political weight as agitations of the flesh, 'the carnal or corporeal dimension of representation'.[32]

While these critics understand the development of democracy and its relationship to sovereignty within the context of the birth of modernity and the concomitant development of technological, bureaucratic and secularising forces often inaugurated or punctuated by a range of critical events such as revolution, regicide or some other historical crisis, a concept of fugitive politics suggests that the conditions for a politics of dissensus that materialises democracy exceed the moments that give them expression and that most often galvanise critical attention. Lefort's influential account of the *'empty place'* of power in modern democracy is related to what I describe as the surplus condition of fugitive politics on Shakespeare's stage. The critical passage in Lefort's 'The Permanence of the Theologico-Political?' is as follows:

> I have for a long time concentrated upon this peculiarity of modern democracy: of all the regimes of which we know it is the only one to have represented power in such a way as to show that power is an *empty place* and to have thereby maintained a gap between the symbolic and the real. It does so by virtue of a discourse which reveals that power belongs to no one; that those who exercise power do not possess it; that they do not, indeed, embody it; that the exercise of power requires a periodic and repeated contest; that the authority of those

vested with power is created and re-created as a result of
the will of the people [. . .] Nor can power be divorced
from the work of division by which society is instituted;
a society can therefore relate to itself only through
the experience of an internal division that proves to be
not a de facto division, but a division that generates its
constitution.[33]

Lefort's theory of modern democracy that locates democratic
politics everywhere and nowhere disincorporates the body as
a site for political contestation: 'There is not power linked
to a body.'[34] While acknowledging the precision with which
disincorporation operates in Lefort's analysis of totalitarian regimes, Ziarek makes clear that 'he fails to investigate
an alternative relation between the body and democracy' in
favour of the 'social construction of historicism'.[35] Lefort's
influential account exaggerates the 'disembodied character
of citizenship' and maintains the fantasy, vigorously challenged in my reading of the theoretical intersections of
Krause, Grosz and Ziarek, that the democratic public sphere
is removed from the corporeal condition of non-sovereign,
intersubjective agency.[36]

Titus Andronicus and *The Winter's Tale* depict the precarious, exposed and vulnerable body intimately woven into
expressions of dissent that establish the parameters of the
productivity of non-sovereign agency central to a concept
of fugitive politics. If, as I am suggesting, the term 'fugitive
politics' describes a divisibility of power disavowed by the
sovereign exception as well as by the consensual politics of
neo-liberalism, then these two plays represent the spectrum
of possibility for intersubjective agency at the expense of the
integrity of the female body. In other words, Shakespeare
probes the limits of fugitive politics by representing the
female body as an object with an agitating force demanding
a response to its fragile condition.

Ay Me, This Object Kills Me

Shakespeare's tragedy *Titus Andronicus* transforms human bodies into commodities; abstracts them into metaphors for the fragile Roman polity; and exposes the often-devastating cost on human bodies of literary and historical tradition. Because of its investment in bodies, the play is especially suited to the type of criticism that construes meaning in body counts and body parts. Titus's severed hand, an extension of his controlling agency, becomes a commodity in his attempt to secure the return of his kidnapped sons; severed to 'purchase [. . .] at an easy price' (3.1.197) his sons' safe return, the hand buys him only their severed heads. Aaron, the play's villain, mocks Titus's exchange: 'and for thy hand / Look by and by to have thy sons with thee. / [*Aside*] Their heads I mean' (199–201). Marcus, Titus's brother, establishes the human body as the central political metaphor for the sovereign state when he invites Titus to become emperor so that he might 'help to set a head on headless Rome' (1.1.189). Yet in contemporary criticism the body of Lavinia, Titus's raped and mutilated daughter, has become the play's central focus;[37] as a spectator and spectacle of violence, Lavinia seems to resemble the subject of the early modern blazon: anatomised and frozen, remaining on stage '*with her hands cut off and her tongue cut out, and ravished*' (2.4. s.d.) for most of the play after her violent assault. The various subject and object positions that her fragmented body occupies after it has been violated, I argue, transform it into a performing object that wrestles agency away from the men who act upon and for her, redefining the trope of the early modern blazon.[38]

In experimental theatre, performing objects are 'material images of humans, animals, or spirits that are created, displayed, or manipulated in narrative or dramatic performance'.[39] While puppets and masks are at the centre of performing object theory, John Bell extends the concept of the performing object to include techniques of performance not labelled puppetry but which share its focus on artificiality and manipulation.[40] Specifically in relation to its depiction of severed hands and heads that become performing objects in the play, *Titus Andronicus* juxtaposes bodily fragmentation and wholeness to examine the limits of human autonomy and agency. Indeed, the fragmented body in the play is often rendered whole at key moments with the rhetoric of the blazon linguistically suturing the bloody site of division. In this toggling back and forth between fragmentation and wholeness, the play balances the divisible body against a body reincorporated by a linguistic prosthesis that generates the sensation of wholeness while simultaneously memorialising the division. With the depiction of the body as performing object, Shakespeare imagines a political body that radically reconfigures the force of its representational effect and, in the process, depicts non-sovereign agency that defines the contested condition of fugitive politics. In Shakespeare's earliest tragedy, thick descriptions of Lavinia's body, especially through the convention of the literary blazon, and her body's insistent visibility on stage certainly draw attention to the informal social and political inequalities and their 'agency-disabling' effects. At the same time, however, her corporeality on stage also highlights the startling vitality of agency in the presence of violent aggression and control that tragically refuse the necessary 'social uptake' of Lavinia's intersubjective demands.[41]

In her account of early modern anatomical blazons, Nancy Vickers asserts that the printed collections of anatomical blazons 'worked [. . .] to emphasize the partiality of the despised or venerated bodily object'.[42] In representing, often on a single page, a body part such as hair, a breast or a foot in a title, text or picture, the blazons tended to 'affirm the power of the part, its potential for action, its devastating effect on helpless admirers'.[43] Vickers understands these anatomical blazons specifically in terms of the power of the body's fragmented condition: 'creating a "total picture" was never the overriding concern [. . .] their subjects were body parts, not bodies'.[44] The printed collections of anatomical blazons often participated in extended 'poetic competition and proliferation' in which 'every description of a part invited further description'.[45] The generative nature of the genre is precisely the condition of the blazon in Shakespeare's play. The body emblazoned in *Titus Andronicus* achieves a temporality that surpasses Marcus's poetic achievement in describing the spectacle of Lavinia's body when he stumbles upon her after her rape and mutilation. Shakespeare's play extends the temporal dimension of the event of the emblazoned body by imbuing Lavinia's body parts and surface with a volatility – a kinetic agitation[46] – that renders moot, and perhaps even critically self-serving, questions about her depth, interiority and subjectivity. In surpassing the desire of the single *blasonneur*, the play imagines vulnerable female corporeality not only as a symptom of patriarchal culture – though it may very well suggest this as one possible meaning – but, more importantly, as Grosz points out, the female body imparts 'forces, intensities, requiring codifications or territorializations and in turn exerting [its] own deterritorializing and decodifying force, systems of compliance and resistance'.[47] Put otherwise, the play's integration of performing objects and performing bodies in its depiction of Lavinia's mutilated presence transforms the literary blazon, with its poetic description of the masculine fantasy of a fragmented female body that reinforces a subject-object binary, into a 'volatile body'.[48] Central to my reading of Lavinia's body is its tactility, its agitating power that poses problems for the way the play's characters and critics attempt to make sense of Lavinia's physical condition as an embodiment of her fractured subjectivity.[49] Instead of interrogating the contours of subjectivity modelled on depth and interiority, the play's complicated depiction of Lavinia's body offers a form of non-sovereign agency and social uptake critical to dissensual politics.

In representing the human body in its fragmented and prostheticised form, Shakespeare's play addresses the damaging consequences of making the corporeal body 'incorporate into Rome' (1.1.464). The play's representation of Lavinia's ravaged body and of Marcus's blazon at the end of act 2, however, are the most sustained explorations of the impossibility of rendering the human body – in particular the body of the female in the play – a docile object, subject to prosthetic wholeness. Marcus's question – 'Who is this – my niece [. . .]?' (2.4.11) – immediately before his extended description of the spectacle of her ravaged body captures the epistemological dilemma created by Lavinia's presence in the play after her rape. Seeing Lavinia's brutalised body, Shakespeare has Marcus attempt to make sense of the traumatic scene:

Speak, gentle niece, what stern ungentle hands
Have lopped and hewed and made thy body bare
Of her two branches, those sweet ornaments
Whose circling shadows kings have sought to sleep in,
And might not gain so great a happiness
As have thy love. Why dost not speak to me?
Alas, a crimson river of warm blood,
Like to a bubbling fountain stirred with wind,
Doth rise and fall between thy rosèd lips,
Coming and going with thy honey breath.
[. . .]
Yet do thy cheeks look red as Titan's face,
Blushing to be encountered with a cloud.
Shall I speak for thee? Shall I say 'tis so?
[. . .]

> O, had the monster seen those lily hands
> Tremble, like aspen leaves upon a lute
> And make the silken strings delight to kiss them,
> He would not then have touched them for his life.
> Or, had he heard the heavenly harmony
> Which that sweet tongue hath made,
> He would have dropp'd his knife, and fell asleep,
> As Cerberus at the Thracian poet's feet.   (2.4.16–51)

The incommensurability between the gruesome spectacle of Lavinia's disfigured body and the Ovidian and Petrarchan poetic discourses that Marcus employs to describe what he sees transforms this scene into a lesson in reading. Lavinia's substance becomes sheer surface, as her uncle and others attempt to read her bleeding body according to their own desires. Katherine Rowe describes Marcus's initial reaction to Lavinia as a 'culmination of a fantasy of *his* own release into expressive tears and anger', and she concludes that Lavinia's family views her '*as* a mirror and *through* a mirror. The flood of masculine tears replaces the flood of Lavinia's blood, while the objects of their gaze – the bloody stains on her cheeks – become the tearful stains on their own.'[50]

While Marcus's blazon is a powerful moment of social inscription that reflects his acculturation into Roman history and culture at the expense of Lavinia's desire, the scene also reinforces the unpredictability of non-sovereign, inter-subjective agency. Like the divisible sovereignty that shapes political dissent in Lezra's account of radical republicanism, Lavinia's sovereignty is divided too, a cleavage embodied in the visceral image of her violated form. The division imagined as fragmentation at this moment, however, is the precondition of dissensual politics, and the social distribution of her agency is subject to the unpredictable uptake of others. Clearly, Demetrius and Chiron privilege language as an expression of agency and intent. For her rapists, the acts of writing and telling are the only ways for her to express her desire. They imagine intention as the defining attribute of agency, and if Chiron and Demetrius can remove the method by which Lavinia communicates with intention, then they render her 'silent' (2.4.8), meaningless and preparing for suicide. They refuse to take seriously, however, the agitations of her volatile body, her 'signs and tokens' (2.4.5), reading them as indicators of weakness. Marcus's acknowledgement of her volatile body, on the other hand, engages Lavinia's desire, but his act of social uptake reveals the fragile condition of body politics in the play, underscoring the necessary political truth that there is no guarantee of the type of social uptake generated in expressions of intersubjective agency. As 'Rome's rich ornament' (1.1.55) and as a lover trafficked between Bassianus and Saturninus, Lavinia's agency is clearly enfolded into the desires of others. Bassianus's claim that 'this maid is mine' (1.1.279) indicates Lavinia's passive position as the object of men's desires. However, the play stages a shift in Lavinia's status as object in the forest before her rape and mutilation, ironically when her body is most vulnerable to the desire of others.

In responding to the scene of violent rape, it is difficult to make the case for Lavinia's agentic capacities, and claims of agency are at times misconstrued as arguments about Lavinia's responsibility for her victimisation. The scene of her rape in act 2 illustrates, however, the potential force of non-sovereign agency as well as the impossibility of guaranteeing the direction of the social uptake of intersubjective desire. As the scene's tension escalates, Bassianus is murdered, and Lavinia begins to understand her vulnerability. Her appeals are for recognition. First, she looks to Tamora, who 'bearest a woman's face' (2.3.136). Tamora's refusal to 'hear her speak' (137) is a reminder of the unpredictability of non-sovereign agency and a refusal of the intersubjective desire required for a politics of dissent. It would seem that Lavinia's attempt to generate a form of group identity in opposition to the oppressive forces of patriarchy fails. Later in the same scene, Lavinia again tries to affiliate with Tamora along gendered terms that divide them from the oppressive patriarchy that controls them. Lavinia implores Tamora to 'be called a gentle queen' (168) and kill her rather than subject her to the brutality of rape and mutilation:

> 'Tis present death I beg, and one thing more
> That womanhood denies my tongue to tell.
> O, keep me from their worse than killing lust,
> And tumble me into some loathsome pit.   (173–6)

Tamora's refusal to participate in this gesture of affiliation denies Lavinia the social uptake necessary for action and identity. Tamora says, 'What begg'st thou then, fond woman? Let me go!' (172). Lavinia is not recognised as a subject at this moment when recognition is necessary, and her attempts for political action go unheeded.

The play revisits Lavinia's expression of non-sovereign, intersubjective agency in act 4 in her instructive encounter with Ovid's *Metamorphoses*. From its opening moment when young Lucius cries out that Lavinia follows him everywhere, though he 'know[s] not why' (4.1.2), the scene explores the process of social uptake and group identity. Echoing Tamora, young Lucius tells his aunt that 'I know not what you mean' (4). Young Lucius's attempt to affiliate with his aunt in opposition to the oppressive forces that marginalise the family and jeopardise Rome is different from Titus's attempts to 'interpret her martyred signs' (Folio 3.2.36) or 'wrest an alphabet' (Folio 3.2.44) from her violated body. Predicated on forgetting the division that defines politics, Titus's desire is appropriative. His macabre pun as he ponders Lavinia's disfigured body indicates this desire: 'O, handle not the theme, to talk of hands, / Lest we remember that we have none' (Folio 3.2.29–30). According to Titus's logic, Lavinia's agentic capacities must reflect his own desire, and her political dissent must reinforce Roman consensus. Young Lucius's affiliation, however, is woven in the fabric of grief and division. His reference to Hecuba as he describes Lavinia's expressive sorrow is evidence of this association. While certainly a figure central to the revenge narrative that unfolds in this particular scene, Hecuba is also associated with the obligation to grieve unimaginable loss. Bethany Packard links the reference to Hecuba to young Lucius's capacity to identify with his grieving aunt. She writes, 'Lavinia educated Lucius, and he is more open to the potential for proliferating narratives than other Andronici. He is part of her collaborative work in this scene,'[51] and incorporates Michael Witmore's observation that '[w]hat is striking about the almost divinatory way in which Lavinia makes use of the boy's book is the collaboration of woman, boy, and text'.[52] Forecasting the political dimension of the affiliation of young Lucius and Lavinia, Packard acknowledges the necessity of social uptake to expressions of agency: 'Lucius' narrative skill and familiarity with *The Metamorphoses* demonstrate Lavinia's influence on the future of her family and of Rome.'[53] Linking young Lucius's social uptake of Lavinia's non-sovereign agency to gender, the scene locates the copy of Ovid's *Metamorphoses* outside the pattern of patriarchal inheritance so central to the play's representation of Roman virtue. The boy tells Titus that his 'mother gave it me' (4.1.43), and Marcus understands the gift as part of the dead mother's legacy: 'For the love of her that's gone, / Perhaps, she culled it from among the rest' (43–4). Unlike Titus's, young Lucius's recognition of Lavinia is not appropriative but intersubjective, facilitated through the object of the book, and suggests that non-sovereign agency is the foundation for political action in opposition to dominant forces of oppression such as Roman patriarchy, masculine desire and an ethos of violence enacted on female bodies.

By stressing affiliation and social uptake, I intend to shift discussions of this scene from Titus's and Marcus's appropriative acts of engagement with Lavinia. The result is to develop alternative ways to understand how power distributes itself in relation to vulnerable bodies, often gendered female, that tend to be relegated to the role of victim on the early modern stage. Even with this objective, however, there is no guarantee that social uptake or the social distribution of non-sovereign agency produces politically efficacious effects. In *Freedom Beyond Sovereignty*, Krause makes this point clear:

> Social uptake matters to agency if efficacy matters because our effects often depend on how others interpret and respond to what we are doing. Individual agency thus needs more than a social context of discursive relations. It needs a community of bearers who can take up the agent's deeds and help bring them to fruition in ways that are constant with her own understanding of her actions and identity.[54]

The sensation of Lavinia's agitating body that is at first so alien to young Lucius and denied social uptake eventually enfolds itself into his perception. He begins this process of social uptake qualifying the effects of social inscription to discipline Lavinia's body throughout the play and that we see most memorably enacted in Marcus's blazon of Lavinia after he discovers her violated body in act 2. What often gets subsumed in discussions of the powerful poetics of the blazon, however, is the degree to which Lavinia's body resists becoming a poetic trope. To view Lavinia solely as a spectacle of violence is to miss the work that her body does on stage as language tries unsuccessfully to manage her unruly corporeality.

Her agitating, agentive body, not her pornographic abjection,[55] gives a cinematic scope and force to this scene. More than any other recent production of the play, Julie Taymor's film adaptation of *Titus Andronicus* (1999) compellingly captures Lavinia's non-sovereign agency, transforming the way we might view her status as victim, martyr or a docile body in the play. In *Shakespeare's Anti-Politics: Sovereign Power and the Life of the Flesh*, Daniel Juan Gil links *Titus Andronicus* to Taymor's film as an account of the transformation of 'the life of the flesh' in the 'early modern political domain' to the body's precarious survival in an 'era of massively powerful corporate states uneasily caught up in the forces of globalization'.[56] At the core of both the play and the film, however, is political conflict enacted on bodies. According to Gil,

> Taymor seems to endorse [the] Schmittian starting point [that rights occur only in the context of the sovereign exception], and her goal is the same as Shakespeare's; namely, to stay with the body as her characters dive into the very heart of raw state power. The strategy of staying with the body as it is transfigured through an encounter with sovereign power accounts for the most distinctive and visual feature of Taymor's film, its campy and gruesome violence. But as in Shakespeare's play, this violence gains philosophical weight by remaining dialectically tied to the issue of state power.[57]

For Gil, the relationship between Shakespeare's play and Taymor's film illustrates that the life of the flesh persists as a political category. Where precarious flesh is the remainder of the 'civic republican critique of absolute sovereignty' on the early modern stage, in Taymor's film it is an indicator of a 'globalized fascism that shatters the traditional liberal ideal of the sacred individual endowed with inalienable rights'.[58] We might describe the 'individual endowed with inalienable rights' as a sovereign subject, a fantasy under assault in Shakespeare's play intent on staging the effect of intersubjective agency in a politics of dissensus. Before turning to Hermione's statue in *The Winter's Tale* as our final foray into Shakespeare's commentary on the essential fragility of intersubjective agency, I want to discuss Taymor's transformative depiction of Lavinia's volatile body as an interpretation that captures the radical unpredictability of a fugitive politics that abjures sovereignty as a primary force. Her experimental cinematic technique highlights the play's investment in body politics and serves as a powerful reminder that Shakespeare's early modern politics is predicated on an aesthetically arresting visual economy.

Such a Sight Will Blind a Father's Eye

Taymor's filmic representation of the blazon that describes Lavinia is in fact an extended image of bodily fragmentation that persists throughout the film, reappearing in experimental non-narrative, dream-like sequences that depict fragmented bodies and body parts. The director's use of prosthetic hands to replace Lavinia's severed limbs also extends the logic of the blazon beyond its status as a singular event at the end of act 2 – when Marcus stumbles upon Lavinia's disfigured body on a tree stump in a swamp. In surpassing its status as a singular poetic event, the extended blazon participates in what Margaret Owens describes as a 'reconfiguration of corporeal semiotics',[59] which she attributes to the cultural transformations ushered in by the

Protestant Reformation. By extending the poetic blazon through cinematic imagery throughout her film, Taymor accentuates how the body may be individuated into parts and surfaces. In doing this, she illustrates how attempts to recover bodily integrity – including psychological depth and wholeness – are at best performed in the service of narrative that exploits female corporeality according to the sovereign logic mitigating against a radical politics defined by antagonism, potentiality and dissent.

Taymor's use of objects such as masks, along with repeated images of bodily fragmentation, reflects her experimental background in theatre and alludes to the early decades of the twentieth century, when avant-garde artists endowed performing objects – masks and artificial body parts – with new meaning.[60] In the film, for example, Taymor includes a scene in which young Lucius locates replacement hands for Lavinia. Set in a carpenter's shop filled with artificial limbs and replicas of dismembered torsos, this scene demonstrates the artificiality of bodily integrity. The relationship between object and subject established as Lavinia replaces her lost hands with the artificial devices is reciprocal in Taymor's vision: just as the new prosthetic limbs animate a renewed sense of bodily integrity and repaired wholeness for Lavinia, she too animates and completes otherwise fragmented, inanimate objects. This reciprocity between inanimate object and animate subject – what Lucian Ghita aptly describes as a 'precarious materiality'[61] – evokes Taymor's abiding interest in the relationship between performing body and performing object, and hints at the political potential in breaking down the subject-object binary to begin to define a new form of non-sovereign agency that informs the body politics in the play.

Taymor's depiction of Marcus's blazon in her film, combined with its representation of the body's desire for relevance extended throughout the film, underscores what Grosz terms 'the productivity of the body, the ways in which social inscriptions of bodies produce the effects of depth'.[62] Transforming Lavinia's body into a stage property, as Taymor's film aggressively does in response to the play that hints at this possibility, is to infuse her victimised form with a transgressive potential emphasised in the movement from violated subject to docile object to 'prosthetic synthesis'. This movement helps to rewrite the body's cultural condition by 'augmenting its powers and capacities through the incorporation into the body's own spaces [. . .] of objects that, while external, are internalized, added to, supplementing and supplemented by the "organic body" [. . .], surpassing the body, not "beyond nature" but in collision with a "nature" that never really lived up to its name'.[63] Reorienting a reading of the play away from what Lavinia's body means – a reading practice encouraged by how we encounter the play as a text to be unpacked – to what her body does, Taymor's film draws attention to the ontological status of the female body that is simultaneously an empty space and an already encoded surface of inscription.[64]

A formal reading of the film's representation of Lavinia's body allows us to bridge a gap between a purely textual interpretation of the play and one informed by performance history. It helps to uncover the body's volatility in a way that the text itself is not able to completely capture. This volatility is best illustrated in the film's depiction of Marcus's blazon after Lavinia's violent rape. The blazon that describes Lavinia's body as an abject object of desire begins, as I've suggested, before Marcus's extended description of her body's 'two branches, those sweet ornaments' (2.4.18) whose 'circling shadows' have seduced kings to 'sleep in' (19). The 'rosèd lips' (24) and 'lily hands' (44) that Marcus emblazons are derided by Chiron and Demetrius immediately before her uncle enters the scene. Demetrius mocks that Lavinia has 'no tongue to call, nor hands to wash, / And so let's leave her to her silent walks' (2.4.7–8). Lavinia's presence as the object of her rapists' derision, then, begins the cinematic blazon that Marcus's poetic description only extends. Taymor's initial depiction of Lavinia's violated body begins with a tracking shot that slowly isolates Lavinia and her two rapists in the middle of a swamp; the tracking shot ends once it establishes the apocalyptic setting and brings Chiron, Demetrius and Lavinia into view. Shot so that Lavinia's back is facing the camera that pans closer to the scene's action, the *mise en scène* encourages the film's viewers to perceive Lavinia as an object – at first not visible in the long tracking shot, and then a faceless spectacle on a tree stump in a scene of humiliation and scorn. The camera's gaze, combined with the shot's slow tracking movement, heightens the desire to witness the condition of Lavinia's brutalised body, yet it defers the revelation of her bloody, dismembered condition by cutting to a scene of her taunting rapists.

By deferring the audience's desire with a cut to Chiron and Demetrius, Taymor draws attention to the scene's insistence that Lavinia's body is an object in a regime of vision with a violent objectifying force. Indeed, the film highlights the precarious condition of Lavinia's body by cutting back to its initial tracking camera, which by this time in the scene's progression focuses on the three figures. Shot over Lavinia's shoulder but with her head and torso in the frame, the medium shot captures the horror of triangulated desire that traffics Lavinia between men in the play. With Lavinia centred in the foreground of the film frame, Chiron and Demetrius stand on opposite sides of her, forming a triangle of mimetic desire and implicating the film's audience, whose expectations to bear witness to the effects of Lavinia's rape have been simultaneously produced and deferred by the scene's structure.

The camera's perspective shifts in the next series of shots, toggling back and forth between images of Lavinia's body from her rapists' point of view and the perspective of a seemingly objective camera that visually seeks to articulate Lavinia's pain. In this series of shots, the audience sees a close-up of Lavinia's face for the first time after her attack. The shot frames her face – eyes closed, head tilted slightly back – in order to establish Lavinia's subjectivity that Chiron and Demetrius have brutally evacuated. The close-up, however, severs subjectivity, located visually in Lavinia's look of anguish, from her body – a body with a volatility that has yet to be completely rendered visible after her rape. Quick cuts from her rapists to the spectacle of Lavinia's body on the stump and the instability of a hand-held camera shot of Lavinia further obfuscate a clear image of Lavinia's ravaged condition. The final shot of this sequence, which returns to a close-up of her face, reinforces the impact of the sequence more generally that subjectivity and emotion are effects severed from the body.

Marcus's arrival in the scene only intensifies the tension between Lavinia as object and subject. The previously objective point of view of the tracking shot earlier in the scene is now clearly aligned with Marcus's perspective. The slow movement of the camera toward Lavinia is sutured to Marcus's vision, as the camera cuts back and forth from Marcus walking toward his niece and the image, from his point of view, of her on the stump. Marcus's vision – indeed, his desire – in retrospect identifies the desire of the audience that had previously aligned its perspective with the establishing shot that appeared removed from Chiron and Demetrius's violent mimetic desire. It is as if Taymor belatedly satisfies viewers' expectations to witness Lavinia's dismembered and tortured body using Marcus as a necessary surrogate – a proxy whose avuncular compassion shields viewers from the implications of their desire. Taymor captures the language of the blazon in the powerful shot that frames Lavinia turning toward Marcus with her arms outstretched, revealing her severed hands replaced with twigs, and opening her tongueless mouth to release a stream of blood. This revelation, however, is distorted by the slow-motion tempo of the sequence that unsettlingly gives the manifestations of her pain an aesthetic quality. The scene then cuts to a reaction shot of Marcus contemplating what he witnesses; the gap of contemplation that separates the immediacy of Lavinia's bloody body and Marcus's efforts to remove Lavinia from the stump is the interstitial that transforms the rhetoric of the blazon into a form of haptic visuality – a moment when vision itself becomes tactile and, as embodied in Marcus's reaction, reveals the 'impression of seeing for the first time, gradually discovering what is in the image rather than coming to the image already knowing what it is'.[65]

Taymor's transformation of the literary blazon into a 'hypertrophy of the visual'[66] sutured to Marcus's contemplative, searching gaze undoes the impression of hermeneutic certainty that characterises aspects of the blazon in early modern literature. In the shot-reaction-shot sequence that structures the scene, the possessiveness and monitory authority of the blazon – its participation in a fetishistic and voyeuristic economy – explodes. Instead of capturing a series of representations, Taymor's cinematic strategy is to insist that Marcus's perception turn back on to him and his body be changed by the tactile, volatile face that looks back. The camera's cut to Marcus at this moment signals the extent to which he is drawn into Lavinia's fragmented materiality. Kaja Silverman's influential account of the cinematic experience asserts that 'there are, of course, no tactile convergences, and the gap between viewer and spectacle remains irreducible'.[67] However, through Taymor's suturing of Lavinia's body to Marcus's searching gaze in the shot-reaction-shot sequence that elides most of Marcus's emblazoning language from Shakespeare's play, the film insists that cinematic vision may be tactile. The cinematic structure of the blazon, according to Taymor's powerful manipulation of it in this scene, establishes 'tactile convergences' as the primary way that Lavinia's volatile body might 'tell' (2.4.1), 'speak' (1), 'bewray' (3), 'scribe' (4) or 'scrawl' (5). As the cut to Marcus's anguished face in the reaction shot suggests, the viewer, carefully manipulated to identify with his angle of vision by the wide tracking shots establishing Lavinia as the object of the gaze, is 'transfixed and transmogrified in consequence of the infectious, visceral contact of images'.[68]

The film's repeated investment in depicting dismembered arms and hands – most associated with a sense of touch – is a cinematic extension of the blazon of Lavinia's body at the end of act 2. The fragmented arms and hands foreground tactility as the ambivalent conduit of desire that spreads contagion in the play. Focusing on the disembodied hand, these moments in Taymor's film capture the process in the play itself by which 'perception becomes a kind of physical affliction, an intensification and disarticulation of bodily sensation'.[69] Walter Benjamin describes this dynamic aspect of the cinematic experience for the spectator as film's 'distracting element' which is also 'primarily tactile'.[70] A reading of the haptic power of Lavinia's image suggests that aesthetic representation may have what, according to Benjamin, is a dynamic or transactional authority. As Steven Shaviro has argued in relation to the body on screen, 'images aren't static or decorative';[71] indeed, a volatile body such as Lavinia's on stage or screen reorients the very notion of identification as the viewer is not allowed to identify with other seemingly sympathetic protagonists; instead, 'the spectator is touched by – drawn into complicitous communication with'[72] – the violated object of 'man's eye' (2.3.177).

In *Titus*, act 2 ends with Marcus helping Lavinia off the stump. His command to his niece, 'Come, let us go and make thy father blind, / For such a sight will blind a father's eye' (2.4.52–3), not only signals an end to his role as Lavinia's *blasonneur*, but it also expresses the play's investment in exploring haptic visuality. Marcus acknowledges the power of an objectified Lavinia and infuses her fragmented, vulnerable body with an infectious agitation. Marcus transforms the productive force of the spectacle into a scene of hyperbolic grief: 'One hour's storm' that drowns the mead is an insufficient metaphor, according to Marcus, to describe the amount of 'whole months of tears' that will issue from Titus's eyes (2.4.54–5) when he physically holds Lavinia in his arms. Marcus's turn to metaphor to describe Lavinia's haptic agency is his attempt to disavow the non-metaphoric power of her condition. In the film, Marcus, holding Lavinia in his arms, looks directly at Lavinia when he describes the power of her condition to blind Titus. However, as Marcus's rhetoric turns to metaphor, he turns away from Lavinia, disavowing the possibility of her corporeal authority by delivering the figurative lines while looking away from the object. After hearing Marcus's metaphoric turn, Lavinia draws attention to her volatile body by noticeably shifting to free herself from her uncle's arms. By agitating in Marcus's arms at the moment when figurative language defers the effect of her status as an agentive object, Lavinia insists that her body not be ignored, and Marcus returns his attention to her face as they make their way out of the swamp.

The female body's kinetic agitation, which reinforces Lavinia's visual tactility, is the subject of her father's first encounter with her in act 3. In the film, Marcus carries Lavinia, described as 'consuming sorrow' (3.1.61), to Titus and Lucius and warns them about the horror of what he is about to show them. Titus responds to Marcus's warning: 'Will it consume me? Let me see it then' (62). The repetition of the pronoun 'it' in Titus's response intensifies Lavinia's objectified status and proleptically frames Lucius's reaction after seeing his sister's maimed body three lines later: 'Ay me, this object kills me' (65). Lavinia's consuming agency – metaphorised as 'sorrow' in Marcus's abstracting discourse – operates simultaneously as an active force, and the effect of the event of the poetic blazon extends beyond act 2 and into the play's futurity. Marcus and Titus's exchange at the moment that Titus sees his daughter captures this temporal effect:

MARCUS. This was thy daughter.
TITUS. Why, Marcus, so she is.   (3.1.63–4)

Marcus's insistence that the agentive potential of Lavinia's body ramifies only in the past is immediately reconfigured in Titus's corrective that Lavinia 'is' his daughter. The exchange infuses her body, which is the spectacle at the centre of this scene, with an immediacy that defies the force of the blazon as a singular event that seeks to regulate, contain and control the unpredictable effects of female corporeality. Despite Marcus's best poetic efforts in act 2 to render docile the volatile female body, the effect of her haptic visuality, hinted at in the text of the play and embodied on stage and screen, persists.

The film accentuates the pervasiveness of the fragmented body, moreover, in an extra-textual scene in which young Lucius visits a carpenter's shop looking for prosthetic hands for his niece. The camera sequence slowly pans around the shop, where the audience sees shelves and tables filled with dismembered hands, feet, heads and torsos being prepared to be used as parts of statues of saints.[73] Taymor's inclusion of this scene reinforces the film's radical portrayal of the literary blazon: by extending the logic of the blazon beyond the scene of its poetic utterance and by demonstrating how the unintended consequences of fragmentation surpass Lavinia's body as the object of man's eye and include other bodies associated with patriarchal authority and tradition, the film reconfigures the object of the blazon. In Taymor's aesthetic world, the poetic device is imbued with the potential to resist the political and ideological force that relegates and regulates the power of the emblazoned body to literary history and convention. The film's radical depiction of the blazon has an immediacy, evoked in Titus's presentist interpretation of Lavinia, 'so she is' (3.1.64), that points to a future for fugitive politics 'open to contingency and to transformation'.[74] It is above all an act of social uptake, fragile, without any guarantees that her non-sovereign agency will generate a commensurate act of non-sovereign responsibility that fosters the sense of ethical accountability yet still acknowledging the myriad ways that human agency disarticulates itself from intentionality and control.[75]

And Lavinia with a Veil over her Face

What Taymor's adaptation of *Titus Andronicus* makes clear is the political valence of tactility that does not contradict a theory of social inscription but that instead explores the intersection of constructivists' claims about political and social identity with non-sovereign agency. According to Krause's non-sovereign view of agency, the 'social construction of identities is only a threat to agency if agency is equated with autonomy and located in the exercise of a self-determined will, or in a choice that is self-generated all the way down. But individual agency is not located exclusively within the will and it is not reducible to the exercise of choice.'[76] Krause stresses that a subject's intention or will has the potential to be at odds with the effects she has in her community. Moments of 'failed and frustrated agency' will 'regularly fail to affirm' who she is.[77] In a similar register, Krause insists that the 'identification of agency with control also is a mistake',[78] and she maintains that 'although the mark of agency is the manifestation of the individual's identity in her deeds, identity is not reducible to the will, and consequently agency sometimes exceeds or counteracts the individual's intentions'.[79] Krause's repeated qualification about the relationship between agency and intention in light of the force of social inscription provides an important way to begin to make sense of Lavinia's problematic role in Titus's dumb show in act 5 that seems to depict Lavinia as an agent in her own death. Once again, Taymor's interpretation of this scene in her film adaptation proves instructive in terms of how the female body remains the site for non-sovereign agency that has the potential to execute the subject's desire, but without any guarantee.

If Lavinia's body – its surface, its fragmented form, its violated boundaries – is the object of the literary blazon central to the play, then her appearance in the play's final act *'with a veil over her face'* (5.3.25–6. s.d.) is, at least, a curious staging decision. The stage directions from Q1 have been adopted by most editors of the play,[80] but the quarto provides no clear direction about when the veil is removed to reveal Lavinia's face. Bate's Arden edition (1995) places this stage direction immediately before Titus utters the lines 'Die, die, Lavinia, and thy shame with thee, / And with thy shame thy father's sorrow die' (5.3.45–6). In this interpretation, Lavinia's exposed face is a visible component of the murder sequence. Taymor adopts Bate's staging suggestion and, in accordance with Q1, Lavinia enters wearing a veil, which she removes immediately before Titus snaps her neck and kills her. The editorial decision to unveil Lavinia at the moment of her execution is motivated, it seems, by the desire to show her stoic expression as she encounters the full weight of literary and cultural tradition seeking justice and retribution through the female body. If we do not emend the stage directions to Q1, however, the scene appears quite different. As an extension of her body and the focal point of Marcus's and Taymor's blazon in act 2, Lavinia's face – obscured from vision by the veil that remains in place for the play's duration – occupies a space '[w]here never man's eye may behold' it (2.3.177).

Lavinia's veiled, faceless condition recalls her objectified status and at the same time invigorates it with a kinetic force that establishes the tactile visuality of her emblazoned body in act 2. The veiled Lavinia is all surface, a prop in act 5 who enters the scene with Titus and remains unacknowledged until Titus names her at the moment he kills her: 'Die, die, Lavinia' (5.3.45). Lavinia's veiled face becomes a vexing source for the fantasy of subjectivity, staging subjectivism as a product of active desires that, once in process, create the impression that it was there from the beginning as the cause.[81] This fantasy removes intersubjective agency as viable in any political intervention that eventually transpires. The veil's complexity represents the impossibility of reconciling social uptake and a subject's intentions. Taymor's decision to unveil Lavinia at the moment of her murder insinuates the desire for a form of corporeal feminism that interprets the body as crucial to understanding agency and to accessing interiority. Veiled, however, Lavinia's body literally remains all surface, and those who gaze on her are forced to recognise this condition of her lived body.

The veil, a prosthetic skin in the scene, agitates in place of her body and highlights the non-sovereign condition of political subjectivity. Saturninus's question to Titus immediately after he kills Lavinia begins the powerful process of inscription that contends with her agentive capacity: 'What hast thou done? Unnatural and unkind!' (5.3.47), and Titus's response that aligns his woe with cultural pattern and precedence continues the process of subjectivism that only retrospectively assumes its status as a natural or essential force: 'Killed her for whom my tears have made me blind. / I am as woeful as Virginius was' (48–9). Titus's turn to cultural history enacts a movement away from the kinetic agitation of the haptic image and towards a vision in which the object is 'separate, complete, objectifiable', and already possessed by Titus, Virginius's surrogate.[82] If, as Q1 suggests, Lavinia's face remains covered, the play is able to reveal the mechanics of subjectivism – acts of inscription that continue to imprint their markings on her body. Thus, her faceless presence serves to emphasise the process of becoming in the play that is central to the evanescence of fugitive politics.

Lavinia's veil is also revelatory for the audience. Remaining in place, the veil is a radicalising prosthetic supplement that reshapes 'experience away from meanings or fixed wholes to its effective components (those singularities which produce meaning)',[83] and what we witness is the powerful logic of the blazon folded back on to itself. Sovereign divisibility is simultaneously enacted and refused. As a performing object with an intensity that surpasses poetic attempts to contain and codify it, Lavinia's emblazoned body – a fragmented spectacle extended in time by its tactile visuality and, more radically, a veiled surface inscribed by Titus's, or a critic's, literary imagination – affirms social inscription as a virtual effect. Hiding nothing underneath, Lavinia's veil, which we seem too eager to remove in the play's final moments, ironically reveals that the dynamism of non-sovereign agency lay in the tactility of the body's prosthetic surfaces, explored vividly in Taymor's film, that pretend, like Marcus's poetic blazon, to suture division and that supplement, but more likely surpass, the penetrating, fragmenting violence of social inscription that grants potency to the sovereign exception.

Mocked with Art: The Politics of Hermione's Prosthetic Body

In turning from *Titus Andronicus* to *The Winter's Tale*, early Shakespeare gives way to late, and violent tragedy gives way to transcendent romance; these two plays, performed almost twenty years apart, however, are linked by their attention to the volatility of the female body – its performing and performative capacities, or, what I have described in relation to Lavinia, its non-sovereign, intersubjective agency. *The Winter's Tale* has become a touchstone for two recent critical trends: one, for theo-political readings that illuminate the impact of reformed religious practices on England's recalcitrant Catholic traditions, and two, for critical responses to the Bodinean concept of indivisible sovereignty.[84] In what immediately follows, I explore several exemplary readings of the play that have shaped how we might understand the claims of theology and politics in Shakespeare's late romance before ending with an examination of the power of non-sovereign agency in the resurrection scene that closes the play.

Julia Reinhard Lupton offers perhaps the most sustained analysis of the theological dynamism of the image in *The Winter's Tale*. In her reading of the statue scene in act 5, Lupton claims that Shakespeare 'stages the visual conditions of Catholic image worship, but only as canceled, with equal emphasis on both the act of staging and the act of cancellation'.[85] In a complex analysis of multiple intersecting discourses on idolatry, Lupton shows how the play's dramatic structure commingles pre-Catholic pagan ritual with Catholicism and residual Catholic ritual still vibrant in reformed England. According to Lupton, the iconographies of the residual religions, 'in their very bankrupting by the Protestant historical vision, together underwrite the hagiographic scheme informing the play'.[86] In arguing that the play stages 'an *iconography of idolatry*, a visual and critical analysis of the religious image in a secular world', Lupton's reading of the statue scene shows how its 'staged mystery' associated with Catholic idolatry is undercut, deflated by Hermione's body itself.[87] Hermione's corporeality assures us, as Lupton writes, that '[n]o heretical transubstantiation or pagan magic [. . .] has in fact taken place'.[88] Lupton's reading of the statue pushes further, however, implicating the actor's body in the hermeneutics of the scene. 'Shakespeare', Lupton writes, 'manages to distract us from the power of his own art: the reassurance that the statue is not "really" Hermione but an actor.'[89] The staging of iconoclasm, according to Lupton, 'is itself only apparent, since another metamorphosis is occurring through the verbal and optical media of the theater – namely, that we take the actor "for" Hermione, as both a representative and a representation, a proxy and a mimesis'.[90] She elaborates on the theatrical effect of the iconographic body in the scene:

> The point is not that we are fooled into thinking that the actor playing Hermione is not really an actor; instead, a particular kind of fictionality emerges as the double negation of both the ritual truth of a sacramental or magical theater [. . .] and the nominalist truth of iconoclastic discourse [. . .] *The Winter's Tale* smashes the Catholic idols in order to draw new wine from their old skins. The presentation of Hermione-as-statue privileges the mimetic

illusion of the icon over the material presence of the idol; when the statue reveals itself as human, the representational icon is reduced once more to the presentational idol, but within the scene of dramatic fiction, whose staging of human bodies recycles the mimetic iconicity and epiphanic idolatry of pagan and Catholic rites.[91]

In her persuasive account, Lupton clarifies how the myth of theological supersession fails to do justice to the vibrancy of residual rituals that compete with emergent reformed practices – practices bound in many cases to the structure and materiality of pagan and Catholic ritual.[92]

In addition to the play's religious themes explored so perspicaciously by Lupton, scholars have revisited the play's rich political dimensions, especially in relation to the force of sovereignty explored by, among others, Carl Schmitt, Giorgio Agamben and Jacques Derrida. Christopher Pye, Bradin Cormack and Philip Lorenz have invigorated political discussions of *The Winter's Tale* with trenchant, original readings of the play's critique of the sovereign decision. Pye's penetrating account of the relationship between the aesthetic and Schmitt's concept of the sovereign decision argues, contra Schmitt, that the realm of the aesthetic is 'where the political, understood as the domain of the act in its purely contingent character, reaches its fullest potential'.[93] For Schmitt, the aesthetic is part of 'liberalism's onslaught against the political'.[94] Pye's challenge to Schmitt on this point understands the aesthetic as much more than a product of the 'multiplication of separate discursive spheres', as Schmitt would have it. For Pye, the aesthetic is instead the principal location within which the concept of indivisibility that characterises sovereignty in the Schmittian sense emerges.[95] Pye concludes, 'Paradoxically, not just the superfluity but the radical contingency of the aesthetic becomes apparent only when it is understood in its relations to its strongest totalizing claims.'[96] In *The Tears of Sovereignty*, Philip Lorenz understands the implications of Pye's discovery of the role of the aesthetic in sovereignty's expression to mean that the 'aesthetic sphere itself can be viewed as a threat to the fantasy of sovereignty, whether of the state or of the self'.[97] In Lorenz's account of the way the play exposes the *process* of sovereign indivisibility, Hermione's statue and its restoration act with an efficacy that he equates with special effects: '*The Winter's Tale* turns in a new direction, reorienting the sovereignty question back, in a way, to where it has been from the start – to the stage, and its machinery of wonder, without which no sovereignty effects would be possible in the first place.'[98] Hermione's movement from art to life, captured in the image of her wrinkle, enacts the 'combination of sameness and difference'[99] that so menaces the notion of indivisible sovereignty desired by Leontes. Tracing the effect of difference throughout the play, Bradin Cormack argues that *The Winter's Tale* is about 'the threat of difference to indivisible sovereignty and, in reverse, the absurdity of indivisibility as a starting point for thinking about power in a world in which power simply is differentiated, and in which meaning simply is distributed'.[100] In Cormack's reading of the play, sovereignty 'erodes from within', vulnerable to the 'differences it is unable properly to manage'.[101]

These powerful theological and political accounts of the play have a common interpretive crux, summarised cogently by Lorenz: 'the crisis of sovereignty is also a crisis of representation'.[102] Put otherwise, in a way that brings us back to the productivity of non-sovereign agency, these critics take seriously the symbolic power of sovereign authority and understand sovereignty as an intersubjective phenomenon, diffused and distributed across subjects and objects.

To employ language from *The Winter's Tale*, a 'co-active' (1.2.141) encounter transforms the putative indivisibility of sovereignty into its inevitable self-betrayal. In relation to Hermione's body – as monument and as flesh – self-betrayal is a sign of non-sovereign agency that hazards intention and consensus in favour of contingency and difference.

The non-sovereign agency that *The Winter's Tale* explores bears the traces of what contemporary theorists of sovereignty and state power describe as authority that is increasingly fragmented. Antonio Negri and Michael Hardt, for example, trace the fragmentation of sovereignty accompanied by an equally dissensual notion of the people as the multitude. For them, 'The multitude is a multiplicity, a plane of singularities, an open set of relations, which is not homogeneous or identical with itself and bears an indistinct, inclusive relation to those outside of it' in contrast to a concept of the people as a sovereign body with a unified, homogeneous identity.[103] According to Negri and Hardt, 'Whereas the multitude is an inconclusive constitutive relation, the people is a constituted synthesis that is prepared for sovereignty.'[104] Hent Kalmo and Quentin Skinner note in the introduction to *Sovereignty in Fragments* how a pluralist view of sovereignty has emerged that accounts for the social reality of 'division and disagreement' that characterise 'the fragmentation of authority'.[105]

Within this particular context, Shakespeare's play is noteworthy because it has not just two but three sovereigns. Like John and Philip in *King John*, whose conflicting claims to the crown trouble the idea of indivisible sovereignty, Leontes' and Polixenes' rival kingships pose questions about sovereignty's relation to difference, and, adding to the complexity, as Cormack points out, Hermione functions as the play's 'third sovereign'.[106] He goes on to identify her power in relation to the two kings this way: 'Hermione's power over Polixenes threatens the primacy of his, Leontes', sovereignty: first, because her speech, not his, has been efficacious; second, because affection, the putative source of that authority, is a principle disruptive of the very possibility of placing events in relation to a uniquely sovereign cause.'[107] Sovereign singularity, writes Cormack, is redistributed 'onto an affective structure that, if anything, is the more intense [. . .] for the generosity of its differentiations'.[108] Leontes' own language betrays the intensity of the redistribution of sovereignty, as he bears witness to the affective force of the sovereign touch – the royal prerogative explored in Chapter 3 with King Henry's 'little touch' in the night – in *The Winter's Tale* reallocated to Hermione's gentle fingers.

Paddling Palms and Pinching Fingers

Echoing Othello's intense reaction to the ocular proof of Desdemona's supposed infidelity with Othello's lieutenant Cassio, Leontes too is '[p]erplexed in the extreme' (*Othello* 5.2.406) as a spectator of the hospitality that Hermione shows Polixenes in act 1. Responding to her husband's demand – 'Tongue-tied, our queen? Speak you' (1.2.28) – to convince the Bohemian king to stay in Sicily for another week, Hermione reluctantly and deliberately enters into the conversation. 'I had thought, sir, to have held my peace until / You had drawn oaths from him not to stay' (1.2.28–9), she says, before she gives her husband advice on the best arguments to make to Polixenes: 'You, sir, / Charge him too coldly. Tell him you are sure / All in Bohemia's well. This satisfaction / The bygone day proclaimed. Say this to him, / He's beat from his best word' (29–33). Perhaps encouraged by her husband's praise ('Well said, Hermione!' (33)), the direction of her address shifts, and she turns from Leontes, her surrogate, directly to Polixenes to make the argument to change his mind.

The scene registers this shift in the change in pronouns in her argument:

> To tell, he longs to see his son, were strong.
> But let him say so then, and let him go;
> But let him swear so, and he shall not stay:
> We'll thwack him hence with distaffs.
> [*To* POLIXENES] Yet of your royal presence I'll adventure
> The borrow of a week. When at Bohemia
> You take my lord, I'll give him my commission
> To let him there a month behind the gest
> Prefixed for's parting. – Yet, good deed, Leontes,
> I love thee not a jar o' the clock behind
> What lady she her lord. – You'll stay?   (34–44)

Hermione shifts from third person pronouns when discussing Polixenes with her husband ('he longs to see his son', 'let him say so', 'let him go') to second person ('your royal presence', 'You take my lord', 'You'll stay'), marking her strategic, physical investment in the scene. Lupton's illuminating reading of this moment identifies the slow progression of Hermione's direct engagement in the exchange within the framework of hospitality and risk. According to Lupton, Hermione begins 'tongue-tied' or captive 'by her mouth's own fullness, by her own verbal gifts'; she moves to 'reserved', speaking to and through Leontes, who acts as her surrogate in the exchange; she then speaks boldly to her husband, criticising him for being too timid in his argument with Polixenes; and finally she speaks directly to Polixenes, 'venturing now to address [him] face to face'.[109] Lupton teases out the implications of Hermione's use of the word 'adventure' (38) in her speech to Polixenes, meaning on one level 'venture, enterprise, the weak/week terms of the loan that she has set'.[110] Yet, for Lupton, the adventure is also more subjective and consequently carries more risk. She writes,

> The adventure here is also, however, subjective, consisting in the shift from mediated missive to direct address, a venture that tenders her very being as collateral to the loan. That is, Hermione's subjectivity guarantees the loan insofar as she appears *as a subject* by virtue of this loan, a venture risked in the changing syntax and dramatic orientation of her enunciation.[111]

Lupton stresses the process by which Hermione becomes public in this scene with her movement from silent observer, to Leontes' ventriloquism, to a physical participant in the exchange. From her intimate, private discussions with Leontes to her public, persuasive speech to Polixenes, the scene transforms Hermione into both a subject, as Lupton argues, and an object subject to others' gaze.

The scene continues to explore Hermione's precarious position as both subject and object – as the agent of the venture that will guarantee that Polixenes remain in Sicily and as the collateral or object that secures the venture. In short, like Lavinia in *Titus Andronicus*, explored so richly in Taymor's adaptation of the play, Hermione is a performing object. And like Lavinia, who begs to be tumbled 'into some loathsome pit, / Where never man's eye may behold [her] body' (2.3.176–7), she understands too late the risk of becoming vibrant matter. Leontes acknowledges that her touch is part of the performance of their marriage vows. Speaking about the two times Hermione spoke most convincingly, he says, 'Ere I could make thee open thy white hand /And clap thyself my love: then didst thou utter / "I am yours for ever"' (1.2.102–4). Coactive in the marriage ritual, the touch of her 'white hand' as she spoke her vow makes her body part of the event. The tactility of the expression of love in his imagination helps to explain his hostile reaction to Hermione's act of persuasion that transforms it into a spectacle. 'Too hot, too hot!' (108) he says as he watches Hermione's body with Polixenes:

> To mingle friendship far is mingling bloods.
> I have tremor cordis on me: my heart dances;
> But not for joy; not joy. This entertainment
> May a free face put on, derive a liberty
> From heartiness, from bounty, fertile bosom,
> And well become the agent; 't may, I grant;
> But to be paddling palms and pinching fingers,
> As now they are, and making practised smiles,
> As in a looking-glass,   (1.2.109–17)

Leontes reacts to the spectacle of the scene of seduction, a scene that sexualises friendship, embodying it in the imagined act of mingling blood. Leontes' 'heart dances' because Hermione's body acts. The threat of her performing body is localised in her hand, the same agentive hand that clapped his in the marriage ceremony, with its 'paddling' palm and 'pinching fingers' now touching Polixenes. His reaction to her body here illustrates the effect of haptic visuality – a form of touching with the eyes, contact between the perceived object and the person perceiving – and at this moment Leontes' haptic vision of Hermione's vibrant body is painful, producing one of the most enigmatic passages in the play:

> Affection, thy intention stabs the centre,
> Thou dost make possible things not so held,
> Communicatest with dreams; – how can this be? –
> With what's unreal thou coactive art,
> And fellow'st nothing. Then 'tis very credent
> Thou mayst co-join with something, and thou dost,
> And that beyond commission, and I find it,
> And that to the infection of my brains
> And hardening of my brows.   (1.2.138–46)

In an attempt to wed reason and passion, Leontes ascribes intention to affection and gives it a potency that wounds. He understands affection as a power that gives presence to the immaterial; as a 'coactive art', affection conjoins with matter ('something') to amplify experience ('commission'), transforming an event into a disease that infects his brain. Put otherwise, affection, according to Leontes, is the force beyond matter that gives matter its potency. By differentiating affection from matter, Leontes tries to reduce the threat that Hermione's body possesses; furthermore, by ascribing intention to affection, he implies that it can be corralled and reallocated. Called 'affection', the haptic image is non-sovereign, incomplete, part dream, part commission, coactive with the unreal but a partner to nothing. By wrestling with affection, he harnesses an element of Hermione's non-sovereign agency that eludes intention and that potentially enables alternative ways of viewing the world.

Leontes must tether its force to reduce the power of its contingency and unpredictability. Looking at his son Mamillius, he says, 'Most dear'st! my collop! Can thy dam? – may't be?' (137). The staccato rhythm of the line, broken by exclamations and questions, generates the tether: his son (dearest), a form of Leontes' flesh (my collop), Mamillius's mother (thy dam), her untamed desire (may't be?). The series of fragments has an as-yet-unrealised narrative force that begins to transmute affect into a libidinal economy that he can manage. 'I am angling now,' he says in an aside, 'Though you perceive me not how I give line' (1.2.179–80). Even as his infected brain and hardened brow register the affective materiality of Hermione's body, he insists on viewing haptic visuality as a form of representation in a narrative about his own sovereign power. Hermione understands just what is at stake in this battle over regimes of knowledge – representational, affective, sovereign and non-sovereign. After Leontes confronts her in her private chamber and calls her an adulteress and a bed-swerver, she responds,

> No, by my life.
> Privy to none of this. How will this grieve you,
> When you shall come to clearer knowledge, that
> You thus have published me!   (2.1.96–9)

Hermione's use of the word 'published' certainly suggests her concern that she has been publicly shamed,[112] and it indicates the precarious condition that results from her public assertion of subjectivity in her engagement with Polixenes. Lupton calls the moment in which Hermione improvises on centre stage in Leontes' drama 'the terrifying contingency of the here and now, a *Jetztzeit* defined by the acknowledging, and potentially misrecognizing, presence of others. Hermione switches, against her better instincts and her own sense of decorum, from hostessing as a social role to hostessing as an existential venture.'[113] Hermione's anger at being 'published' is her acknowledgement of the vulnerability that she intuited would result if she spoke for the king. She tells Leontes after he commands his 'tongue-tied' queen to speak in act 1: 'I had thought, sir, to have held my peace until / You had drawn oaths from him not to stay' (1.2.28–9). Public performances of subjectivity notwithstanding, however, to be 'published' is also associated with property and goods. The *Oxford English Dictionary* lists as one of its definitions 'to make public property; to confiscate (goods)'. Hermione's anxiety, informed by the contingency of the cultural moment that accommodates her public role, is also an acknowledgement of her object-ness – of her ability to be turned into property.

Leontes defines Hermione's object-ness as confirmation of her vile participation with Polixenes. Before the court guards take her away, he says, 'You have mistook, my lady, / Polixenes for Leontes: O thou thing / Which I'll not call a creature of thy place' (2.1.83–5). Here, Leontes strips Hermione of her social identity, reducing her to a form of life that vexes categorical distinction between 'the prince and the beggar' (88). In her thing-ness, Hermione resembles what Giorgio Agamben calls bare life, a form of life with all political and social distinctions erased, leaving only biological existence (*zoe*). Ziarek's definition of bare life informs how we might view this moment in the play: she is 'damaged life, stripped of its political significance, of its specific form of life'.[114] Stripped of political and social forms of life, Hermione is an object standing trial, whose truthful voice bears no impact on Leontes' sovereign decision or on the Oracle's pronouncement of her chastity that promises to restore her political and social identity. For Hermione at this point in the play, being published is to endure a bare life, to become an object in circulation 'on every post' (3.2.99). It is, as she reminds her husband, empty: 'no life', she says, 'I prize it not a straw' (106–7). Her lament over her public condition echoes Lavinia's in *Titus Andronicus*, whose futile request to be left 'where never man's eye may behold [her] body' (2.3.177) collapses her subjectivity into utter object-ness.

In the comparison that this chapter is making between Lavinia and Hermione, both characters are reduced to objects that possess agency, and it is through this comparison that we see the role of contingency in defining the radical potential of fugitive politics. Lavinia's vibrant body becomes a stage prop for Titus's final performance, a critical object possessing the power of non-sovereign agency that feeds Rome's desire for historical continuity and Titus's appetite for revenge. The non-sovereign force of Hermione's vibrant body, however, functions differently. Although, like Lavinia, a stage prop in a final performance, Hermione's body is cared for by Paulina, whose ameliorative touch 'tenderly appl[ies] to her / Some remedies for life' (3.2.149–50). In stipulating their sixteen-year relationship after Hermione's death, the play suggests that non-sovereign agency redistributes subjective force and transforms it into a plenary power. With its emphasis on Hermione's volatile body in Paulina's hands, the play challenges claims of the disembodied character of citizenship – that a political public sphere is somehow removed from the corporeal condition of what Krause calls non-sovereign, intersubjective agency. Where Agamben's view of absolute power understands the body as 'always already a biopolitical body and bare life', which for him means that 'nothing in it [. . .] seems to allow us to find solid ground on which to oppose the demands of sovereign power',[115] Shakespeare's depiction of Hermione's body in act 5 shows that bare life is not always determined by the sovereign decision and is indeed not always bare, but may be contested, antagonistic to and within the exception, and coordinate with new forms of political life articulated through and by the female body.

Life as Lively Mocked as Ever

Hermione's resurrection from a statue in act 5 transforms the concept of tragic overliving into an event with an emancipatory political valence. If tragic overliving involves elements that resemble the condition of bare life – the desire to be invisible, the body as burden, the loss of selfhood, and the depiction of life as living death – then Hermione's act of overliving reconfigures the condition, exposing sovereign power's reliance on bare life – that is, reliance on a body already dead but that actively threatens and provokes. The play's final scene begins with what appears to be another acknowledgement of the sovereign exception. Paulina tells Leontes that her 'poor house to visit, / It is a surplus of your grace, which never / My life may last to answer' (5.3.6–8). Paulina's 'services' – her hospitality, her home, her life – are the gifts of the sovereign, an amplification and extension of his absolute authority. The scene quickly balances the surplus sovereignty, however, with a description of Hermione's statue: 'As she lived peerless, / So her dead likeness, I do well believe, / Excels whatever yet you looked upon / Or hand of man hath done' (14–17). The statue's perfection, as an embodiment of Hermione's peerless life, exceeds all other works of art; this excess is surplus too, more lively than Hermione's own flesh, 'life as lively mocked as ever / Still sleep mocked death' (19–20). The duelling surpluses – one a condition of sovereignty and the other a condition of its rival – dialectically structure the encounter, but more than a scene of resistance to absolutism, the antagonism between sovereign power and the sovereign body that shapes the encounter reconfigures absolutism, dividing it by infecting its boundaries, by exposing it to Hermione's volatile, reanimated body.

Leontes responds to the statue in a series of opposites that capture his wonder at what he sees. After Paulina explains the wrinkles on Hermione's face as an image of her '[a]s she lived now' (32), Leontes says,

> As now she might have done,
> So much to my good comfort, as it is
> Now piercing to my soul. Oh, thus she stood,
> Even with such life of majesty – warm life,
> As now it coldly stands – when first I wooed her.
> I am ashamed: does not the stone rebuke me
> For being more stone than it?   (32–8)

His description of 'good comfort' is followed by the 'piercing' to his soul, and her 'warm life' is opposite her stone body, which 'coldly stands'. Echoing Marcus's turn to metaphor when he first sees Lavinia after she has been raped and mutilated, Leontes' use of synoeciosis at this moment suggests his wonder at what he witnesses. A form of antithesis, synoeciosis brings together opposites to reconcile them, to render them familiar to each other. Rather than a sign of exclusion and a result of the sovereign exception, Hermione's statue, the residue of bare life, is reconciled with the figure of the sovereign.

Leontes' shame at being rebuked by the stone is a sign of the affection that conjoins the two seeming opposites. Leontes is described as being 'wrought', 'transported' and 'stirred' by his encounter with the statue, and now the affection that so vexed him in act 2 is transformed into an 'affliction' that 'has a taste as sweet / As any cordial comfort' (76–7). The volatile body that he punished earlier in the play, reducing it to bare life, now possesses a tactility – a taste, a touch – that the sovereign demands: 'what fine chisel / Could ever yet cut breath? Let no man mock me, / For I will kiss her' (78–80). Paulina repeats the threat of infection at this moment, asking Leontes to 'forbear: The ruddiness upon her lip is wet; / You'll mar it if you kiss it, stain your own / With oily painting' (80–2). Paulina's warning expresses the reciprocity of desire that I argue divides sovereignty at this moment in the play, transforming the exception into non-sovereign agency. His lips will damage the wet paint on the statue, and in the process his own lips will be stained with oily paint.

The play reinforces a sense of divided sovereignty after Hermione's resurrection in the act of touch. Paulina asks Leontes, 'present your hand: / When she was young you wooed her; now in age / Is she become the suitor?' (107–9). The royal touch wavers at this moment, its efficacy now challenged by the magic of the metamorphosis that Leontes has just witnessed. Without clarifying who touches whom first at the moment of Hermione's descent, Leontes acknowledges once again the affliction that is affection, as her warmth penetrates his body: 'Oh, she's warm!' (109), he exclaims. The result of the penetration of the sovereign body – its piercing, its feeling of shame, its sense of warmth – is to render its absolutism divisible and to create the potential for a new form of political life. Leontes acknowledges this new form in the play's final passage. Although it begins with what appears to be a sovereign command that some might argue is a sign of sovereignty's reconstitution, Leontes' sovereign consent as to whom Paulina will marry is clearly interpenetrated with her own act of consent: 'Thou shouldst a husband take by my consent, / As I by thine a wife. This is a match, / And made between's by vows' (136–8). His sovereign prerogative is now an expression of intersubjective, non-sovereign agency, matching his consent with Paulina's gift.

Another way to view the miraculous events that close *The Winter's Tale* is to understand them as Paulina's wager. She wagers that to resuscitate a consequential, political form of life she would have to render Hermione lifeless. She would have to inhabit actively and deliberately – and aesthetically – bare life that is the result of Leontes' sovereign exception. With this wager, Paulina considers fugitive politics from the perspective of bare life – that is, from the 'perspective of the impossible'.[116] As with every wager, its outcome is unpredictable and contingent. Lavinia's fate in *Titus Andronicus* is a stark reminder of what is at stake in Paulina's gamble that from the excluded residue of the sovereign exception a new form of political life might emerge.

The sixteen-year period between Hermione's death and her resurrection is notable because of the inactivity of its political exiles. The 'wide gap of time' (5.3.154) remains a mystery at the end of the play; in fact, Paulina insists that she and Hermione not disclose what transpires during the interim. At Polixenes' request that Paulina 'make it manifest' (113) what occurred during the period and exactly how her reanimation happened, Paulina hedges, 'That she is living, / Were it but told you, should be hooted at / Like an old tale: but it appears she lives' (115–17). Hermione too wonders what occurred in the interim. She says to her daughter, Perdita: 'Tell me, mine own, / Where hast thou been preserved? Where lived? How found / Thy father's court?' (123–5). Postponing this inquiry into how things came to pass for Perdita, Paulina interrupts the mother-daughter exchange: 'There is time enough for that, / Lest they desire upon this push to trouble / Your joys with like relation' (128–30). As the play ends, the desire for a story to make sense of the unknowable events is a preoccupation. The demand for information closes the play, in fact; Leontes tells Paulina,

Lead us from hence, where we may leisurely
Each one demand an answer to his part
Performed in this wide gap of time since first
We were dissevered.   (152–5)

Paulina's deferral of the narrative that unravels time and clarifies how and why events transpire indicates the degree to which a new political form of life is nurtured by contingency, something that explanatory stories would undo. Paulina knows that to narrate events, to fill in the 'wide gap of time' with logic, reason, and cause and effect, is to risk the potency of potential: 'That she is living, / Were it but told you,' she says, 'should be hooted at / Like an old tale' (115–17). The 'wide gap of time' offers refuge from the dichotomous politics of resistance characterised by active and passive agency. By occluding bodies, the interim ironically exposes the extreme cost that the sovereign exception exerts on female bodies. The 'wide gap of time' is noteworthy because of the way it negates the exclusion, the way it enables Paulina and Hermione to transform the condition of bare life. In this 'wide gap of time', they are both subject and object, sovereign and exile. This is Paulina's wager: that she and Hermione can wield the unanticipated and unformed authority of a new political dispensation by mocking the life of the body, 'To see the life as lively mocked as ever' (5.3.19). Paulina's wager is that by severing the sovereign exception from the tyrant who wields it, she might redefine sovereignty itself from indivisible absolutism to a form of non-sovereignty that Ziarek describes 'as interconnection and yet nonidentity between form and life, human and inhuman, which makes their separation and unification equally impossible'.[117]

Historical continuity and the desire for revenge erode the contingency that fuels fugitive politics in *Titus Andronicus*. To be '[i]ncorporate in Rome' (1.1.464), as Tamora becomes, is to abide by the sovereign exception and to render indivisible absolutism's claims over forms of political life. *The Winter's Tale*, however, presents us with a new form of sovereignty – one that is divided from itself by the force of exclusion that only appears to make it cohesive. Its form is precarious, its efficacy uncertain. At the close of the play, Paulina calls the politics of this new dispensation a 'push' (5.3.129). She warns Hermione about the precariousness of the new political moment. 'Lest they desire upon this *push* to trouble / Your joys with like relation' (129–30, italics mine), she tells Hermione, who seeks explanations for the events in front of her. A push is a critical or decisive moment in time, an event to which the outcome is very much in doubt – in other words, a contingent event with potential to thwart intentions just as easily as to fulfil them. The push that Paulina identifies is the expression of the political in the play. The push registers agency but menaces intention; it acknowledges desire but troubles fulfilment, and it recognises sovereign power as it severs it from its execution. The push is the site where fugitive politics divides the sovereign exception. Like Paulina, Leontes understands the politics of the push at the play's end. His demand to know all the events performed in the 'wide gap of time since first / We were dissevered' (5.3.154–5) is either an acknowledgement of sovereign divisibility – to dissever is to divide – or his desire to put sovereignty back together again, to suture the 'wide gap of time' that enables Paulina's wager. But, like the contingency of the social uptake that constitutes non-sovereign agency, it is impossible for us, or Paulina, to know for sure.

EPILOGUE: TURNING AWAY

In *Shakespeare's Fugitive Politics*, I have argued that the political in Shakespeare is more important than politics. In making this case with readings of plays that span the trajectory of Shakespeare's dramatic career, I hope to have demonstrated that his plays were incubators for a political philosophy that considered the expression of politics to be evanescent rather than formal, fugitive rather than sustained, and antagonistic rather than consensual. Each of the book's chapters has demonstrated that Shakespeare imagined sovereign power as a productive force for political contestation and that the consequence of the sovereign exception was a divided absolutism – the breach that reallocates sovereign power to enable alternative political communities.

The political in the plays examined in *Shakespeare's Fugitive Politics* coalesces into an archive of dramatic characters and theatrical action. Characters discover themselves to be the subject of time and history, or, in the Bastard's own language from *King John*, find themselves 'bastard[s] to the time' (1.1.207) – a process of exposure to the political as it is remembered and recreated on the stage in Shakespeare's London. Mark Wenman describes this type of exposure as 'a certain precedence of human freedom' and an indication of the 'priority of constituent power',[1] even in the face of sovereign power that renders life bare. Each chapter discovers fugitive politics in Shakespeare through close readings of plays that expose the imbricated relationship between fractured sovereignty and forms of non-sovereign agency central to creating new forms of political life – a funeral effigy in *Julius Caesar*, friendship in *Coriolanus*, bureaucratic sovereignty in *King John*, touch in *Henry V*, and volatile bodies in *Titus Andronicus* and *The Winter's Tale*. This productive dissensus between sovereign power and non-sovereign agency forges new ways of being in the early modern world responsive to a democratic calculus augmenting power beyond the bare life and the sovereign exception. Echoing Hannah Arendt and Thomas Paine on political action, fugitive politics enables subjects to become political actors and to possess the power to reimagine the world and begin it anew. This is what we see in the closing scene of *The Winter's Tale* with Hermione's resurrection, and this is what we see in *Henry V* with Catherine's sugar touch. The direction and outcome of the political is contingent and unpredictable, frustrating those critics who seek a systematic form of political action resistant to absolutism. As Bonnie Honig reminds us, however, the fragility of the political moment is necessarily 'spontaneous, novel, creative, and perhaps most disturbing, always self-surprising',[2] and, as this book has suggested, almost always asymmetrical. The power of asymmetrical politics is that it refuses what Honig calls the 'subsumptive logic'[3] of the dialectical framework that misrecognises expressions of political innovation, viewing these moments 'not in terms of the new worlds they may bring into being but rather in terms of their appositeness to molds and models already in place: incomplete, but definitive in their contours'.[4] In this way, the fugitive in Shakespeare's politics is the political invention that antagonism produces.

The book's central premise – one that perhaps to some readers will be disturbing – has been that fugitive politics emerges within sovereign power, not necessarily as ancillary or as a reaction to it. This may invite a critical response similar to that which has developed around Chantal Mouffe's evolving understanding of necessity of order and unity as a 'precondition of agonism'.[5] This reading of Mouffe, as Wenman has pointed out, aligns her with the neo-conservative belief that the first order of politics is to provide security from the 'threat of privation, which is supposedly rooted in the human condition'.[6] As our explorations of Shakespeare's political philosophy suggest, however, the sovereign exception that arbitrates survival also paradoxically menaces sovereignty's own claims to absolutism, allowing for what Wenman calls 'agonistic augmentation', an 'ongoing and open-ended resistance to, and redirection of, the law'.[7] Paulina's wager in *The Winter's Tale* – the push that so menaces Leontes' sovereign desire – illustrates both a form of resistance and redirection, a confrontation and a turn away.

The redirection of sovereign power describes movement more than dialectical resistance. The political fugitive is in transition, moving beyond boundaries and borders that seek to conscribe her. On Shakespeare's stage, movement becomes focused, and lines of flight telescope into turns of the body, nearly imperceptible moments of embodied politics in which the body's movement, its touch, its turn or turning away, illustrates the non-sovereign force of the political. In *Dorsality*, David Wills argues that the human becomes technological at the moment the body deviates from its human condition by 'turning that way', a turning to the back 'in the simplest or most minimal fashion [. . .] just a little to the left or right'.[8] His argument deconstructs the binary that separates the human and technology by showing how the dorsal turn that characterises bodies resists technological inevitability and advancement.

The dorsal turn is 'resistance precisely to a technology that defines itself as straightforward, as straight and forward, straight-ahead linear advance, the totally concentrated confidence and pure technological fiat of an unwavering liftoff propelled by naked combustible force. We should preserve the right to *hold back* [. . .]'.[9] For Wills, the turn back, or dorsal turn, is a dissident movement, a form of resistance emerging from within the already technological body – a movement he calls 'the dorsal chance'.[10]

Shakespeare's Fugitive Politics has explored the dorsal chance that calls into question the abiding absolutism of the sovereign exception. Wills's work allows us to think differently about Thomas Hobbes's argument in *Leviathan* that insists on the artificiality of sovereign power. Hobbes insists that Nature is 'by the *art* of man' imitated, and therefore produces 'an artificial animal'. Prefiguring Wills's claim about the technological body, Hobbes goes on to suggest that all life is in some way like '*automata*' – artificial, the heart a spring, the nerves strings, the joints wheels. Hobbes follows his description of man as an artificial animal by associating man's artifice to the sovereign state, 'which is but an artificial man'.[11] The challenge for the subject of sovereign power is not to survive the power of the state, but to find a space beneath, beyond, indeed even within Leviathan that, as Peter DeGabriele has argued, 'has not been, and cannot be, captured by the contract with sovereign power'.[12] Reading Hobbes, Wills might say that technological man encounters an artificial sovereign, and the contest poignantly enacts the vanishing point of sovereign authority and the beginning of fugitive politics in which the object of sovereign power reclaims her humanity with the dorsal chance.

Coriolanus 'turns [his] back' (3.3.138) on Rome toward a 'world elsewhere' (139); the Bastard turns on commodity, the bias of the world; Catherine turns away from Henry's kiss, withholding consent until Burgundy makes it so; Lavinia 'turn'st away thy face' (2.4.28) in shame from Marcus after her rape; Paulina tells Hermione to 'turn' toward Perdita at the moment of her reanimation. Looking more closely at Hermione's turn in *The Winter's Tale*, we see how the gap between Hermione's technological body – the statue that stirs – and her corporeal body collapses, producing the dorsal turn that is, at the same time, a form of political dissent. When Hermione descends from her pedestal in act 5, Paulina says,

> Start not; her actions shall be holy as
> You hear my spell is lawful: do not shun her
> Until you see her die again; for then
> You kill her double. Nay, present your hand:
> When she was young you wooed her; now in age
> Is she become the suitor? (5.3.104–9)

Paulina warns Leontes not to turn away from a reanimated Hermione, reversing the logic of the dorsal turn that kills Euridyce a second time in book 10 of Ovid's *Metamorphoses*. Ovid writes, 'anxious for another look at her, he turned his eyes so he could gaze upon her. Instantly she slipped away. He stretched out to her his despairing arms, eager to rescue her, or feel her form, but could hold nothing save the yielding air.'[13] Orpheus's turn, born of deep love and the persistent memory of the pain of his original loss, is acquisitive, joined to a gaze like Marcus's in *Titus Andronicus* that fails in the end to confirm the truth of the body it so earnestly seeks. Paulina knows the power of the dorsal turn that would kill Hermione 'double', and she reverses its potency. In this new political and aesthetic dispensation, Hermione 'become[s] the suitor', who, like Orpheus, turns. Her movement from the pedestal away from Leontes is interpreted by the men in the scene as a turn toward her husband. Polixenes says, 'She embraces him' (111), and Camillo describes what he sees: 'She hangs about his neck' (112). The scene implies that Hermione reunites with Leontes by turning toward him and touching him. His trauma over her death, a potential remnant of Orpheus's anguish at holding nothing 'save the yielding air', is avoided in this scene by her outstretched arms, eager to feel his form, or so the story goes.

I'd like to think that Hermione's touch of Leontes at this moment is one of utility, not unity, and antagonism, not intimacy. She uses him to descend from the pedestal, but her gaze is moving in another direction. Paulina redirects Hermione, who turns *away* from Leontes and *toward* her daughter, Perdita. 'Turn, good lady; / Our Perdita is found' (120–1), commands Paulina. This is the dorsal turn that fuels fugitive politics. If Paulina's wager is that Hermione's lifeless body articulates a viable political form of life within the sovereign exception, Hermione's turn away from Leontes and toward Perdita at this moment transforms the reanimated queen into the fugitive who balances separation and unification. They leave the stage 'together', according to Paulina, yet, as the play concludes, they are also 'dissevered' and 'hastily lead away'. Shakespeare's late romance stages non-sovereign agency, fractured sovereignty and fugitive politics – all incubators for a democratic politics at risk of being usurped by the suturing forces of consensus that, as Paulina warns, 'trouble / [. . .] joys with like relation'. The echo of consensus that negates politics closes the play, as Leontes leaves for another place 'where we may leisurely / Each one demand an answer to his part' (152–3) in the events leading up to Hermione's dorsal turn. Although our own most earnest critical intentions may coincide with Leontes' desire to know how each part contributes to the whole, *Shakespeare's Fugitive Politics* remains resistant to the 'like relation' conjured in the sovereign demand. It turns instead toward Paulina, who expresses a political form of life that answers the sovereign demand obliquely, asymmetrically and without direct address, turning its attention elsewhere.

NOTES

Chapter 1

1. All references to Shakespeare's plays are to *The Norton Shakespeare*, 3rd edn, ed. Stephen Greenblatt et al. (New York: W. W. Norton & Company, 2016).
2. Wolin, 'Fugitive Democracy', p. 11.
3. Ibid., p. 23.
4. Ibid.
5. See Gil, *Shakespeare's Anti-Politics*, for an illuminating counter-reading of this moment in the play. Gil describes the rioters' anger and motivation as 'anti-public rage, a rage against a certain version of political publicity' (p. 31) and an example of the 'kind of anti-political vision that the play articulates' (p. 33). While my argument intersects with and has been informed by many aspects of Gil's excellent analysis, I understand the 'alternative mode of sociability that operates at the level of bodies' (p. 33) as political in relation to the sovereign body whose mythic and corporeal presence informs the multiple ways non-sovereign agents experience and articulate power. I deal with the concept of non-sovereign, intersubjective agency explicitly in Chapter 5.
6. For an account of non-sovereign freedom in literature of the Roman republic, see Connolly, *The Life of Roman Republicanism*, especially chapters 3 and 4, pp. 115–72. Connolly argues that the Ciceronian citizen 'can live in a

world where the drive to achieve *concordia* or *consensus* thrives with a framing of politics as conflict' (p. 156).

7. The reading of friendship that is foundational to the fugitive politics explored throughout this book is taken from Derrida, *The Politics of Friendship*.

8. Quoted in Xenos, 'Momentary Democracy', in Botwinick and Connolly (eds), *Democracy and Vision*, p. 31.

9. Wolin, *Politics and Vision*, pp. 602–3.

10. Turner, 'The Problem of the More-than-One', p. 413.

11. Ibid., p. 414. See also Wootton, 'Oxbridge Model', p. 7, pp. 9–10.

12. Wolin, *Politics and Vision*, p. 603.

13. Ibid.

14. Ibid.

15. Ibid., pp. 604–5.

16. Ibid., p. 604.

17. Ibid. For a recent account of sovereignty and civil society shaped by the theories of Agamben and Schmitt, see Gil: 'As far as Agamben is concerned, the precondition for any social life is a prior sovereign decision about the limits and nature of human being [. . .] By making this decision, sovereign power stamps an existential identity onto some human bodies and thus elevates those human bodies to the personhood that is the precondition for what liberal-communitarian theory misrecognizes as extra-political community life' (*Shakespeare's Anti-Politics*, p. 4).

18. Ibid., p. 2.

19. Ibid. Gil is careful to qualify Shakespeare's political commitment to what he calls civic republicanism, calling it 'essentially self-annihilating' and claiming that 'it criticizes the monarchical order for the demeaning effects of dependence on raw sovereign power without finding a way to define a political and social order that itself escapes being dependent on raw sovereign power' (p. 8).

20. In this, *Shakespeare's Fugitive Politics* is in conversation with Lezra, *Wild Materialism*. Lezra has been especially valuable in shaping my understanding of the relationship between forms of sovereignty and other, more democratic, expressions of the political. See especially pp. 15–19 and 'Chapter 2: *Phares*; or, Divisible Sovereignty', pp. 63–87. Other scholarship in this conversation includes, but is not limited to, Nyquist, *Arbitrary Rule*, DeGabriele, *Sovereign Power and the Enlightenment*, and Netzley, *Lyric Apocalypse*.
21. Wills, *Dorsality*, p. 212.
22. Ibid., p. 239.
23. Ibid., p. 237.
24. Ibid., p. 238.
25. Wolin, *Politics and Vision*, pp. 605–6.
26. In 'What Revolutionary Action Means Today', Wolin rejects the notion of a passive political subject in favour of a political being that he describes as drawing 'its sustenance from circumscribed relationships: family, friends, church, neighborhood, workplace, community, town, city. These relationships are the sources from which political beings draw power—symbolic, material, psychological—and that enable them to act together. For true political power involves not only acting so as to affect decisive changes; it also means the capacity to receive power, to be acted upon, to change, and to be changed' (p. 27).
27. The political affect described here resembles the concept of 'tacit knowledge' that Wolin identifies as fundamental to political philosophy: 'intuitions, feelings, and perceptions' that 'rarely find explicit expression in formal theory' ('Political Theory as Vocation', pp. 1,073–4). Wolin's political philosophy of fugitive democracy has been the subject of much criticism. For a comprehensive assessment of the theory in relation to his important

work *Politics and Vision*, see Botwinick and Connolly (eds), *Democracy and Vision*. For a sustained critical appraisal of Wolin's important essay that takes issue with its nihilistic implications from *Democracy and Vision*, see especially George Kateb, 'Wolin as Critic of Democracy' (pp. 39–57). Kateb contends that for Wolin 'fugitive democracy then becomes acceptable in itself' (p. 47), and concludes that his 'passion is a noble passion, noble as it is futile. It is Marx's passion, but because it is without Marx's hope, it becomes Sorelian. The democratic energies of creation are redirected to destruction' (p. 56).

28. Mouffe, *Agonistics*, p. xii. In this study, Mouffe clarifies concepts explored in *Hegemony and Socialist Strategy*, specifically the importance of the radical negativity of antagonism to politics that seeks to impede the 'full totalization of society and forecloses the possibility of a society beyond division and power' (p. 1).

29. Ibid., p. 7.

30. Ibid., p. 9, p. 15. For Mouffe's account of the difference between political antagonism and agonism, see pp. 9–15.

31. See Sumi, *Ceremony and Power*. Caesar leaves the bulk of his estate to his family, but includes a significant gift to the *plebs*, which includes a small amount of money to Roman citizens living in the city and his suburban estate across the Tiber to be used as a public park (pp. 98–9). His will, according to Sumi, ratifies his relationship with the Roman people in a 'formal, legal framework' (p. 99), guaranteeing his legacy.

32. A typical aristocratic Roman funeral would include the display of the corpse at home, where it would lie in state for family, friends, and household slaves and freedmen to observe. From the family home, the body would be carried in procession (*pompa funebris*) by relatives, slaves,

freedmen, *clients* and actors, the latter who were hired to dress as Caesar in his triumphal gown, during the walk to the Forum. The processional to the Forum often included the parade of *imagines* or funeral busts of the deceased's ancestors. At the Forum, the body would be displayed on the Rostra, where speeches in praise of the deceased were delivered as well as the singing of the dirge. Then the body would be removed for burial or cremation (see Sumi, *Ceremony and Power*, pp. 101–4).

33. Gil, *Shakespeare's Anti-Politics*, pp. 30–1.

34. For an important account of this type of agency within a postcolonial context, see Haynes and Prakash, 'Introduction: The Entanglement of Power and Resistance'; see also O'Hanlon, 'Recovering the Subject'. For an account of non-sovereign agency in relation to the postcolonial female subject, see Kamra, 'Self-Making through Self-Writing'.

35. Krause, *Freedom Beyond Sovereignty*. In this book, Krause echoes Wolin, who claims that to be a political subject 'means the capacity to receive power, to be acted upon, to change, and to be changed' ('What Revolutionary Action Means Today', p. 28).

36. See Weinstock, *Divus Julius*, pp. 346–55 for the most authoritative scholarly account of the complete ritual, combining descriptions from Appian, Suetonius, Cicero, Livy and Plutarch.

37. Plutarch, *Plutarch's Lives*, vol. 7, p. 212.

38. Sumi, *Ceremony and Power*, p. 107. See Appian, *Roman History*, vol. 2, pp. 497–9.

39. Sumi, *Ceremony and Power*, p. 108. See also Weinstock, *Divus Julius*, p. 353.

40. Appian, *Roman History*, vol. 2, p. 499. Sumi calls this moment in the funeral a '*deus ex machina*', and it was unprecedented in representing the body as it looked after its violent death (*Ceremony and Power*, p. 107).

Caesar's body would have been laid out flat on his bier on the Rostra sò that it would not have been seen by the crowd; Weinstock identifies a wax effigy on the couch in place of Caesar's violated body since the corpse could not be used in the ritual. The effigy is attested in other Roman funerals, especially in a *funus imaginarium* – funeral with an image – though generally this device occurs much later in history. The effigy on the couch, however, would not have represented Caesar's wounds, nor would it have been able to rotate mechanically, as the second effigy appearing suddenly near the end of the ceremony seems to do.

41. See Agamben, *Homo Sacer*, for the essential articulation of this paradox: 'nothing in Roman *consecratio* allowed one to place the emperor's effigy in relation to what is sovereignty's clearest feature, its perpetual nature. The macabre and grotesque rite in which an image was first treated as a living person and then solemnly burned gestured instead toward a darker and more uncertain zone, which we will now investigate, in which the political body of the king seemed to approximate – and even to become indistinguishable from – the body of *homo sacer*, which can be killed but not sacrificed [. . .] And it is here that the body of the sovereign and the body of *homo sacer* enter into a zone of indistinction in which they can no longer be told apart' (p. 58).

42. See Anderson, *Performing Early Modern Trauma from Shakespeare to Milton*, pp. 170–1 for a discussion of the early modern descriptions of the effigies of Prince Henry and Elizabeth I. See also Owens, 'John Webster, Tussaud Laureate' and '*The Revenger's Tragedy* as *Trauerspiel*'. Susan Zimmerman writes in *The Early Modern Corpse in Shakespeare's Theatre* that '[t]o imagine a corpse inside a statue is to evoke a fearsome, uncanny double' (p. 183).

43. See Horowitz, *Sustaining Loss*, p. 139.
44. Kottman, *A Politics of the Scene*, p. 115.
45. Hammill and Lupton (eds), *Political Theology and Early Modernity*, p. 2.
46. Ibid., p. 3.
47. Hammill, *The Mosaic Constitution*, p. 23.
48. Lorenz, *The Tears of Sovereignty*, p. 25.

Chapter 2

1. Here, I draw on Rancière's understanding of politics as 'specifically opposed to the police'. In 'Ten Theses on Politics', he writes that 'The essence of politics, then, is to disturb this arrangement by supplementing it with a part of the no-part identified with the community as a whole. Political litigiousness/struggle is that which brings politics into being by separating it from the police that is, in turn, always attempting its disappearance either by crudely denying it, or by subsuming that logic to its own. Politics is first and foremost an intervention upon the visible and the sayable.' In a politics of dissensus, the political makes visible that which the sensible had erased from view; 'it lodges one world into another'.
2. For an example of recent criticism that emphasises the productive nature of discord in the play, see Pfannebecker, 'Cyborg *Coriolanus*/Monster Body Politic'. She concludes that existence in the play is necessarily 'communal and political' (p. 128), but that it is 'always bounded by multiple and often contradictory relations of force [. . .] Politics, *Coriolanus* also suggests, are determined by boundaries which, like all boundaries, require violence. There are no politics without treading on someone, somebody, something' (pp. 128–9).
3. Cavell, 'Who Does the Wolf Love?', p. 7.
4. Ibid., p. 7.

5. Ibid., p. 18.
6. Ibid.
7. De Montaigne, *The Essays of Montaigne*, p. 188.
8. Derrida, *Of Hospitality*, p. 123.
9. Ibid., p. 125.
10. Derrida, *The Politics of Friendship*, p. 1, hereafter cited parenthetically according to page number.
11. Shannon, *Sovereign Amity*, p. 3.
12. Ibid.
13. Ibid., p. 5.
14. Ibid.
15. Ibid., p. 8.
16. Derrida affiliates explicitly with Carl Schmitt's dictum that politics is possible only through the sovereign state of exception that establishes, and makes war with, an avowed enemy. The absence of an enemy would mean the end of politics – the beginning of depoliticisation. According to Schmitt, 'The specific political distinction to which political actions and notions can be reduced is the distinction between friend and enemy' (*The Concept of the Political*, p. 26). Derrida's concept of hospitality is informed by the same paradox that I claim characterises friendship in the play. In *Of Hospitality*, Derrida describes the guest receiving hospitality as also a foreigner: 'Anyone who encroaches on my "at home" [. . .] on my power of hospitality, on my sovereignty as host, I start to regard as an undesirable foreigner, and virtually as an enemy. This other becomes a hostile subject, and I risk becoming their hostage' (pp. 54–5). The intervention that this essay makes in politico-friendship theory is also indebted to Tom Roach's illuminating discussion of the concept in *Friendship as a Way of Life: Foucault, AIDS, and the Politics of Shared Estrangement*. Roach writes, 'When the most troubling aspects of relationships become the

very foundation of a friendship, however, new subjective, communal, and political forms can be imagined' (p. 8). He continues, 'Friendship [. . .] bespeaks the anarchical contingency of all relationality. In its very nature it is *anti*-institutional, indeed it cannot congeal into an epistemological object known as "society." It is excessive of self-identity, and hence contrary to Aristotle's claim, structurally incapable of grounding social forms. I find it nonetheless necessary to run the risk of seeking out communal and political forms that approximate friendship: ones that acknowledge the impossibility of the social as such, ones that embrace the contradiction of relating at the point of unrelatability' (p. 13). I hope to show that Coriolanus and Aufidius's relationship resembles an approximate friendship that redefines the communal in their battle against it.

17. Quoted in Shannon, *Sovereign Amity*, p. 3.
18. Elyot, *The Boke Named the Governour*, p. 130.
19. Grimald, 'Of Frendship', p. 145.
20. Quoted in Shannon, *Sovereign Amity*, p. 4.
21. Ibid.
22. De Montaigne, *The Essays of Montaigne*, p. 188.
23. Ibid., p. 191.
24. Ibid., p. 189.
25. Ibid., p. 190.
26. Elyot, *The Boke Named the Governour*, p. 134.
27. Cicero, *De Senectute, De Amicitia, De Divinatione*, p. 155.
28. Chernaik, *The Myth of Rome*, p. 8.
29. Spencer, 'Shakespeare and the Elizabethan Romans', p. 32.
30. Hadfield, *Shakespeare and Republicanism*, p. 95, p. 100, p. 143, p. 155. Hadfield's response to David Scott Wilson-Okamura is perhaps the most cogent defence of the claim that the concept of republicanism need not be held hostage by literary critics who claim it is not a

political force until the decade of the revolution. Hadfield rebuts Wilson-Okamura's major counter-claim that
what modern readers see as pre-1640 republicanism is
a challenge to different types of tyranny so that ancient
aristocratic forms of government are restored. Hadfield
defines republicanism during this period as a constellation of ideas and arguments about the potential form of
government in relation to an increasingly autonomous
multitude (p. 282). See also Hadfield, 'Was Spenser
Really a Republican After All?'; see Wilson-Okamura,
'Republicanism, Nostalgia, and the Crowd', for a challenge to Hadfield's claim.

31. Patterson, *Shakespeare and the Popular Voice*, p. 10.

32. Ibid., p. 132. In this, Patterson agrees with Anne Barton
that Shakespeare emphasises what is 'hopeful, communal and progressive' in a very young republic (p. 124).
Specifically, Barton argues that *Coriolanus* is unique in
Shakespeare's canon for the 'tolerance and respect it
accords an urban citizenry' (see 'Livy, Machiavelli and
Shakespeare's *Coriolanus*', p. 140).

33. See Cheney, 'Introduction: Marlowe in the Twenty-First
Century', p. 16.

34. Ibid.

35. Hammill, '"The thing / Which never was"', p. 166.

36. Ibid.

37. Ibid., p. 167.

38. See Kuzner, *Open Subjects*, p. 106, p. 107. I will have
more to say about Kuzner's account of republicanism and
vulnerable subjectivity (pp. 10–24), which is exemplary.

39. Ibid., p. 109.

40. In this effort, his work is aligned with that of scholars such as Victoria Kahn, Patrick Collinson and Alan
Cromartie. Just as Collinson and Cromartie broaden
our understanding of how an evolving England's monarchy comes to accommodate anti-monarchical, indeed

republican, desires, Kahn rereads Machiavelli to show that his influential account of republicanism incorporates, even requires, anti-republican values such as coercion and fraud. See Kahn, *Machiavellian Rhetoric.*

41. Nelson, 'Shakespeare and the Best State of the Commonwealth', p. 268.
42. Armitage et al., 'Introduction', p. 16.
43. Chernaik, *The Myth of Rome*, p. 245.
44. Ibid.
45. Ibid., pp. 245–6; Armitage et al., 'Introduction', p. 6, and chapters by Condren (pp. 157–75), Richards (pp. 176–98) and Peltonen (pp. 234–52). See also Howard, 'Dramatic Traditions in Shakespeare's Political Thought', p. 136.
46. Armitage et al., 'Introduction', p. 15.
47. Ibid., p. 21.
48. Rahe, *Against Throne and Altar*, p. 10.
49. Ibid., pp. 10–11.
50. Roe, *Shakespeare and Machiavelli*, p. 4. For a resistant reading of the power of Roe's claim, see Richard Strier's review of *Shakespeare and Machiavelli.*
51. Rahe, *Against Throne and Altar*, pp. 11–12. For an exception to this line of argument, see Mayer, *Thomas Starkey and the Commonweal.*
52. Rahe, *Against Throne and Altar*, p. 12.
53. Pocock, 'Machiavelli and Rome', p. 145.
54. Kahn, 'Machiavelli's Afterlife and Reputation', p. 241.
55. Ibid., p. 243.
56. Bodin, *The Six Bookes of the Commonweale*, vol. 4, p. 702. See also Gilbert, *Machiavelli and Guicciardini*, p. 90 for a discussion of the ambivalence in the political treatises about republican and monarchical forms of government in the period.
57. Machiavelli, *Discourses.* Hereafter cited parenthetically.
58. See Huffman, *Coriolanus in Context*, p. 109.
59. Ibid., p. 110.

60. See Skinner, 'Machiavelli's *Discorsi*', p. 135, p. 136.
61. Del Lucchese, *Conflict, Power, and Multitude in Machi-avelli and Spinoza*, p. 4.
62. Vatter, *Between Form and Event*, p. 93.
63. Lefort, *Travail de l'oeuvre*, p. 475. See Vatter's introduction to *Between Form and Event*, pp. 1–23.
64. For a compelling account of the belly metaphor that stresses linguistic revolt in addition to civic strife, see Riss, 'The Belly Politic'. See also Eastman, 'The Rumbling Belly Politic', Garganigo, '*Coriolanus*, the Union Controversy, and Access to the Royal Person', and Gurr, '*Coriolanus* and the Body Politic'.
65. Schweitzer, *Perfecting Friendship*, p. 9.
66. For a discussion of potentiality as a political force in relation to notions of an unbounded community, see Agamben, *The Coming Community*, and Nancy, *The Inoperative Community*.
67. Derrida describes the logic of hospitality in its absolute form as a type of perversion: 'The guest takes and receives [. . .] We thus enter from the inside: the master of the house is at home, but nonetheless he comes to enter his home through the guest – who comes from the outside'; see *Of Hospitality*, p. 125.
68. Lupton, *Citizen-Saints*, p. 60.
69. Hammill, *The Mosaic Constitution*, p. 121.
70. Ibid., p. 23.
71. See Kuzner, 'Unbuilding the City', p. 175. Other recent work that explores representations of political alliances in the play includes Archer, *Citizen Shakespeare*, pp. 142–59, Arnold, *The Third Citizen*, and Shrank, 'Civility and the City in *Coriolanus*'.
72. See Kaegi, '"How apply you this?"', for a discussion of the underlying force of consensus in the citizens' voices in the fable of the belly.

73. Goh, 'Rejecting Friendship', p. 103. See also Goh, *The Reject*.

74. Kuzner, *Open Subjects*, pp. 101–3.

75. Goh describes this process: 'In relation to friendship, a figure of the *reject* would not only be a solitary one, the one who stands apart from friendship, but also the one who raises the impasse or abyss of friendship before friendship, raising it before the other *and* against himself or herself, constantly plunging friendship into that abyss' ('Rejecting Friendship', p. 104).

76. Derrida, *The Politics of Friendship*, p. 1.

77. Goh calls this form of rejection a 'preemptive measure against lapsing into the all-too-human weakness for some amicability' ('Rejecting Friendship', p. 106).

78. Ibid.

79. The term 'motility of division' is Jacques Lezra's. For his illuminating discussion of this concept, see *Wild Materialism*, pp. 63–87.

80. See Cavell, 'Who Does the Wolf Love?', p. 3. His understanding of Shakespeare's use of the word 'clusters' here is informed by Brecht's production.

81. See Thomson, *Deconstruction and Democracy*, pp. 12–30.

82. I am indebted to David Wills for introducing me to the concept of asymmetrical friendship in his illuminating account of the concept in 'Full Dorsal: Derrida's *Politics of Friendship*'. Wills writes about Derrida's concept of friendship: 'But it is also, obviously, a figure of catastrophic inversion, a disruption of the symmetry and closure of a love or friendship that is presumed to function only in the face-to-face, and which therefore remains open to the politics of enmity' (para 30). See also Wills, *Dorsality: Thinking Back through Technology and Politics*.

83. Schmitt, *The Concept of the Political*, p. 35.

84. The servingmen's preference for war as a reaction to the strange eruption of hospitality between the two rival warriors illustrates yet another limit to a politics of friendship characterised by fraternity. The servingmen's exclusion from the alliance points to the force of exclusion at the core of a democratic community emerging from fraternity. Derrida bases his critique of the fraternal democratic community on its gendered homogeneity – 'although the figure of the friend, so regularly coming back on stage with the features of the *brother* – who is critically at stake in this analysis – seems spontaneously to belong to a *familial, fraternalist,* and thus *androcentric* configuration of politics' (*The Politics of Friendship*, p. vii). The hospitality exchanged between Aufidius and Coriolanus reproduces this exclusion in terms of gender to be sure, but for the servingmen the force of exclusion is also in terms of social hierarchy, qualifying friendship's radical potential dramatised in the scene.

85. Schmitt, *The Concept of the Political*, p. 35.

Chapter 3

1. A selection of the important scholarship on this topic includes Christopher Pye, *The Regal Phantasm: Shakespeare and the Politics of Spectacle*; Leonard Tennenhouse, *Power on Display: The Politics of Shakespeare's Genres*; David Scott Kastan, 'Proud Majesty Made a Subject: Shakespeare and the Spectacle of Rule'; Laurie Shannon, 'The False Prince and the True Subject: Friendship and Public Institutions in *Edward II* and *The Henriad*', in *Sovereign Amity: Figures of Friendship in Shakespearean Contexts*, pp. 156–84; Stephen Greenblatt, 'Invisible Bullets: Renaissance Authority and its Subversion in *Henry IV*

and *Henry V*'; Norman Rabkin, 'Rabbits, Ducks, and *Henry V*'; Richard Helgerson, *Forms of Nationhood: The Elizabethan Writing of England*; and Jonathan Dollimore and Alan Sinfield, 'History and Ideology: The Instance of *Henry V*'.

2. Schmitt, *Political Theology*, p. 5.
3. See Agamben, *Homo Sacer*, esp. pp. 28–9.
4. Ibid., pp. 32–3.
5. See Pettit, *Republicanism*, pp. 21–7. Pettit defines freedom as non-domination in the republican tradition. This moment in the play clearly engages proto-republican concepts of liberty and freedom played out in a geopolitical context as war between France and England. Pettit shows how liberty can be lost without actual interference, which makes domination the central antagonist to liberty (p. 35). Pettit adds, 'interference occurs without any loss of liberty when the interference is not arbitrary and does not represent a form of domination' (p. 35).
6. Ibid., p. 21.
7. Lezra, *Wild Materialism*, p. 18.
8. Moshenska, *Feeling Pleasures*, p. 3.
9. Taylor, *A Secular Age*, p. 140.
10. Ibid., p. 10. For an account that explores the nostalgia embedded in the accounts of disenchantment in which a pre-modern past retrospectively acquires the sense of enchantment, see Asad, *Formations of the Secular*, pp. 13–14.
11. Moshenska, *Feeling Pleasures*, p. 12.
12. The scholarship on political theology and secularisation in early modern England is vast and includes prominently Julia Reinhard Lupton, *Citizen-Saints: Shakespeare and Political Theology* and *Thinking with Shakespeare: Essays on Politics and Life*; Jacques Lezra, *Wild Materialism: The Ethic of Terror and the*

Modern Republic; Graham Hammill, *The Mosaic Constitution: Political Theology and Imagination from Machiavelli to Milton*; Hammill and Lupton (eds), *Political Theology and Early Modernity*; Victoria Kahn, *The Future of Illusion: Political Theology and Early Modern Texts, Wayward Contracts: Literature, Political Theory, and the Crisis of Political Obligation in England, 1640–1674* and 'Political Theology and Fiction in *The King's Two Bodies*'; Stephen Greenblatt, *Hamlet in Purgatory*; Anselm Haverkamp, '*Richard II*, Bracton, and the End of Political Theology'; Ken Jackson, '"Is it God or the Sovereign Exception?" Giorgio Agamben's *Homo Sacer* and Shakespeare's *King John*'; Philip Lorenz, *The Tears of Sovereignty: Perspectives of Power in Renaissance Drama*; Jennifer Rust, *The Body in Mystery: The Political Theology of the Corpus Mysticum in the Literature of Reformation England*; Debora Kuller Shuger, *Political Theologies in Shakespeare's England: The Sacred and the State in 'Measure for Measure'*; and Richard McCoy, *Alterations of State: Sacred Kingship in the English Reformation*. On political theology and secularism more generally, see Hent de Vries and Lawrence E. Sullivan (eds), *Political Theologies: Public Religions in a Post-Secular World*.

13. Schmitt, *Political Theology*, p. 66.
14. Peltonen, *Classic Humanism and Republicanism in English Political Thought, 1570–1640*, p. 18.
15. Sidney, *Discourses Concerning Government*, pp. 389–90.
16. Ibid., p. 484.
17. Ibid.
18. Ibid., pp. 484–5.
19. Peltonen, *Classic Humanism*, p. 19.
20. Griffiths, 'The Sonnet in Ruins', para 30.
21. Ibid.

22. Hadfield, *Shakespeare and Republicanism*, p. 13. See Rahe, *Against Throne and Altar*, pp. 19–55 for an account of English republicanism that claims it was not a viable political force in the Elizabethan and Jacobean periods. James Kuzner takes issue with readings of early modern drama that speak to proto-liberal empowerment or, by contrast, to monarchical hegemony. For an approach with similar concerns, see Arnold, *The Third Citizen*. For a discussion of how the Tudor stage remained throughout the sixteenth century a viable space from which to explore republican political sentiment in the form of the public or social imaginary, see Howard and Strohm, 'The Imaginary Commons'. I am making the case that fugitive politics expresses itself from within the body of the sovereign. In this, I agree with Howard and Strohm, who show that because the 'public weal' is 'intersubjective, underarticulated, and, in many respects, unsponsored or unofficial, it cannot predict or know its own conditions of enunciation' (p. 551). In a related argument, Etienne Balibar argues that '*After the subject comes the citizen. The citizen* [. . .] is that "nonsubject" who comes after the subject, and whose constitution and recognition put an end (in principle) to the subjection of the subject' ('Citizen Subject', pp. 38–9). For a discussion of Balibar's analysis, which pertains to political developments in the late eighteenth century, within an early modern political and cultural context, see Archer, *Citizen Shakespeare*, pp. 2–3; he writes, 'Yet citizenship did not cancel out subjecthood in a linear fashion, for the monarchical subject survived "within" the citizen [. . .] Instead of an evolution from subject to citizen, we have alterations, overlappings, and doublings-back in the history of what Balibar [. . .] calls "subjectivation"' (p. 3).

23. See Pocock, *The Machiavellian Moment*.

24. Collinson, *Republica Anglorum*, pp. 23–4.

25. Ibid., p. 24.
26. Peltonen, *Classic Humanism*, p. 54.
27. Ibid., p. 76. See Canny, 'Edmund Spenser and the Development of an Anglo-Irish Identity', p. 7.
28. Arendt, *On Revolution*, pp. 256–7.
29. Arendt, *The Origins of Totalitarianism*, p. 464.
30. See Santner, *The Royal Remains*.
31. Arendt, *The Origins of Totalitarianism*, p. 465.
32. Ibid., p. 464.
33. Ibid., p. 465.
34. Lezra, *Wild Materialism*, p. 28.
35. Ibid., pp. 28–9.
36. Ibid., p. 29.
37. Ibid.
38. Badiou, *Being and Event*, p. 180.
39. This phrase comes from Quentin Meillassoux's 'History and Event in Alain Badiou', p. 9.
40. Badiou, *Being and Event*, p. 180.
41. Žižek, *Event*, pp. 179–80.
42. Netzley, *Lyric Apocalypse*, p. 8.
43. Ibid.
44. Ibid., p. 7. While I disagree with Netzley's most aggressive claims about the limits of recognition in taking account of the political in literature, Netzley's commitment to the force of immanent events has helped shape my own sense of the nature of eventful politics in Shakespeare.
45. Manning, *Politics of Touch*, p. xiii.
46. Ibid., p. xv.
47. Ibid., p. 114.
48. Ibid.
49. Santner, *The Royal Remains*, p. 81.
50. Manning, *Politics of Touch*, p. 115.
51. Ibid. For an argument about the unique force of national time, see Shapiro, *For Moral Ambiguity*, pp. 112–38.

52. Ibid., pp. 122–3.

53. Rancière describes politics as an 'interruption', a moment in which incommensurability becomes apparent in the fabric of an existing social order that exposes the process of subjectification. See 'Ten Theses on Politics'.

54. See Toynbee, 'Charles I and the King's Evil', for a discussion of the King's Evil in Shakespeare. Moshenska argues that the king's ability to cure scrofula through touch 'was an important way in which English monarchs had publicly legitimated their status throughout the Middle Ages, though they did not do so without some nervousness in the seventeenth century' (*Feeling Pleasures*, p. 230).

55. See Brogan, *The Royal Touch in Early Modern England*. Brogan's study is an important addition to scholarship on the royal touch and should be included in subsequent research. My own book was at press before I was able to integrate Brogan's historical account and analysis into my own thinking about sovereignty, touch and *Henry V*. See also Barlow, *The English Historical Review*, p. 27. Barlow details both the King's Evil and the ceremony of touching from their recorded origins to the late medieval period. See also Bloch, *The Royal Touch*.

56. Barlow, *The English Historical Review*, p. 25.

57. Barlow suggests that the practice of the royal touch ended in England 'not by the skepticism of the people but by the rationalism of the Hanoverian kings and their advisers' (ibid., p. 27).

58. Levin, '"Would I Could Give You Help and Succour"', p. 195. Elizabeth's relation with Rome was a central concern in 1570, after the pope's papal bull excommunicating her. Levin writes that 'English Protestants publicly discounted the papal bull on the grounds that Elizabeth still had the God-given ability of a true monarch to cure by touch, and even English Catholics as

well as Protestants continued to go to Elizabeth to be healed by her touch' (p. 201).

59. Ibid.
60. Ibid.
61. Willis, 'The Monarch and the Sacred', p. 166.
62. Ibid.
63. Ibid.
64. Ibid.
65. F. J. Furnivall (ed.), *Robert Laneham's Letters*, p. 35.
66. Crawfurd, *The King's Evil*, pp. 71–2.
67. Cited in Crawfurd, *The King's Evil*, p. 72.
68. Ibid., p. 74.
69. Clowes, *A right frutefull treatise for the artificiall cure of struma*, p. 50.
70. Timothy Rosendale argues that this speech 'depicts a skeptical but now ultimately constructive view of royal authority [. . .] Hal's soliloquy simultaneously recognizes both his genuine commonality with all his subjects and the genuine difference made by the representational order of power. Richard [II] felt his mortality only out of despair; Henry V reworks it into an enabling condition of his power' ('Sacral and Sacramental Kingship in the Lancastrian Tetralogy', p. 133).
71. Moshenska, *Feeling Pleasures*, p. 39.
72. Ibid.
73. Lezra, *Wild Materialism*, p. 29, pp. 63–87.
74. Ibid., p. 79.
75. Ibid., p. 72. See Derrida, *Without Alibi*, p. xix. For an account of sovereignty similar to the one established in *Without Alibi*, see Derrida, *Rogues*, p. 101.
76. Lezra, *Wild Materialism*, p. 75.
77. Ibid.
78. Ibid., p. 109.
79. For an interpretation of the fable of the beehive in the play that puts the simile in the context of Henry's reputation as the mirror of Christian kings, see Gurr,

'*Henry V* and the Bees' Commonwealth'. Gurr points out the fable's appearance in Virgil, Erasmus and Elyot. As a fable for the most strategic execution of war with France, Shakespeare's use of it in *Henry V* contradicts the simile's more common function to contain sovereign power within the limits of the commonwealth.

80. Schmitt, *Political Theology*, p. 36.
81. Hollingsworth, *Poetics of the Hive*, pp. 193–4.
82. Rancière, *Disagreement*, p. 42. Informing how I interpret the beehive simile within the contexts of the force of sovereignty in the play, Rancière writes in *Disagreement* that 'Politics ceases wherever this gap no longer has any place, wherever the whole of the community is reduced to the sum of its parts with nothing left over' (p. 123).
83. Lezra, *Wild Materialism*, pp. 74–5.
84. Campana, 'The Bee and the Sovereign?', p. 108. See also Brown, 'Introduction: Reading the Insect', and Hollingsworth, *Poetics of the Hive*, pp. 192–4.
85. Campana, 'The Bee and the Sovereign?', p. 108.
86. Lezra, *Wild Materialism*, pp. 86–7.
87. Lezra's description of divisible sovereignty is apt. It is '[t]he emergence, in short, of a secularized, mobile, incomplete, and radically republican sovereign imaginary' (ibid., p. 87).
88. Rancière, *Disagreement*, p. 15.
89. Quoted in Manning, *Politics of Touch*, p. 108.
90. Žižek, *The Ticklish Subject*, p. 188.
91. DeGabriele, *Sovereign Power and the Enlightenment*, p. 26.
92. Elaine Scarry argues that the body becomes a particular point of emphasis during moments of cultural crisis: 'It will gradually become apparent that at particular moments when there is within a society a crisis of belief – that is, when some central idea or ideology or cultural construct has ceased to elicit a population's belief either because it is manifestly fictitious or because it has for some reason been

divested of ordinary forms of substantiation – the sheer
material factualness of the human body will be borrowed
to lend that cultural construct the aura of "realness" and
"certainty"' (*The Body in Pain*, p. 14).

93. See Hendrick, 'Advantage, Affect, History, *Henry V*', which
argues that Catherine's agency 'is exemplified through
her body [. . .] [H]er mode of speech becomes the body'
(pp. 482–3). Hendrick's essay engages a wide range of
scholarly interest on this scene, including Jean Howard and
Phyllis Rackin, *Engendering a Nation: A Feminist Account
of Shakespeare's English Histories*; Claire McEachern,
'*Henry V* and the Paradox of the Body Politic'; Phyllis
Rackin, *Stages of History: Shakespeare's English Chronicles*; Lance Wilcox, 'Katherine of France as Victim and
Bride'; Marilyn Williamson, 'The Courtship of Katherine and the Second Tetralogy'; Corinne S. Abate, '"Once
more unto the breach": Katharine's Victory in *Henry V*';
and Helen Ostovich, '"Teach you our princess English?"
Equivocal Translation of the French in *Henry V*', p. 156.

94. Rancière, *The Philosopher and His Poor*, p. 226.

95. Her lack of voiced consent need not be a sign of her
surrender or lack of agency. For persuasive accounts
of the relation between silence and agency, see Luckyj,
'"A Moving Rhetoricke"', p. 37, and Goldberg, 'Shakespearean Inscriptions', p. 130.

96. Rancière, *Disagreement*, p. 116.

97. In arguing that touch transforms regimes of perception,
I draw on Davide Panagia's account of the dissensual
politics of sensibility: 'dissensus is an aesthetic-political
moment that results in the reconfiguration of the regimes
of perception that seize our attention, so that we can no
longer assume the legislative authority (or logical priority) of any one form of perception' (*The Political Life of
Sensation*, p. 42).

98. Rancière, *Disagreement*, p. 101.
99. Kamuf, 'Introduction: Event of Resistance', p. 15.
100. Ziarek, *An Ethics of Dissensus*, p. 8.
101. Ibid., p. 23. In comparing the body with the prison, Judith Butler writes, 'The prison comes to be only within the field of power relations, but more specifically, only to the extent that it is invested or saturated with such relations, that such a saturation is itself formative of its very being. Here the body is not an independent materiality that is invested by power relations external to it, but it is that for which materialization and investiture are coextensive' (*Bodies That Matter*, p. 34).

Chapter 4

1. In *Shakespeare's Anti-Politics: Sovereign Power and the Life of the Flesh*, Daniel Juan Gil explores the emergence of bureaucratic agencies that, on one level, work in tandem with absolute sovereign power defined by Schmitt and Agamben. He notes how the sovereign 'who defines and guarantees a way of life is veiled by the early modern development and expansion of quasi-autonomous, bureaucratic administrative agencies that increasingly do the work of government without the actual, personal involvement of the king or queen' (p. 7). Gil explores the balance of the absolutist perspective that incorporates a concept of bureaucracy functioning most efficiently as a surrogate for the sovereign power but that also responds to the 'oppositional discourse of civic republicanism' (p. 7).
2. Weber, *From Max Weber: Essays in Sociology*, p. 214.
3. Bennett, *The Enchantment of Modern Life*, p. 105. In a reading of Kafka's stories, Bennett finds more than the 'negative or unnerving effect of interacting with official

complexities' (p. 106). For Bennett, Kafka's stories reveal 'bureaucratic entanglement to be both maddening *and* attractive' (p. 106).

4. With this claim, I am amplifying Gil's argument about how the ethos of civic republicanism in Shakespeare accommodates the force of the sovereign exception in defining the parameters of political community, but also how those independent agents of the king play at least a 'consultative role in political life' (*Shakespeare's Anti-Politics*, p. 7). In *Representing the Professions*, Edward Gieskes reads *King John* in a way that productively complicates the Bastard's role, arguing that his career 'represents choosing a profession rather than the recognition of a vocation' (p. 61). Gieskes tacitly links the Bastard to the historical figures Thomas Cromwell and Lord Burghley, sixteenth-century administrators who consolidated the Crown's staff of bureaucrats, culminating in the Elizabethan Privy Council's 'executive ascendency' by the end of the sixteenth century (p. 69). Gieskes's conclusion about this historical parallel is instructive: 'The fact that [. . .] the Bastard's job duties parallel those of the figures like Burghley suggests less that Shakespeare was creating a deliberate allegory than that the Tudor functionary was a recognizable type with publicly recognized tasks' (p. 96). For his complete reading of the play in relation to the emerging bureaucratic institutions of law, political administration and theatre, see *Representing the Professions: Administration, Law, and Theater in Early Modern England*, especially Chapters 1 and 2, pp. 38–113.

5. Ibid., p. 43. According to Gieskes, professions generated 'new modes of self-recognition and principles of the social field' (p. 43). Following Jean-Christophe Agnew in *Worlds Apart*, Gieskes shows how economic transformation that

made markets 'free of traditional constraints of place, time and ritual' transformed social life, giving it, according to Agnew, a 'transactional quality' that precipitated 'new strategies to cope with anxieties about the self and the society' (p. 43). See Agnew, *Worlds Apart*, p. 4.

6. Knapp, *The Bureaucratic Muse*, p. 2 n. 4.

7. See Elton, *Studies in Tudor and Stuart Politics and Government*. Penry Williams and G. L. Harriss's 'A Revolution in Tudor History?' modified Elton's influential account by questioning his claim that Tudor history is a period for revolutionary developments in English government. Williams and Harriss clarify Elton's narrative of bureaucratic formation in the early modern period by pointing out moments when the administrative apparatus briefly returned to the royal household in the early sixteenth century. In *Revolution Reassessed: Revisions in the History of Tudor Government and Administration* Christopher Coleman and David Starkey offer another re-examination of Elton's major claims about the development of Tudor government. See Brown, 'The Reign of Henry IV', p. 21, and *The Governance of Late Medieval England*, p. 2. For a discussion of bureaucracy in a modern context with relevance to the political context of early modern England, see Lefort, *The Political Forms of Modern Society*, esp. pp. 89–121 and pp. 292–306.

8. Brown, *The Governance of Late Medieval England*, p. 2.

9. Slavin, 'The Tudor State, Reformation and Understanding Change', esp. p. 243. See Gieskes, *Representing the Professions*.

10. Brown, *The Governance of Late Medieval England*, p. 2.

11. Slavin, 'The Tudor State, Reformation and Understanding Change', p. 241.

12. Brown, *The Governance of Late Medieval England*, p. 2.

13. Knapp, *The Bureaucratic Muse*, p. 182.

14. Ibid., p. 185.
15. See Brown, *The Governance of Late Medieval England*, p. 59; also see Arendt, *The Origins of Totalitarianism*, p. 243. Arendt elaborates on this new form of authority: 'There are no general principles which simple reason can understand behind the decree, but ever-changing circumstances which only an expert can know in detail. People ruled by decree never know what rules them because of the impossibility of understanding decrees in themselves' (p. 244).
16. Gieskes, *Representing the Professions*, p. 43.
17. Brown, *The Governance of Late Medieval England*, p. 60.
18. Gieskes, *Representing the Professions*, p. 110.
19. Braddick, *State Formation in Early Modern England*, p. 24.
20. Elton has commented that England was a monarchy limited by specific conditions: 'the real limitations on monarchy sprang from political realities that rendered the king dependent on others for advice, cooperation, and effectiveness in rule' (*Studies in Tudor and Stuart Politics and Government*, p. 35); see especially pp. 149–77. For a similar position, see also Geremek, *Poverty: A History*, p. 16. MacCaffrey asserts that the 'fateful weakness of [Elizabeth's] fragile regime was its lack of coercive power', and he maintains that the 'stability of the system demanded arduous and constant wooing of the body politic' ('Place and Patronage in Elizabethan Politics', p. 97). These assertions proved foundational to the new historicists' understandings of how power operated in the period. See also MacCaffrey's *Elizabeth I: War and Politics 1588–1603*, where he reasserts the aspects of English culture that make it an 'underdeveloped polity', such as the absence of a standing army, limited powers of taxation, England's compact size and its excellent internal communications, and the intimacy generated by its monarchs and by its varied aristocratic social and

familial relations (p. 20). However, he notes that in the sixteenth century the Western European political world was 'in the first phases of becoming modern, impersonalized, and bureaucratic' (pp. 17–18), and that England was 'by no means untouched by the processes of adaptation that were altering all Western European societies' (p. 20). His book, in large part, traces the impact of these alterations on Elizabethan society. Writing about the tension between 'quasi-autonomous bureaucratic agencies' and the 'exceptional power of the king' (*Shakespeare's Anti-Politics*, p. 131 n. 11), Gil notes that the developing legal system most clearly reflects the balance of administrative and absolute power: 'common law seems to run without any deference to the king but where its functioning is silently structured by the presence of an alternative system of justice – namely the prerogative equity courts, including the Chancellor's Court and Star Chamber – which are explicitly seen as an expression of the king's absolute power' (pp. 131–2 n. 11).

21. See Stewart, *The English Ordinance Office*, p. 34.
22. Woodbridge, *Vagrancy, Homelessness, and English Renaissance Literature*, p. 152.
23. Ibid.
24. Ibid., p. 22. See Gil, *Shakespeare's Anti-Politics*, pp. 42–67 for an argument about the sovereign relation to administrative developments in the legal and police system in *Measure for Measure*. His conclusion that the play demonstrates how 'to engineer forms of community that flourish in the shadow of sovereignty' (p. 67) recognises the productive nature of constraint that is central to my analysis of the Bastard's role in *King John*.
25. According to Gieskes in *Representing the Profession*, the Bastard's 'education and career [. . .] represent a dramatic refraction of the skills and practices necessary for a Tudor bureaucrat' (p. 108).
26. Lezra, *Wild Materialism*, p. 79.

27. Finnerty, '"Both are alike, and both alike we like"', p. 38. According to Finnerty, early modern friendship counter-balances the 'pervasive skepticism about transcendent values and moral absolutes, its emphasis on human fallibility and corruption, and its focus on personal isolation' (p. 38). See also Bray, *The Friend*, esp. pp. 13–41, for a description of the historical challenge that feudal notions of friendship present, especially as they inform policy and transform into modern expressions of friendship by the sixteenth century.

28. Finnerty, '"Both are alike, and both alike we like"', pp. 38–9.

29. Quoted in Wills, *Prosthesis*, p. 199.

30. According to Wills, Ambroise Paré's medical treatises on artificial body parts provide an analogue for Wilson's rhetorical primer. Paré's prosthetic bodies exist 'because the surgical interventions that made possible the wearing of modern prosthetic devices, for which the paradigm remains the artificial limb, brought into particular focus the competing discourses of the organicist and mechanistic conceptions of the human body, putting the machine into a close and uneasy relation with the organic' (*Prosthesis*, p. 246).

31. Ibid., p. 247.

32. In *Narrative Prosthesis: Disability and the Dependencies of Discourse*, David Mitchell and Sharon Snyder examine the concept of prosthesis in terms of the powerful cultural desires for what counts as a 'normal' body. In their account of the implications of the concept of prosthesis for disability studies, they show how the prosthesis restores a 'deficient' body into a fiction of wholeness and integrity. In response to this fiction, Mitchell and Snyder write that the purpose of their study '*is to make the prosthesis show, to flaunt its imperfect supplement*

as an illusion' (p. 8). See also Mitchell and Snyder (eds), *The Body and Physical Difference*, pp. 1–31.

33. It is perhaps noteworthy, or just coincidental, that the Bastard expresses his dismay using the prosthetic trope, turning 'thumped' into 'bethumped'. I want to thank my colleague Peter DeGabriele for drawing my attention to this detail.

34. Rancière clarifies this point in *Disagreement*: 'politics exists wherever the count of parts and parties of society is disturbed by the inscription of a part of those who have no part [. . .] Politics ceases wherever this gap no longer has any place, wherever the whole of the community is reduced to the sum of its parts with nothing left over' (p. 123).

35. See Hobson, 'A Comment on Roy Battenhouse': 'The ensuing deal between John and Philip, itself canceled by the arrival of Pandulph, implicitly acknowledges that the sacral claims of kingship are either empty or, at best, unknowable' (p. 72).

36. See Griffiths, 'Sovereignty, Synecdoche', for an argument that prosthetic hands in the play challenge sovereign action: 'The play unravels these knotty questions by asking us repeatedly to consider what it means to have a "hand" in something. The vision of sovereign power that results from this sees it as constantly shifting, moved from hand to hand through a succession of compromised transactions' (p. 40).

37. See Harper-Bill, 'John and the Church of Rome'. John's own claim of sacred authority registers a long history of animosity toward Rome and Pope Innocent III, which, according to many historians, serves as a significant, if incomplete, precursor to the religious transformations of the sixteenth century. Harper-Bill summarises the prevailing interpretation this way: 'the king is blamed not

so much for tyranny, political miscalculation or even the loss of his French provinces, as for his surrender, after a promising start which prefigured Henry VIII's militant stance, to the aggression and the blandishments of the church of Rome' (p. 289).

38. C. J. Gordon points out that the language at this critical moment seems to point to the marriage between the Church and Christ the Bridegroom, which has here been generalised to apply to the alliance between states as corporate entities. For Gordon, this appears as an expansion, not a contraction, of political theology and sacramentality (email message to author, 25 March 2015).

39. Agamben, *The Kingdom and the Glory*, p. 3.

40. Schmitt, *Political Theology*, p. 36.

41. Agamben, *The Kingdom and the Glory*, p. 3.

42. Ibid.

43. Ibid., p. 108.

44. Sterne, 'Bureaumentality', pp. 111–12.

45. Ibid., p. 112.

46. See Bennett, 'Culture and Governmentality'.

47. Weber, *From Max Weber: Essays in Sociology*, p. 215.

48. Foucault, *Security, Territory, Population*, p. 76.

49. Ibid., p. 235. In his analysis of Arendt's account of the rise of totalitarian bureaucracies, Santner identifies the convergence of the 'quasi-naturalness of the people and the anonymous, machinelike functioning of bureaucratic administration' that 'transformed all state institutions into one form or other of *thanato-political biocracy*' (*The Royal Remains*, p. 53).

50. Agamben, *The Kingdom and the Glory*, p. 111.

51. Ibid., pp. 118–19.

52. Arendt, *The Origins of Totalitarianism*, p. 243.

53. Agamben, *The Kingdom and the Glory*, pp. 142–3. Agamben is clear about how collateral effects are consubstantial with every governmental act: 'Governing means allowing

the particular concomitant effects of a general "economy" to arise, an economy that would remain in itself wholly ineffective, but without which no government is possible. It is not so much that the effects (the Government) depend on being (the Kingdom), but rather that being consists of its effects: such as the vicarious and effectual ontology that defines the acts of government' (p. 142). For a discussion that brings an understanding of governmentality, political theology and the rhetoric of theo-political sovereignty into conversation, see Hammill, 'Blumenberg and Schmitt on the Rhetoric of Political Theology'.

54. Critics of *King John* generally agree that the socio-political apparatus absorbs the subversive potential of the Bastard Faulconbridge, despite the real threat that his unnatural birth poses to the systems of patriarchy that constitute the culture of the play. Consistent with Arendt's description of the accidental agent in bureaucracy, Peter Womack reads the Bastard as a 'hybrid figure' that is both a 'rootless swaggerer and national champion, cynical and noble, illegitimate and royal' ('Imagining Communities', p. 114). Womack argues that he embodies a contradiction between identification with metropolitan forms of power that were marginal to centralised royal control and an identification with the 'ambitions and illusions of a national centre' (p. 115). He concludes that *King John* demonstrates an absolutist theatre in which the 'monstrous many-headedness of the multitude is evoked, in the last analysis, in order to be resolved in, and so to substantiate, the all-embracing oneness of the monarch' (p. 138). Womack ends his essay suggesting that 'the last analysis' is not, in fact, the end to an early modern theatrical effect that might disrupt sovereignty's hold on power: 'Even if the royal orientation of that identity prevented the full expression of an autonomous "national consciousness"

within the text, the experience in the theatre will have made it possible to imagine that too' (p. 138). Virginia Vaughan notes that the 'subversion of patrilineal inheritance that was so clear in act 1 lingers in our minds as we watch so much being made of Henry's lineal claim to the throne. Primogeniture works only when there are no obfuscations, no illegitimate sons, and no rival claimants' ('*King John*: Subversion and Containment', p. 74). I draw on Vaughan's work from an important collection of essays on *King John* from 1989. In *A Companion to Shakespeare's Works: The Histories*, Vaughan argues against the binarism that structured her original argument about the play, claiming that the play's conclusion suggests the modern conception of a 'mixed' form of government, in which the loyalty and consent of the nobles are major ingredients of the king's authority ('*King John*', p. 393).

55. See Anderson, '"Legitimation, Name, and All Is Gone"', for a discussion of how the legacy of the important discoveries of new historicism has produced an understanding of power that enables a useful yet limited critique of early modern sovereignty. This chapter has significantly expanded the context and claims of the original essay. Few critics have observed a similar historical register of bureaucracy in the play. Christopher Pye has argued that the early modern theatre represents the power of the sovereign in the king's futile attempt to preserve traditional structures of power against 'the gradual emergence of mobile free labor' (*The Regal Phantasm*, p. 6). James Saeger finds in the play a vision of an 'independent identity that draws upon historically emergent conceptions of the self' ('Illegitimate Subjects', p. 1). He argues that the Bastard is a more 'independent, autonomous, and authentic identity' (p. 1) than one based on genealogical claims. He concludes that the play 'asserts

individual autonomy while drawing on traditional genealogically-based forms of authorization' (p. 20). Edward Gieskes argues that the Bastard inhabits and embodies a limited type of meritocracy in which he is able to function in various positions within the social hierarchy. The play's representation of the Bastard's status is informed by changing notions of profession during the period: 'Personally chosen profession begins to succeed divinely ordained vocation' ('"He is but a bastard to time"', p. 794). My argument extends his conclusion that the play 'represents a changing understanding of service and legitimacy in government' (p. 794). Yet even Gieskes's perspicacious reading of the play hints at a subversive quality in the Bastard that is ultimately contained by royal or aristocratic authority. He understands the Bastard's final speech as a moment that represents 'the fullness of his assimilation to the ranks of the nobility while it still bears the trace of his origins' (p. 793); in 'The Four Voices of the Bastard', Michael Manheim has identified a 'new Machiavellianism' that characterises the 'new politics' being articulated in the play and argues that the Bastard is 'in the process of learning a new political ethos and unlearning an old one' (p. 133).

56. Garber, 'Descanting on Deformity', p. 89.
57. Rose, *States of Fantasy*, p. 9.
58. Arendt, *The Origins of Totalitarianism*, p. 244.
59. Gallagher, *Medusa's Gaze*, p. 27. See also Anderson, *Performing Early Modern Trauma from Shakespeare to Milton*, pp. 57–66. These events underscore the fact that the act of execution was a sovereign mandate with details that were beyond the sovereign's control, structured by a bureaucracy filled with middle managers like Hubert or the Scrivener who were increasingly abstracted from royal authority.

60. In Curtis Breight's account, in *Surveillance, Militarism and Drama in the Elizabethan Era*, the state ceases to be a static object of study and is more a shifting formation produced by a constant process of legitimation. Legitimation is achieved and maintained not so much through the act or ritual of policy enforcement, but through other means. In *The Great Arch: English State Formation as Cultural Revolution*, Philip Corrigan and Derek Sayer argue, 'It is not so much the fine detail of enforcement of this or that statute or proclamation that matters, as the steady, exemplary and cumulative weight of growing state regulation' (p. 70).

61. Findlay, *Illegitimate Power*, pp. 253–7. Findlay estimates that bastardy figures as a subject in over one hundred plays in the period.

62. Neill, '"In Everything Illegitimate"', p. 273. For other work on bastardy, see Gooding, '"The Plague of Custom"', and Laslett, Oosterveen and Smith (eds), *Bastardy and its Comparative History*. Michael Neill has provided a general account of many of the shifting meanings of the ubiquitous figure in Renaissance drama. For an interrogation of bastardy within a single play, see Neill, 'Bastardy, Counterfeiting, and Misogyny in *The Revenger's Tragedy*'.

63. Neil, '"In Everything Illegitimate"', p. 273.

64. Findlay, *Illegitimate Power*, p. 4.

65. Ibid., p. 25.

66. See Arendt, *The Origins of Totalitarianism*, pp. 243–5. Arendt makes the distinction between laws and decrees that helps makes sense of the bureaucratic logic emerging in *King John*: 'government by bureaucracy is government by decree, and this means that power [. . .] becomes the direct source of all legislation. Decrees moreover remain anonymous (while laws can always be traced to specific men or assemblies), and therefore seem

to flow from some over-all ruling power that needs no justification [. . .] The administrator considers the law to be powerless because it is by definition separated from its application. The decree, on the other hand, does not exist at all except if and when it is applied; it needs no justification except applicability' (pp. 243–4). The Bastard was 'born' by sovereign decree, and if blood establishes status, as the debate over his origins suggests, this bureaucratic birthright creates the space for an altered relationship to the crown.

67. Breight, *Surveillance, Militarism and Drama in the Elizabethan Era*, p. 237.

68. MacCaffrey, 'Place and Patronage in Elizabethan Politics', p. 104.

69. Hobson, 'Bastard Speech', p. 109.

70. Ibid.

71. I employ Breight's use of Cohen's analysis of consent. For a more detailed account of the concept, see Cohen, *The Manipulation of Consent*, pp. 76–7.

72. Brown, *The Governance of Late Medieval England*, p. 52.

73. See Saeger, 'Illegitimate Subjects', who claims that in the end the Bastard is the 'voice of English nationalism' (p. 16). In '"So Jest with Heaven"', Dorothy Kelher makes a similar argument, claiming that the 'bellicose nationalism' of the final speech 'is the new faith in Shakespeare's vision of the modern political world' (p. 111). Both David Scott Kastan and Philip Edwards have offered suggestive counters to Kelher's conclusion. Kastan claims that the speech is, at most, qualified support in a fluid political environment, noting that the nobility would soon be disloyal to the new king (*Shakespeare and the Shapes of Time*, p. 53). Edwards reads the Bastard's speech as a frustrated articulation of the loss of true royalty in the national community, as 'new

ambitions [are] extinguishing old sanctity' (*Threshold of a Nation*, p. 122). His argument, however, stresses the Bastard's self-abnegation, noting that he does not press his own claim to the crown. Edwards cites the moment in act 5 when John 'gives up' – in effect providing the Bastard with his final 'commission': 'With this commission, the Bastard works brilliantly. The all-embracing need is the integrity of England, and on behalf of England and the royal blood that is in him he put up the magnificent pretence that there is a fierce and war-like John behind him' (p. 121). The deteriorating royal body (not the maintained fiction of a fierce corpse), I argue, is central to the new authority of the Bastard, as it reconfigures his relationship from the personal to the impersonally bureaucratic.

74. Agnew, *Worlds Apart*, p. 42.
75. Ibid., p. 113.
76. In *Inwardness and Theater in the English Renaissance*, Katharine Maus claims that the figure of the Bastard in *King John* functions as a 'machiavel', personifying a 'radical, unprincipled estrangement of internal truth from external manifestation' (p. 35). This claim, however, posits inwardness as a priori to the social context of its expression – an assumption that the notion of a bureaucratic subjectivity complicates. Phyllis Rackin has characterised the Machiavellian figure as a site in which the 'Protean, shape-shifting actor, the ruthless image of the Florentine and the new commercial adventurer merge in a single figure that combines subversive threat with theatrical power' (*Stages of History*, p. 74). The subversion that Rackin identifies in this figure comes from the disruption of 'old generic categories that reduce individuals to representations of their classes'. In her formulation, 'strikingly individualized characters represent the

emergence of individual subjectivity in a changing world'
(p. 74). She associates the emergence of the new subjectivity to 'the lawless forces' that 'motivate the action and
move the plot' of *King John* (p. 66). Rackin's speculations emphasise individual subjectivity at the expense of
the evolving social and political developments that continue to play a role in the formation of identity during
bureaucratic developments in the early modern period.
Amplifying Rackin, Maus suggests that the machiavel
often 'exploits his self-awareness by undertaking a *coup
d'état*' (p. 55). Of course, the self-awareness of the Bastard manifests itself precisely in the desire not to rebel. In
'Mingling Vice and "Worthiness" in *King John*', Robert
Weimann notes this reversal in the play and connects it to
the play's rewriting of Vice as a worthy figure. According
to Weimann, Shakespeare 'seeks to redeem the unbridled
energy of the valiant performer on behalf of his arduous
task in the building of, historically speaking, an anachronistic image of the nation-state' (p. 110). The bureaucratic subject figured in the character of the Bastard
reveals most vividly its contingent force instrumental to
but not defined by its relationship to the sovereign.
77. Agamben, *The Kingdom and the Glory*, p. 135.
78. Ibid., p. 142.
79. Manning, *Politics of Touch*, p. xxii.

Chapter 5

1. Watson, *Mocked with Death*, p. 164.
2. For an exceptional analysis of the relationship between
   language and animation in the play, see Lynn Enterline's
   '"You speak a language that I understand not"'.
3. Krause, *Freedom Beyond Sovereignty*, p. 46.
4. Ibid., p. 37.

5. Ibid.
6. Frost, *Lessons from a Materialist Thinker*, p. 140. See also van Mill, *Liberty, Rationality, and Agency in Hobbes's Leviathan*. Van Mill claims that 'Hobbes requires a theory of rationality that is intersubjective but not in a deliberatively democratic manner' (p. 75). For a strong counter-reading of Hobbes that puts significant pressure on this concept of agency as 'social' or 'intersubjective', see DeGabriele, *Sovereign Power and the Enlightenment*, pp. xviii–xxx and pp. 8–14.
7. Frost, *Lessons from a Materialist Thinker*, p. 139.
8. Ibid., p. 11, pp. 10–11.
9. Ibid., p. 140.
10. Krause, *Freedom Beyond Sovereignty*, p. 46.
11. Ibid. See also Frost, *Lessons from a Materialist Thinker*, p. 139. Krause's understanding of power and agency is informed by but ultimately contradicts Hannah Arendt's formulation of individual agency explored in *The Human Condition*. According to Krause, Arendt 'neglects the importance of the connection between the agent's understanding of the action and its social reception' (*Freedom Beyond Sovereignty*, p. 36). See pp. 32–46 for her analysis of Arendt's position.
12. See Brown, 'Wounded Attachments'.
13. Ibid., pp. 390–1.
14. Ibid., p. 391.
15. Ibid.
16. Ibid., p. 407.
17. Ibid.
18. Ibid.
19. Ziarek, *An Ethics of Dissensus*, p. 8. See also Coole, 'Rethinking Agency'. Coole's work on a phenomenological concept of agency is pertinent to the idea of intersubjective sovereignty explored here. While maintaining that a form of agency with potency to produce effects and reflexivity to promote concern about those effects

is the *sine qua non* of politics, Coole describes agentic capacities that are contingent and that emerge 'imperfectly within an intercorporeal lifeworld' (p. 126). The argument takes issue with Habermas over the insistence that rationality is the distinguishing characteristic of agents, who remain individuals responsible for 'the communicative task' (p. 126) of reaching understanding, cooperation and consensus.

20. Ziarek, *An Ethics of Dissensus*, p. 8.
21. Ibid., p. 13.
22. See Krause, *Freedom Beyond Sovereignty*, p. 186.
23. Ziarek, *An Ethics of Dissensus*, p. 116.
24. Grosz, *Volatile Bodies*, p. 10.
25. Ibid., p. 8.
26. Ibid., p. 9.
27. Ibid., pp. 12–13.
28. Ibid., p. 165.
29. Ibid.
30. Santner, *The Royal Remains*, p. 4.
31. Melzer and Norberg (eds), *From the Royal to the Republican Body*, pp. 10–11; quoted in Santner, *The Royal Remains*, p. 4.
32. Santner, *The Royal Remains*, pp. 4–5.
33. Lefort, 'The Permanence of the Theologico-Political?', pp. 159–60.
34. Lefort, *The Political Forms of Modern Society*, p. 303. See also Copjec, 'The Subject Defined by Suffrage' and *Read My Desire*, pp. 160–1.
35. Ziarek, *An Ethics of Dissensus*, p. 139.
36. See Connolly, *Why I Am Not a Secularist*, for an argument about embodiment and intersubjectivity that resembles my own. See also Ziarek, *An Ethics of Dissensus*, p. 139.
37. For critics whose work focuses substantially on Lavinia, see Pascale Aebischer, *Shakespeare's Violated Bodies: Stage and Screen Performance*; Thomas P. Anderson, "'What

Is Written Shall Be Executed": "Nude Contracts" and "Lively Warrants" in *Titus Andronicus*'; Lisa Dickson, '"High" Art and "Low" Blows: *Titus Andronicus* and the Critical Language of Pain'; Douglas Green, 'Interpreting "Her Martyr'd Signs": Gender and Tragedy in *Titus Andronicus*'; Coppélia Kahn, *Roman Shakespeare: Warriors, Wounds, and Women*, pp. 46–76, esp. p. 48; Marion Wynne-Davies, '"The Swallowing Womb": Consumed and Consuming Women in *Titus Andronicus*'; Karen Robertson, 'Rape and the Appropriation of Progne's Revenge in Shakespeare's *Titus Andronicus*, or "Who Cooks the Thyestean Banquet?"'; Emily Detmer-Goebel, 'The Need for Lavinia's Voice: *Titus Andronicus* and the Telling of Rape'; and Kim Solga, 'Rape's Metatheatrical Return: Rehearsing Sexual Violence among the Early Moderns'. Solga's conclusion about Julie Taymor's cinematic representation of Lavinia hints at the kinetic quality of her body in the play: 'The confusion and anxiety Lavinia's body incites has less to do with what it may symbolically reveal than with its performative limits, which in turn mark the limits of its ability to return evidence [. . .] Her audience can only watch in distress as an otherwise clear picture of her experience dissolves, leaving emptiness in place of a surfeit of symbol' (p. 65).

38. In claiming that Lavinia's body is a performing object, I draw on scholarship on early modern objects and stage props, including Jonathan Gil Harris, *Untimely Matter in the Time of Shakespeare*; Francis Teague, *Shakespeare's Speaking Properties*; Jonathan Gil Harris and Nasha Korda, *Staged Properties in Early Modern English Drama*; Margreta de Grazia, Maureen Quilligan and Peter Stallybrass (eds), *Subject and Object in Renaissance Culture*; and Will Fisher, *Materializing Gender in Early Modern English Literature and Culture*. Lena

Orlin notes in her assessment of the study of early modern objects that 'the cultural project of things' now rivals the body as a crucial site of inquiry in Renaissance studies ('The Performance of Things in *The Taming of the Shrew*', p. 179).

39. Prochan, 'The Semiotic Study of Puppets, Masks, and Performing Objects', p. 4.

40. Bell, 'Puppets, Masks, and Performing Objects at the End of the Century', p. 16.

41. See Krause, *Freedom Beyond Sovereignty*, p. 97, and for a discussion of the necessary force of social uptake in expressions of non-sovereign agency, see pp. 36–9.

42. Vickers, 'Members Only: Marot's Anatomical Blazons', p. 8. See also Uman and Morrison (eds), *Staging the Blazon in Early Modern English Theater*, for a collection of essays that historically and theoretically reconsiders the literary convention.

43. Vickers, 'Members Only: Marot's Anatomical Blazons', p. 8.

44. Ibid., p. 9.

45. Ibid.

46. I adopt this term from Shaviro, *The Cinematic Body*, p. 4.

47. Grosz, *Volatile Bodies*, p. 180.

48. Ibid.

49. My argument about the tactility of Lavinia in Julie Taymor's film is indebted to the work of Jacques Derrida, *On Touching – Jean-Luc Nancy*; Steven Shaviro, *The Cinematic Body*; Laura U. Marks, *The Skin of the Film*; and Elizabeth Grosz, *Volatile Bodies*.

50. Rowe, 'Dismembering and Forgetting in *Titus Andronicus*', p. 295.

51. Packard, 'Lavinia as Coauthor of Shakespeare's *Titus Andronicus*', p. 292.

52. Witmore, *Pretty Creatures*, p. 148.

53. Packard, 'Lavinia as Coauthor of Shakespeare's *Titus Andronicus*', p. 292.
54. Krause, *Freedom Beyond Sovereignty*, p. 83.
55. See Marshall, 'The Pornographic Economy of *Titus Andronicus*'.
56. Gil, *Shakespeare's Anti-Politics*, p. 127.
57. Ibid.
58. Ibid., p. 128.
59. Owens, *Stages of Dismemberment*, p. 16.
60. See Bell, 'Puppets, Masks, and Performing Objects at the End of the Century', p. 16. Lucian Ghita understands Taymor's vision as an exploration of the 'interface between bodies and objects'; see 'Aesthetics of Fragmentation in Taymor's *Titus*', p. 208. For an extended analysis of Taymor's relationship to Disney and the avant-garde, see Anderson, '*Titus*, Broadway, and Disney's Magic Capitalism, or the Wonderful World of Julie Taymor'.
61. Ghita, 'Aesthetics of Fragmentation in Taymor's *Titus*', p. 207.
62. Grosz, *Volatile Bodies*, p. xiii.
63. Grosz, *Volatile Bodies*, p. 188.
64. See Ziarek, 'Bare Life', who calls for a more developed critical conversation about the ontology of potentiality that is related to Agamben's understanding of bare life. Ziarek writes in response to Agamben's notion of the limits imposed by bare life: 'another reason Agamben does not consider the practice of liberation in greater depth is that his ontology of potentiality is developed to undermine sovereign will and not to transform bare life into a site of contestation and political possibility' (p. 204).
65. Marks, *The Skin of the Film*, p. 178, pp. 162–3. Marks distinguishes the haptic from the optical in this way: 'The haptic image forces the viewer to contemplate the

image itself instead of being pulled into narrative [. . .] Optical visuality, by contrast, assumes that all resources the viewer requires are available in the image [. . .] [I]t affords the illusion of completeness that lends itself to narrative' (p. 163). Haptic visuality is especially appropriate to the film *Titus* since its source play is concerned with how literary intertext and historical narrative help to justify Titus's retributive violence that disposes of Lavinia as a form of necessary collateral damage.

66. Shaviro, *The Cinematic Body*, p. 9.
67. Silverman, *The Acoustic Mirror*, p. 6.
68. Shaviro, *The Cinematic Body*, p. 53.
69. Ibid., p. 52.
70. Benjamin, *Illuminations*, pp. 238–40. He describes the 'distracting' elements of the Dadaists as a precursor to the demand for tactile appropriation in film (p. 238).
71. Shaviro, *The Cinematic Body*, p. 4.
72. Ibid., p. 53.
73. Cartelli and Rowe argue that because the prosthetic devices 'seem to have been carved as the hands of saints, and because they serve to express Titus' meanings as much or more than her own, they remain ambiguous interpolations: part compensatory tools, part reminder of Lavinia's conversion into a figure or sign, a symbol of martyred innocence and "pattern, president, and lively warrant" of the moral authority of the Andronici (5.3.44)' (*New Wave Shakespeare on Screen*, p. 85).
74. Grosz, 'Deleuze's Bergson', p. 229.
75. See Krause, *Freedom Beyond Sovereignty*, p. 41.
76. Ibid., p. 60.
77. Ibid., p. 61.
78. Ibid., p. 82.
79. Ibid., p. 83.
80. See Bate (ed.), *Titus Andronicus: The Arden Shakespeare*, p. 267 n. 44.1.

81. See Colebrook, 'A Grammar of Becoming'.
82. Marks, *The Skin of the Film*, p. 187.
83. Geller, 'The Cinematic Relations of Corporeal Feminism'.
84. In *The Tears of Sovereignty: Perspectives of Power in Renaissance Drama*, pp. 326–41, Philip Lorenz directs us to the most recent scholarship that has established these lines of inquiry into the play. Critics exploring the play's investment in a critique of sovereignty include Bradin Cormack, 'Shakespeare's Other Sovereignty: On Particularity and Violence in *The Winter's Tale* and the Sonnets'; Christopher Pye, 'Against Schmitt: Law, Aesthetics, and Absolutism in Shakespeare's *The Winter's Tale*'; and Julia Reinhard Lupton, 'Hospitality and Risk in *The Winter's Tale*', in *Thinking with Shakespeare*, pp. 161–86. For scholars who explore the play's interest in the impact of the reformed theology in early modern England, see Ken Jackson, '"Grace to boot": St. Paul, Messianic Time, and Shakespeare's *The Winter's Tale*'; Richard Wilson, 'The Statue of our Queen: Shakespeare's Open Secret'; Huston Diehl, '"Strike All that Look Upon with Marvel": Theatrical and Theological Wonder in *The Winter's Tale*'; Chloe Porter, 'Idolatry, Iconoclasm and Agency: Visual Experience in Works by Lyly and Shakespeare'; and Julia Reinhard Lupton, '*The Winter's Tale* and the Gods: Iconographies of Idolatry'. For recent scholarship that bridges the gap between a theological and a political reading of the play, see James Kuzner, '*The Winter's Tale*: Faith in Law and the Law of Faith'.
85. Lupton, '*The Winter's Tale* and the Gods', p. 216.
86. Ibid., p. 177.
87. Ibid.
88. Ibid., p. 216.
89. Ibid., p. 217.
90. Ibid.

91. Ibid.
92. Building on Lupton's influential account of iconography in the play, Chloe Porter reassesses iconoclastic acts, such as Hermione's resurrection, arguing that they provide 'an important context for the relationship between the viewer and the viewed encouraged in the early modern playhouse' ('Idolatry, Iconoclasm and Agency', p. 12). Her work unpacks 'an interactive relationship between audience and performance' that is the result of the intersection of 'pre-Reformation approaches to images' and 'a perception of visual representations as items of ambiguous status subject to direct, physical interrogation by the viewer' (p. 14). Understanding the force of Hermione's statue to generate a new type of agency in the theatre, Porter writes, 'early modern English drama is rooted in a developing visual culture in which pre- and post-Reformation visual experiences were [. . .] in the process of "re-formation"' (p. 14). Porter calls attention to the force of Hermione's statue beyond its reflection and enactment of new modes of signification ushered in by reformed religious practices in the sixteenth century, a process hinted at in Lupton's inclusion of the dynamism of the actor's body in her reading of the scene. For a reading of the effect that the actor's live body has on how we might understand dramatic objects such as a statue or effigy, see Anderson, 'Surpassing the King's Two Bodies'.
93. Pye, 'Against Schmitt', p. 212.
94. Schmitt, *Political Theology*, p. 65.
95. Pye, 'Against Schmitt', p. 213.
96. Ibid. Pye's work is informed by a concept of aesthetics explored in Kahn, *Wayward Contracts*, pp. 6–24.
97. Lorenz, *The Tears of Sovereignty*, p. 229.
98. Ibid., p. 233.
99. Ibid.

100. Cormack, 'Shakespeare's Other Sovereignty', p. 490.
101. Ibid.
102. Lorenz, *The Tears of Sovereignty*, p. 17.
103. Negri and Hardt, *Empire*, p. 103.
104. Ibid.
105. Kalmo and Skinner, 'Introduction: A Concept in Fragments', p. 15. See, for example, Bellamy, *Rethinking Liberalism*. Skinner is sceptical about claims that a concept of the state or sovereignty is no longer functional in an era of globalisation. For him, the decision about 'who gets what and in what circumstances' is only made more critical; see his 'The Sovereign State: A Genealogy', p. 18.
106. Cormack, 'Shakespeare's Other Sovereignty', p. 493.
107. Ibid., p. 510.
108. Ibid., p. 511. Cormack identifies the force that causes a redistribution of sovereignty as love: 'In opposition to the sovereign who cannot admit in the other that which makes the other sovereign, Shakespeare represents love as allowing for difference as an essential part of the experience of the beloved and of erotic desire. In the lover's attention to the beloved, Shakespeare invents an alternative model for sovereignty to the one nurtured by Leontes in the political realm' (p. 497).
109. Lupton, *Thinking with Shakespeare*, p. 171.
110. Ibid.
111. Ibid.
112. See ibid., pp. 171–2. Lupton argues that this public shaming is coupled with 'a more existential process of publication' that involves Leontes' role as 'both director and audience, while casting Hermione as his player queen' (p. 171). Her performance in this capacity is in tension with her desire for retirement, according to Lupton, 'before the eyes of a royal dictator' (p. 172). In

Lupton's insightful reading of this moment in relation to Hannah Arendt's view of the public sphere in politics, Hermione's more spontaneous, less formal mode of performance becomes paradoxically the more public, 'at once *self-authored* (produced by Hermione from out of her own verbal reserve) and *self-authoring* (she appears as a subject to those who witness her, including her husband)' (p. 171).

113. Ibid., p. 174.
114. Ziarek, 'Bare Life', p. 195.
115. Agamben, *Homo Sacer*, p. 187.
116. See Ziarek, 'Bare Life', p. 203.
117. Ibid., p. 208. Ziarek's conclusion has been fundamental to my interrogation of sovereignty in the play: 'In the context of the revolutionary paradigm, the excess of bare life over the constituted forms of life not only does not authorize the sovereign decision on the state of exception but in fact marks openness to what is yet to come – a possibility of political transformation, a creation of new forms of life, an arrival of a more expansive conception of freedom and justice. In so doing, it transforms impossibility into contingency in political life' (pp. 208–9).

Epilogue: Turning Away

1. Wenman, *Agonistic Democracy*, p. 6.
2. Honig, *Political Theory and the Displacement of Politics*, p. 80.
3. Honig, 'Law and Politics in the New Europe', p. 110.
4. Ibid.
5. Wenman, *Agonistic Democracy*, p. 215.
6. Ibid.
7. Ibid., p. 243.

8. Wills, *Dorsality*, p. 4.
9. Ibid., p. 6.
10. Ibid., p. 7.
11. Hobbes, *Leviathan*, p. 3.
12. DeGabriele, *Sovereign Power and the Enlightenment*, p. 3.
13. Ovid, *Metamorphoses*; see Perseus Digital Library, <http://data.perseus.org/citations/urn:cts:latinLit:phi0959.phi006.perseus-eng1:10.1-10.85> (last accessed 16 March 2016).

BIBLIOGRAPHY

Abate, Corinne S., '"Once more unto the breach": Katharine's Victory in *Henry V*', *Early Theatre* 4 (2001): 73–85.

Aebischer, Pascale, *Shakespeare's Violated Bodies: Stage and Screen Performance* (Cambridge: Cambridge University Press, 2004).

Agamben, Giorgio, *The Coming Community*, trans. Michael Hardt (Minneapolis: University of Minnesota Press, 1993).

Agamben, Giorgio, *Homo Sacer: Sovereign Power and Bare Life*, trans. Daniel Heller-Roazen (Stanford: Stanford University Press, 1998).

Agamben, Giorgio, *The Kingdom and the Glory: For a Theological Genealogy of Economy and Government*, trans. Lorenzo Chiesa (Stanford: Stanford University Press, 2011).

Agnew, Jean-Christophe, *Worlds Apart: The Theatre and the Market in Anglo-American Culture, 1550–1750* (New York: Cambridge University Press, 1986).

Anderson, Thomas P., '"Legitimation, Name, and All Is Gone": Bastardy and Bureaucracy in Shakespeare's *King John*', *Journal for Early Modern Cultural Studies* 4.2 (2004): 35–61.

Anderson, Thomas P., *Performing Early Modern Trauma from Shakespeare to Milton* (Burlington, VT: Ashgate Publishing, 2006).

Anderson, Thomas P., 'Surpassing the King's Two Bodies: The Politics of Staging the Royal Effigy in Marlowe's *Edward II*', *Shakespeare Bulletin* 32.4 (2014): 585–611.

Anderson, Thomas P., '*Titus*, Broadway, and Disney's Magic Capitalism, or the Wonderful World of Julie Taymor', *College Literature* 40.1 (2013): 66–95.

Anderson, Thomas P., '"What Is Written Shall Be Executed": "Nude Contracts" and "Lively Warrants" in *Titus Andronicus*', *Criticism* 45.3 (2004): 301–21.

Appian, *Roman History*, vol. 2, ed. and trans. Brian McGing, Loeb Classical Library 3 (Cambridge, MA: Harvard University Press, 1912).

Archer, John, *Citizen Shakespeare: Freeman and Aliens in the Language of the Plays* (New York: Palgrave Macmillan, 2005).

Arendt, Hannah, *On Revolution* (New York: Penguin Books, 1990).

Arendt, Hannah, *The Origins of Totalitarianism* (New York: Harcourt Brace & Company, 1975).

Armitage, David, Conal Condren and Andrew Fitzmaurice, 'Introduction', in David Armitage, Conal Condren and Andrew Fitzmaurice (eds), *Shakespeare and Early Modern Political Thought* (Cambridge: Cambridge University Press, 2009), pp. 1–24.

Arnold, Oliver, *The Third Citizen: Shakespeare's Theater and the Early Modern House of Commons* (Baltimore: Johns Hopkins University Press, 2007).

Asad, Talal, *Formations of the Secular: Christianity, Islam, Modernity* (Stanford: Stanford University Press, 2003).

Badiou, Alain, *Being and Event*, trans. Oliver Feltham (New York: Continuum, 2006).

Balibar, Etienne, 'Citizen Subject', in Eduardo Cadava, Peter Connor and Jean-Luc Nancy (eds), *Who Comes After the Subject?* (New York: Routledge, 1991), pp. 33–57.

Barlow, Frank, *The English Historical Review* 95.374 (January 1980): 3–27.

Barton, Anne, 'Livy, Machiavelli and Shakespeare's *Coriolanus*', in *Essays, Mainly Shakespearean* (Cambridge: Cambridge University Press, 1994), pp. 136–60.

Bate, Jonathan (ed.), *Titus Andronicus: The Arden Shakespeare* (London: Routledge, 1995).

Bell, John, 'Puppets, Masks, and Performing Objects at the End of the Century', *The Drama Review* 43.3 (1999): 15–27.

Bellamy, Richard, *Rethinking Liberalism* (New York: Continuum, 2000).

Benjamin, Walter, *Illuminations*, trans. Harry Zohn, ed. Hannah Arendt (New York: Schocken Books, 1969).

Bennett, Jane, *The Enchantment of Modern Life: Attachments, Crossings, and Ethics* (Princeton: Princeton University Press, 2001).

Bennett, Tony, 'Culture and Governmentality', in Jack Z. Bratich, Jeremy Packer and Cameron McCarthy (eds), *Foucault, Cultural Studies, and Governmentality* (Albany, NY: SUNY Press, 2003), pp. 47–66.

Bloch, Marc, *The Royal Touch: Sacred Monarchy and Scrofula in England and France* (London: Routledge & Kegan Paul Ltd, 1973).

Bodin, Jean, *The Six Bookes of the Commonweale*, vol. 4, trans. Richard Knolles, ed. Kenneth McCrae (Cambridge, MA: Harvard University Press, 1962).

Botwinick, Aryeh and William E. Connolly (eds), *Democracy and Vision: Sheldon Wolin and the Vicissitudes of the Political* (Princeton: Princeton University Press, 2001).

Braddick, Michael, *State Formation in Early Modern England, 1550–1700* (Cambridge: Cambridge University Press, 2000).

Bray, Alan, *The Friend* (Chicago: University of Chicago Press, 2003).

Breight, Curtis, *Surveillance, Militarism and Drama in the Elizabethan Era* (New York: St. Martin's Press, 1996).

Brogan, Stephen, *The Royal Touch in Early Modern England: Politics, Medicine and Sin* (Woodbridge: Boydell Press, 2015).

Brown, A. L., *The Governance of Late Medieval England, 1272–1461* (Stanford: Stanford University Press, 1989).

Brown, A. L., 'The Reign of Henry IV: The Establishment of the Lancastrian Regime', in S. B. Chrimes, C. D. Ross and R. A. Griffiths (eds), *Fifteenth-Century England, 1399–1509: Studies in Politics and Society* (Manchester: Manchester University Press, 1972), pp. 1–28.

Brown, Eric, 'Introduction: Reading the Insect', in Eric Brown (ed.), *Insect Poetics* (Minneapolis: University of Minnesota Press, 2006), pp. ix–xxiii.

Brown, Wendy, 'Wounded Attachments', *Political Theory* 21.3 (1993): 390–410.

Butler, Judith, *Bodies That Matter: On the Discursive Limits of Sex* (New York: Routledge, 1993).

Campana, Joseph, 'The Bee and the Sovereign? Political Entomology and the Problem of Scale', *Shakespeare Studies* 41 (2013): 94–113.

Canny, Nicholas, 'Edmund Spenser and the Development of an Anglo-Irish Identity', *Yearbook of English Studies* 13 (1983): 1–19.

Cartelli, Thomas and Katherine Rowe, *New Wave Shakespeare on Screen* (Cambridge: Polity, 2007).

Cavell, Stanley, 'Who Does the Wolf Love? Reading *Coriolanus*', *Representations* 3 (Summer 1983): 1–20.

Cheney, Patrick, 'Introduction: Marlowe in the Twenty-First Century', in Patrick Cheney (ed.), *The Cambridge Companion to Marlowe* (Cambridge: Cambridge University Press, 2004), pp. 1–23.

Chernaik, Warren, *The Myth of Rome in Shakespeare and his Contemporaries* (Cambridge: Cambridge University Press, 2011).

Cicero, William, *De Senectute, De Amicitia, De Divinatione*, trans. William Falconer (Cambridge, MA: Harvard University Press, 1928).

Clowes, William, *A right frutefull treatise for the artificiall cure of struma* (London, 1602).

Cohen, Youssef, *The Manipulation of Consent: The State and Working-Class Consciousness in Brazil* (Pittsburgh: University of Pittsburgh Press, 1989).

Colebrook, Claire, 'A Grammar of Becoming: Strategy, Subjectivism, and Style', in Elizabeth Grosz (ed.), *Explorations in Time, Memory, and Futures* (Ithaca, NY: Cornell University Press, 1999), pp. 117–40.

Coleman, Christopher and David Starkey (eds), *Revolution Reassessed: Revisions in the History of Tudor Government and Administration* (Oxford: Clarendon, 1986).

Collinson, Patrick, *Republica Anglorum, or History with the Politics Put Back* (Cambridge: Cambridge University Press, 1990).

Condren, Conal, 'Unfolding "The Properties of Government": The Case of *Measure for Measure* and the History of Political Thought', in David Armitage, Conal Condren and Andrew Fitzmaurice (eds), *Shakespeare and Early Modern Political Thought* (Cambridge: Cambridge University Press, 2009), pp. 157–75.

Connolly, Joy, *The Life of Roman Republicanism* (Princeton: Princeton University Press, 2015).

Connolly, William E., *Why I Am Not a Secularist* (Minneapolis: University of Minnesota Press, 1999).

Coole, Diane, 'Rethinking Agency: A Phenomenological Approach to Embodiment and Agentic Capacities', *Political Studies* 53 (2005): 124–42.

Copjec, Joan, *Read My Desire: Lacan Against the Historicists* (Boston: MIT Press, 1994).

Copjec, Joan, 'The Subject Defined by Suffrage', *lacanian ink* 7 (1993): 47–58.

Cormack, Bradin, 'Shakespeare's Other Sovereignty: On Particularity and Violence in *The Winter's Tale* and the Sonnets', *Shakespeare Quarterly* 62.4 (2011): 485–513.

Corrigan, Philip and Derek Sayer, *The Great Arch: English State Formation as Cultural Revolution* (Oxford: Basil Blackwell, 1985).

Crawfurd, Raymond, *The King's Evil* (Oxford: Clarendon Press, 1911).

de Grazia, Margreta, Maureen Quilligan and Peter Stally-brass (eds), *Subject and Object in Renaissance Culture* (Cambridge: Cambridge University Press, 1996).

de Montaigne, Michel, *The Essays of Montaigne*, trans. E. J. Trechmann (Oxford: Oxford University Press, 1935).

de Vries, Hent and Lawrence E. Sullivan (eds), *Political Theologies: Public Religions in a Post-Secular World* (New York: Fordham University Press, 2006).

DeGabriele, Peter, *Sovereign Power and the Enlightenment: Eighteenth-Century Literature and the Problem of the Political* (Lewisburg, PA: Bucknell University Press, 2015).

Del Lucchese, Filippo, *Conflict, Power, and Multitude in Machiavelli and Spinoza: Tumult and Indignation* (London: Continuum, 2009).

Derrida, Jacques, *Of Hospitality*, trans. Rachel Bowlby (Stanford: Stanford University Press, 2000).

Derrida, Jacques, *On Touching – Jean-Luc Nancy*, trans. Christine Irizarry (Stanford: Stanford University Press, 2005).

Derrida, Jacques, 'Politics of Friendship', *American Imago* 50.3 (1993): 353–90.

Derrida, Jacques, *The Politics of Friendship*, trans. George Collins (New York: Verso, 2005).

Derrida, Jacques, *Rogues: Two Essays in Reason*, trans. Pascale-Anne Brault and Michael Naas (Stanford: Stanford University Press, 2005).

Derrida, Jacques, *Without Alibi*, ed. and trans. Peggy Kamuf (Stanford: Stanford University Press, 2002).

Detmer-Goebel, Emily, 'The Need for Lavinia's Voice: *Titus Andronicus* and the Telling of Rape', *Shakespeare Studies* 22 (2001): 75–92.

Dickson, Lisa, '"High" Art and "Low" Blows: *Titus Andronicus* and the Critical Language of Pain', *Shakespeare Bulletin* 26.1 (2008): 1–22.

Diehl, Huston, '"Strike All that Look Upon with Marvel": Theatrical and Theological Wonder in *The Winter's Tale*', in Bryan Reynolds and William N. West (eds), *Rematerializing Shakespeare: Authority and Representation on the Early Modern English Stage* (New York: Palgrave Macmillan, 2005), pp. 19–34.

Dollimore, Jonathan and Alan Sinfield, 'History and Ideology: The Instance of *Henry V*', in John Drakakis (ed.), *Alternative Shakespeares* (London: Methuen, 1985), pp. 206–27.

Eastman, Nate, 'The Rumbling Belly Politic: Metaphorical Location and Metaphorical Government in *Coriolanus*', *Early Modern Literary Studies* 13.1 (May 2007): 21–39.

Edwards, Philip, *Threshold of a Nation* (Cambridge: Cambridge University Press, 1979).

Elton, G. R., *Studies in Tudor and Stuart Politics and Government: Papers and Reviews 1983–1990*, vol. 4 (Cambridge: Cambridge University Press, 1992).

Elyot, Thomas, *The Boke Named the Governour*, ed. Foster Watson (New York: Everyman, 1907).

Enterline, Lynn, '"You speak a language that I understand not": The Rhetoric of Animation in *The Winter's Tale*', in *The Rhetoric of the Body from Ovid to Shakespeare* (Cambridge: Cambridge University Press, 2000), pp. 198–226.

Findlay, Allison, *Illegitimate Power: Bastards in Renaissance Drama* (Manchester: Manchester University Press, 1994).

Finnerty, Páraic, '"Both are alike, and both alike we like":
Sovereignty and Amity in Shakespeare's *King John*',
Literature & History 20.1 (2011): 38–58.

Fisher, Will, *Materializing Gender in Early Modern English
Literature and Culture* (Cambridge: Cambridge University Press, 2006).

Foucault, Michel, *The Birth of Biopolitics: Lectures at the
Collège de France, 1978–1979*, trans. Graham Burchell
(New York: Palgrave Macmillan, 2008).

Foucault, Michel, *Security, Territory, Population: Lectures
at the Collège de France, 1977–1978*, trans. Graham
Burchell (New York: Picador, 2009).

Frost, Samantha, *Lessons from a Materialist Thinker:
Hobbesian Reflections on Ethics and Politics* (Stanford:
Stanford University Press, 2005).

Furnivall, F. J. (ed.), *Robert Laneham's Letters: Describing
a Part of the Entertainment unto Queen Elizabeth at the
Castle of Kenilworth in 1575* (New York: Chatto and
Windus, 1907).

Gallagher, Lowell, *Medusa's Gaze: Casuistry and Conscience
in the Renaissance* (Stanford: Stanford University Press,
1991).

Garber, Marjorie, 'Descanting on Deformity: *Richard III* and
the Shape of History', in Heather Dubrow and Richard
Strier (eds), *The Historical Renaissance: New Essays on
Tudor and Stuart Literature and Culture* (Chicago: University of Chicago Press, 1988), pp. 79–103.

Garganigo, Alex, '*Coriolanus*, the Union Controversy, and
Access to the Royal Person', *SEL: Studies in English Literature 1500–1900* 42.2 (2002): 335–59.

Geller, Theresa L., 'The Cinematic Relations of Corporeal
Feminism: Towards a Feminist Cinematographic Philosophy', *Rhizomes: Cultural Studies in Emerging Knowledge*
11/12 (2005/2006), <http://rhizomes.net/issue11/geller.
html> (last accessed 22 February 2016).

Geremek, Bronislaw, *Poverty: A History*, trans. Agnieszka Kolakowska (Cambridge, MA: Blackwell, 1994).

Ghita, Lucian, 'Aesthetics of Fragmentation in Taymor's *Titus*', in Alexander C. Y. Huang and Charles S. Ross (eds), *Shakespeare in Hollywood, Asia, and Cyberspace* (West Lafayette, IN: Purdue University Press, 2009), pp. 207–17.

Gieskes, Edward, '"He is but a bastard to time": Status and Service in *The Troublesome Raigne of John* and Shakespeare's *King John*', *ELH* 65.4 (1998): 779–98.

Gieskes, Edward, *Representing the Professions: Administration, Law, and Theater in Early Modern England* (Newark, DE: University of Delaware Press, 2006).

Gil, Daniel Juan, *Shakespeare's Anti-Politics: Sovereign Power and the Life of the Flesh* (New York: Palgrave, 2013).

Gilbert, Felix, *Machiavelli and Guicciardini* (New York: Norton, 1984).

Goh, Irving, *The Reject: Community, Politics, and Religion after the Subject* (New York: Fordham University Press, 2015).

Goh, Irving, 'Rejecting Friendship: Towards a Radical Reading of Derrida's *Politics of Friendship* for Today', *Cultural Critique* 79 (2011): 94–124.

Goldberg, Jonathan, 'Shakespearean Inscriptions: The Voicing of Power', in Patricia Parker and Geoffrey Hartman (eds), *Shakespeare and the Question of Theory* (New York: Methuen, 1985), pp. 116–37.

Gooding, Lela Moore, '"The Plague of Custom": Illegitimacy in Elizabethan Drama and Society', unpublished dissertation, Vanderbilt University, 1991.

Green, Douglas, 'Interpreting "Her Martyr'd Signs": Gender and Tragedy in *Titus Andronicus*', *Shakespeare Quarterly* 40 (1989): 317–26.

Greenblatt, Stephen, *Hamlet in Purgatory* (Princeton: Princeton University Press, 2001).

Greenblatt, Stephen, 'Invisible Bullets: Renaissance Authority and its Subversion in *Henry IV* and *Henry V*', in Jonathan Dollimore and Alan Sinfield (eds), *Political Shakespeare* (Manchester: Manchester University Press, 1994), pp. 18–47.

Griffiths, Huw, 'The Sonnet in Ruins: Time and the Nation in 1599', *Early Modern Culture* (2007), <http://emc.eserver.org/1-6/griffiths.html> (last accessed 22 February 2016).

Griffiths, Huw, 'Sovereignty, Synecdoche, and the Prosthetic Hand in *King John*', *Exemplaria* 28.1 (2016): 21–43.

Grimald, Nicholas, 'Of Frendship', in Richard Tottel (ed.), *Tottel's Miscellany* (London, 1867), p. 145.

Gross, Kenneth, *The Dream of the Moving Statue* (Ithaca, NY: Cornell University Press, 1992).

Grosz, Elizabeth, 'Deleuze's Bergson: Duration, the Virtual and a Politics of the Future', in Ian Buchanan and Claire Colebrook (eds), *Deleuze and Feminist Theory* (Edinburgh: Edinburgh University Press, 2000), pp. 214–34.

Grosz, Elizabeth, *Volatile Bodies: Toward a Corporeal Feminism* (Bloomington: Indiana University Press, 1994).

Gurr, Andrew, '*Coriolanus* and the Body Politic', *Shakespeare Survey* 28 (1975): 63–9.

Gurr, Andrew, '*Henry V* and the Bees' Commonwealth', *Shakespeare Survey* 30 (1977): 61–72.

Hadfield, Andrew, *Shakespeare and Republicanism* (New York: Cambridge University Press, 2005).

Hadfield, Andrew, 'Was Spenser Really a Republican After All? A Response to David Scott Wilson-Okamura', *Spenser Studies* 17 (2003): 275–90.

Hammill, Graham, 'Blumenberg and Schmitt on the Rhetoric of Political Theology', in Graham Hammill and Julia Reinhard Lupton (eds), *Political Theology and Early Modernity* (Chicago: University of Chicago Press, 2012), pp. 84–101.

Hammill, Graham, *The Mosaic Constitution: Political Theology and Imagination from Machiavelli to Milton* (Chicago: University of Chicago Press, 2012).

Hammill, Graham, '"The thing / Which never was': Republicanism and *The Ruins of Time*', *Spenser Studies* 18 (2003): 165–83.

Hammill, Graham and Julia Reinhard Lupton (eds), *Political Theology and Early Modernity* (Chicago: University of Chicago Press, 2012).

Harper-Bill, Christopher, 'John and the Church of Rome', in S. D. Church (ed.), *King John: New Interpretations* (Woodbridge: Boydell & Brewer, 2003), pp. 289–315.

Harris, Jonathan Gil, *Untimely Matter in the Time of Shakespeare* (Philadelphia: University of Pennsylvania Press, 2009).

Harris, Jonathan Gil and Nasha Korda, *Staged Properties in Early Modern English Drama* (Cambridge: Cambridge University Press, 2002).

Haverkamp, Anselm, '*Richard II*, Bracton, and the End of Political Theology', *Law & Literature* 16.3 (2005): 313–26.

Haynes, Douglas and Gyan Prakash, 'Introduction: The Entanglement of Power and Resistance', in Douglas Haynes and Gyan Prakash (eds), *Contesting Power: Resistance and Everyday Social Relations in South Asia* (New Delhi: Oxford University Press, 1991), pp. 1–22.

Helgerson, Richard, *Forms of Nationhood: The Elizabethan Writing of England* (Chicago: University of Chicago Press, 1992).

Hendrick, Donald, 'Advantage, Affect, History, *Henry V*', *PMLA* 118.3 (2003): 470–87.

Hobbes, Thomas, *Leviathan: Or the Matter, Forme, and Power of a Commonwealth Ecclesiasticall and Civil*, ed. Michael Oakeshott (New York: Simon & Schuster, 1962).

Hobson, Christopher, 'Bastard Speech: The Rhetoric of "Commodity" in *King John*', *Shakespeare Yearbook* 2 (1991): 95–114.

Hobson, Christopher, 'A Comment on Roy Battenhouse: Religion in *King John*: Shakespeare's View', *Connotations* 2.1 (1992): 69–75.

Hollingsworth, Cristopher, 'Introduction: Reading the Insect', in Eric Brown (ed.), *Insect Poetics* (Minneapolis: University of Minnesota Press, 2006), pp. 192–4.

Hollingsworth, Cristopher, *Poetics of the Hive: The Insect Metaphor in Literature* (Iowa City: University of Iowa Press, 2001).

Honig, Bonnie, 'Law and Politics in the New Europe', in Robert Post (ed.), *Another Cosmopolitanism* (Oxford: Oxford University Press, 2006), pp. 102–27.

Honig, Bonnie, *Political Theory and the Displacement of Politics* (Ithaca, NY: Cornell University Press, 1993).

Horowitz, Gregg, *Sustaining Loss: Art and Mournful Life* (Stanford: Stanford University Press, 1998).

Howard, Jean, 'Dramatic Traditions in Shakespeare's Political Thought', in David Armitage (ed.), *British Political Thought in History, Literature and Theory, 1500–1800* (Cambridge: Cambridge University Press, 2006), pp. 129–44.

Howard, Jean and Phyllis Rackin, *Engendering a Nation: A Feminist Account of Shakespeare's English Histories* (London: Routledge, 1997).

Howard, Jean and Paul Strohm, 'The Imaginary Commons', *Journal of Medieval and Early Modern Studies* 37.3 (2007): 550–77.

Huffman, Clifford, *Coriolanus in Context* (Lewisburg, PA: Bucknell University Press, 1971).

Jackson, Ken, '"Grace to boot": St. Paul, Messianic Time, and Shakespeare's *The Winter's Tale*', in Paul Cefalu and

Brian Reynolds (eds), *The Return of Theory in Early Modern Studies: Tarrying with the Subjunctive* (New York: Palgrave Macmillan, 2011), pp. 102–210.

Jackson, Ken, '"Is it God or the Sovereign Exception?" Giorgio Agamben's *Homo Sacer* and Shakespeare's *King John*', *Religion & Literature* 38.3 (2006): 85–100.

Kaegi, Ann, '"How apply you this?" Conflict and Consensus in *Coriolanus*', *Shakespeare* 4.4 (2008): 362–78.

Kahn, Coppélia, *Roman Shakespeare: Warriors, Wounds, and Women* (New York: Routledge, 1997).

Kahn, Victoria, *The Future of Illusion: Political Theology and Early Modern Texts* (Chicago: University of Chicago Press, 2014).

Kahn, Victoria, 'Machiavelli's Afterlife and Reputation to the Eighteenth Century', in John Najemy (ed.), *The Cambridge Companion to Machiavelli* (Cambridge: Cambridge University Press, 2010), pp. 239–55.

Kahn, Victoria, *Machiavellian Rhetoric: From the Counter-Reformation to Milton* (Princeton: Princeton University Press, 1994).

Kahn, Victoria, 'Political Theology and Fiction in *The King's Two Bodies*', *Representations* 106.1 (2009): 77–101.

Kahn, Victoria, *Wayward Contracts: Literature, Political Theory, and the Crisis of Political Obligation in England, 1640–1674* (Princeton: Princeton University Press, 2004).

Kalmo, Hent and Quentin Skinner, 'Introduction: A Concept in Fragments', in Hent Kalmo and Quentin Skinner (eds), *Sovereignty in Fragments: The Past, Present and Future of a Contested Concept* (Cambridge: Cambridge University Press, 2010), pp. 1–25.

Kamra, Lipika, 'Self-Making through Self-Writing: Non-Sovereign Agency in Women's Memoirs from the Naxalite Movement', *South Asia Multidisciplinary Academic Journal* 7 (2013): 1–12.

Kamuf, Peggy, 'Introduction: Event of Resistance', in Jacques Derrida, *Without Alibi*, trans. Peggy Kamuf (Stanford: Stanford University Press, 2002), pp. 1–27.

Kastan, David Scott, 'Proud Majesty Made a Subject: Shakespeare and the Spectacle of Rule', *Shakespeare Quarterly* 37.4 (1986): 459–75.

Kastan, David Scott, *Shakespeare and the Shapes of Time* (Hanover, NH: University Press of New England, 1982).

Kateb, George, 'Wolin as Critic of Democracy', in Aryeh Botwinick and William E. Connolly (eds), *Democracy and Vision: Sheldon Wolin and the Vicissitudes of the Political* (Princeton: Princeton University Press, 2001), pp. 39–57.

Kelher, Dorothy, '"So Jest with Heaven": Deity in *King John*', in *King John: New Perspectives* (Newark, DE: University of Delaware Press, 1989), pp. 99–113.

Knapp, Hugh, *The Bureaucratic Muse: Thomas Hoccleve and the Literature of Late Medieval England* (University Park: Pennsylvania State University Press, 2001).

Kottman, Paul, *A Politics of the Scene* (Stanford: Stanford University Press, 2008).

Krause, Sharon R., *Freedom Beyond Sovereignty: Reconstructing Liberal Individualism* (Chicago: University of Chicago Press, 2015).

Kuzner, James, *Open Subjects: English Renaissance Republicans, Modern Selfhoods and the Virtue of Vulnerability* (Edinburgh: Edinburgh University Press, 2011).

Kuzner, James, 'Unbuilding the City: *Coriolanus* and the Birth of Republican Rome', *Shakespeare Quarterly* 58.2 (2007): 174–99.

Kuzner, James, '*The Winter's Tale*: Faith in Law and the Law of Faith', *Exemplaria* 24.3 (2012): 260–81.

Laclau, Ernesto and Chantal Mouffe, *Hegemony and Socialist Strategy: Towards a Radical Democratic Politics* (London: Verso, 2014).

Laslett, Peter, Karla Oosterveen and Richard Smith (eds), *Bastardy and its Comparative History* (Cambridge, MA: Harvard University Press, 1980).

Lefort, Claude, 'The Permanence of the Theologico-Political?', trans. David Macey, in Hent de Vries and Lawrence E. Sullivan (eds), *Political Theologies* (New York: Fordham University Press, 2006), pp. 148–87.

Lefort, Claude, *The Political Forms of Modern Society: Bureaucracy, Democracy, Totalitarianism*, ed. John Thompson (Cambridge, MA: MIT Press, 1986).

Lefort, Claude, *Travail de l'oeuvre* (Paris: Gallimard, 1972).

Levin, Carole, '"Would I Could Give You Help and Succour": Elizabeth I and the Politics of Touch', *Albion* 21.2 (1989): 191–205.

Lezra, Jacques, *Wild Materialism: The Ethic of Terror and the Modern Republic* (New York: Fordham University Press, 2010).

Lienwand, Theodore, *Theatre, Finance and Society in Early Modern England* (Cambridge: Cambridge University Press, 1999).

Lorenz, Philip, *The Tears of Sovereignty: Perspectives of Power in Renaissance Drama* (New York: Fordham University Press, 2013).

Luckyj, Christine, '"A Moving Rhetoricke": Women's Silences and Renaissance Texts', *Renaissance Drama* 24 (1993): 33–56.

Lupton, Julia Reinhard, *Citizen-Saints: Shakespeare and Political Theology* (Chicago: University of Chicago Press, 2005).

Lupton, Julia Reinhard, *Thinking with Shakespeare: Essays on Politics and Life* (Chicago: University of Chicago Press, 2011).

Lupton, Julia Reinhard, '*The Winter's Tale* and the Gods: Iconographies of Idolatry', in *Afterlives of the Saints: Hagiography, Typology and Renaissance Literature* (Stanford: Stanford University Press, 1996), pp. 175–218.

MacCaffrey, Wallace, *Elizabeth I: War and Politics 1588–1603* (Princeton: Princeton University Press, 1992).

MacCaffrey, Wallace, 'Place and Patronage in Elizabethan Politics', in S. T. Bindoff, J. Hurstfield and C. H. Williams (eds), *Elizabethan Government and Society: Essays Presented to Sir John Neale* (London and Toronto: Athlone, 1961), pp. 95–126.

McCoy, Richard, *Alterations of State: Sacred Kingship in the English Reformation* (New York: Columbia University Press, 2002).

McEachern, Claire, '*Henry V* and the Paradox of the Body Politic', in Ivo Kamps (ed.), *Materialist Shakespeare: A History* (London: Verso, 1995), pp. 292–319.

Machiavelli, *Discourses on the First Ten Books of Titus Livius*, trans. Christian E. Detmold, The On-Line Library of Liberty, <https://www.marxists.org/reference/archive/machiavelli/works/discourses> (last accessed 22 February 2016).

Manheim, Michael, 'The Four Voices of the Bastard', in Deborah T. Curren-Aquino (ed.), *King John: New Perspectives* (Newark, DE: University of Delaware Press, 1989), pp. 126–35.

Manning, Erin, *Politics of Touch: Sense, Movement, Sovereignty* (Minneapolis: University of Minnesota Press, 2007).

Marks, Laura U., *The Skin of the Film: Intercultural Cinema, Embodiment, and the Senses* (Durham, NC: Duke University Press, 2000).

Marshall, Cynthia, 'The Pornographic Economy of *Titus Andronicus*', in *The Shattering of the Self: Violence, Subjectivity, and Early Modern Texts* (Baltimore: Johns Hopkins University Press, 2002), pp. 106–37.

Maus, Katharine, *Inwardness and Theater in the English Renaissance* (Chicago: University of Chicago Press, 1995).

Mayer, Thomas, *Thomas Starkey and the Commonweal* (Cambridge: Cambridge University Press, 1989).

Meillassoux, Quentin, 'History and Event in Alain Badiou', trans. Thomas Nail, *Parrhesia* 12 (2011): 1–11.

Melzer, Sara and Kathryn Norberg (eds), *From the Royal to the Republican Body: Incorporating the Political in Seventeenth- and Eighteenth-Century France* (Berkeley: University of California Press, 1998).

Mitchell, David and Sharon Snyder (eds), *The Body and Physical Difference: Discourses of Disability* (Ann Arbor: University of Michigan Press, 1997).

Mitchell, David and Sharon Snyder, *Narrative Prosthesis: Disability and the Dependencies of Discourse* (Ann Arbor: University of Michigan Press, 2001).

Moshenska, Joseph, *Feeling Pleasures: The Sense of Touch in Renaissance England* (Oxford: Oxford University Press, 2014).

Mouffe, Chantal, *Agonistics: Thinking the World Politically* (New York and London: Verso, 2013).

Nancy, Jean-Luc, *The Inoperative Community*, trans. Peter Connor, Lisa Garbus, Michael Holland and Simona Sawhney (Minneapolis: University of Minnesota Press, 1991).

Negri, Antonio and Michael Hardt, *Empire* (Cambridge, MA: Harvard University Press, 2000).

Neill, Michael, 'Bastardy, Counterfeiting, and Misogyny in *The Revenger's Tragedy*', *SEL: Studies in English Literature 1500–1900* 36.2 (1996): 397–416.

Neill, Michael, '"In Everything Illegitimate": Imagining the Bastard in Renaissance Drama', *The Yearbook of English Studies* 23 (1993): 270–92.

Nelson, Eric, 'Shakespeare and the Best State of the Commonwealth', in David Armitage, Conal Condren and Andrew Fitzmaurice (eds), *Shakespeare and Early Modern Political*

Thought (Cambridge: Cambridge University Press, 2009), pp. 253–70.

Netzley, Ryan, *Lyric Apocalypse: Milton, Marvell, and the Nature of Events* (New York: Fordham University Press, 2014).

North, Thomas, *Lives of Noble Grecians and Romanes* (London: Nonesuch Press, 1929).

Nyquist, Mary, *Arbitrary Rule: Slavery, Tyranny, and the Power of Life or Death* (Chicago: University of Chicago Press, 2013).

O'Hanlon, Rosalind, 'Recovering the Subject: Subaltern Studies and the Histories of Resistance in Colonial South Asia', in Vinayak Chaturvedi (ed.), *Mapping Subaltern Studies and the Postcolonial* (London: Verso, 2000), pp. 72–115.

Orlin, Lena, 'The Performance of Things in *The Taming of the Shrew*', *Yearbook of English Studies* 23 (1993): 167–88.

Ostovich, Helen, '"Teach you our princess English?" Equivocal Translation of the French in *Henry V*', in Richard C. Trexler (ed.), *Gender Rhetorics: Postures of Dominance and Submission in History* (Birmingham: Centre for Medieval and Early Renaissance Studies, 1994), pp. 147–61.

Ovid, *Metamorphoses*, trans. Brookes More (Boston: Cornhill Publishing Co., 1922).

Owens, Margaret E., 'John Webster, Tussaud Laureate: The Waxworks in *The Duchess of Malfi*', *ELH* 79.4 (Winter 2012): 851–77.

Owens, Margaret E., '*The Revenger's Tragedy* as *Trauerspiel*', *SEL: Studies in English Literature 1500–1900* 55.2 (2015): 403–21.

Owens, Margaret E., *Stages of Dismemberment: The Fragmented Body in Late Medieval and Early Modern Drama* (Newark, DE: University of Delaware Press, 2005).

Packard, Bethany, 'Lavinia as Coauthor of Shakespeare's *Titus Andronicus*', *SEL: Studies in English Literature 1500–1900* 50.2 (2010): 281–300.

Panagia, Davide, *The Political Life of Sensation* (Durham, NC: Duke University Press, 2009).

Patterson, Annabel, *Shakespeare and the Popular Voice* (Oxford: Basil Blackwell, 1989).

Peltonen, Markku, *Classic Humanism and Republicanism in English Political Thought, 1570–1640* (Cambridge: Cambridge University Press, 1995).

Peltonen, Markku, 'Political Rhetoric and Citizenship in *Coriolanus*', in David Armitage, Conal Condren and Andrew Fitzmaurice (eds), *Shakespeare and Early Modern Political Thought* (Cambridge: Cambridge University Press, 2009), pp. 234–52.

Pettit, Philip, *Republicanism: A Theory of Freedom and Government* (Oxford: Clarendon Press, 1990).

Pfannebecker, Mareile, 'Cyborg *Coriolanus*/Monster Body Politic', in Stefan Herbrechter and Ivan Callus (eds), *Posthumanist Shakespeares* (New York: Palgrave Macmillan, 2012), pp. 114–32.

Plutarch, *Plutarch's Lives, Englished by Sir Thomas North in Ten Volumes*, vol. 7 (London: J. M. Dent, 1910).

Pocock, J. G. A., 'Machiavelli and Rome: The Republic as Ideal and as History', in John Najemy (ed.), *The Cambridge Companion to Machiavelli* (Cambridge: Cambridge University Press, 2010), pp. 144–56.

Pocock, J. G. A., *The Machiavellian Moment: Florentine Political Thought and the Atlantic Republican Tradition* (Princeton: Princeton University Press, 1975).

Porter, Chloe, 'Idolatry, Iconoclasm and Agency: Visual Experience in Works by Lyly and Shakespeare', *Literature & History* 18.1 (2009): 1–15.

Prochan, Frank, 'The Semiotic Study of Puppets, Masks, and Performing Objects', *Semiotica* 47 (1983): 3–46.

Pye, Christopher, 'Against Schmitt: Law, Aesthetics, and Absolutism in Shakespeare's *The Winter's Tale*', *South Atlantic Quarterly* 108.1 (2009): 197–217.

Pye, Christopher, *The Regal Phantasm: Shakespeare and the Politics of Spectacle* (New York: Routledge, 1990).

Rabkin, Norman, 'Rabbits, Ducks, and *Henry V*', *Shakespeare Quarterly* 28 (1977): 279–96.

Rackin, Phyllis, *Stages of History: Shakespeare's English Chronicles* (Ithaca, NY: Cornell University Press, 1990).

Rahe, Paul, *Against Throne and Altar* (New York: Cambridge University Press, 2008).

Rancière, Jacques, *Disagreement: Politics and Philosophy* (Minneapolis: University of Minnesota Press, 1999).

Rancière, Jacques, *The Philosopher and His Poor*, trans. Andrew Parker (Durham, NC: Duke University Press, 2004).

Rancière, Jacques, 'Ten Theses on Politics', *Theory & Event* 5.3 (2001).

Richards, Jennifer, 'Shakespeare and the Politics of Co-authorship: *Henry VIII*', in David Armitage, Conal Condren and Andrew Fitzmaurice (eds), *Shakespeare and Early Modern Political Thought* (Cambridge: Cambridge University Press, 2009), pp. 176–98.

Riss, Arthur, 'The Belly Politic: *Coriolanus* and the Revolt of Language', *English Literary History* 59 (1992): 53–75.

Roach, Tom, *Friendship as a Way of Life: Foucault, AIDS, and the Politics of Shared Estrangement* (Albany, NY: SUNY Press, 2012).

Robertson, Karen, 'Rape and the Appropriation of Progne's Revenge in Shakespeare's *Titus Andronicus*, or "Who Cooks the Thyestean Banquet?"', in Elizabeth Robertson and Christine M. Rose (eds), *Representing Rape in Medieval and Early Modern Literature* (New York: Palgrave Macmillan, 2001), pp. 213–37.

Roe, John, *Shakespeare and Machiavelli* (Cambridge: D. S. Brewer, 2002).

Rose, Jacqueline, *States of Fantasy* (Oxford: Clarendon, 1996).

Rosendale, Timothy, 'Sacral and Sacramental Kingship in the Lancastrian Tetralogy', in Dennis Taylor and David Beauregard (eds), *Shakespeare and the Culture of Christianity in Early Modern England* (New York: Fordham University Press, 2003), pp. 121–40.

Rowe, Katherine, 'Dismembering and Forgetting in *Titus Andronicus*', *Shakespeare Quarterly* 45.3 (1994): 279–303.

Rust, Jennifer, *The Body in Mystery: The Political Theology of the Corpus Mysticum in the Literature of Reformation England* (Chicago: Northwestern University Press, 2013).

Saeger, James, 'Illegitimate Subjects: Performing Bastardy in *King John*', *Journal of English and Germanic Philology* 100.1 (2001): 1–21.

Santner, Eric, *The Royal Remains: The People's Two Bodies and the Endgames of Sovereignty* (Chicago: University of Chicago Press, 2011).

Scarry, Elaine, *The Body in Pain: The Making and Unmaking of the World* (New York: Oxford University Press, 1985).

Schmitt, Carl, *The Concept of the Political: Expanded Edition* (Chicago: University of Chicago Press, 2007).

Schmitt, Carl, *Political Theology: Four Chapters on the Concept of Sovereignty*, trans. George Schwab (Cambridge, MA: MIT Press, 1985).

Schweitzer, Ivy, *Perfecting Friendship: Politics and Affiliation in Early American Literature* (Chapel Hill: University of North Carolina Press, 2006).

Shakespeare, William, *The Norton Shakespeare*, 3rd edn, ed. Stephen Greenblatt et al. (New York: W. W. Norton & Company, 2016).

Shannon, Laurie, *Sovereign Amity: Figures of Friendship in Shakespearean Contexts* (Chicago: University of Chicago Press, 2002).

Shapiro, Michael, *For Moral Ambiguity: National Culture and the Politics of the Family* (Minneapolis: University of Minnesota Press, 2001).

Shaviro, Steven, *The Cinematic Body* (Minneapolis: University of Minnesota Press, 1993).

Shrank, Cathy, 'Civility and the City in *Coriolanus*', *Shakespeare Quarterly* 54.4 (2003): 406–23.

Shuger, Debora Kuller, *Political Theologies in Shakespeare's England: The Sacred and the State in* Measure for Measure (Basingstoke: Palgrave, 2001).

Sidney, Algernon, *Discourses Concerning Government* (Edinburgh: Hamilton and Balfour, 1750).

Silverman, Kaja, *The Acoustic Mirror: The Female Voice in Psychoanalysis and Cinema* (Bloomington: University of Indiana Press, 1988).

Skinner, Quentin, 'Machiavelli's *Discorsi* and the Pre-Humanist Origins of Republican Ideas', in Gisela Bock, Quentin Skinner and Maurizio Viroli (eds), *Machiavelli and Republicanism* (Cambridge: Cambridge University Press, 1990), pp. 121–41.

Skinner, Quentin, 'The Sovereign State: A Genealogy', in Hent Kalmo and Quentin Skinner (eds), *Sovereignty in Fragments: The Past, Present and Future of a Contested Concept* (Cambridge: Cambridge University Press, 2010), pp. 26–46.

Slavin, A. J., 'The Tudor State, Reformation and Understanding Change: Through the Looking Glass', in Paul A. Fideler and T. F. Mayer (eds), *Political Thought and the Tudor Commonwealth: Deep Structure, Discourse and Disguise* (New York: Routledge, 1992), pp. 229–59.

Solga, Kim, 'Rape's Metatheatrical Return: Rehearsing Sexual Violence among the Early Moderns', *Theatre Journal* 58.1 (2006): 53–72.

Spencer, T. J. B., 'Shakespeare and the Elizabethan Romans', *Shakespeare Survey* 10 (1957): 27–38.

Sterne, Jonathan, 'Bureaumentality', in Jack Z. Bratich, Jeremy Packer and Cameron McCarthy (eds), *Foucault, Cultural Studies, and Governmentality* (Albany, NY: SUNY Press, 2003), pp. 101–33.

Stewart, Richard, *The English Ordinance Office: A Case Study in Bureaucracy* (Woodbridge: Boydell Press, 1996).

Strier, Richard, Review of *Shakespeare and Machiavelli* by John Roe, *Shakespeare Quarterly* 55.4 (2004): 480–4.

Sumi, Geoffrey S., *Ceremony and Power: Performing Politics in Rome between Republic and Empire* (Ann Arbor: University of Michigan Press, 2005).

Taylor, Charles, *A Secular Age* (Cambridge, MA: Harvard University Press, 2007).

Teague, Francis, *Shakespeare's Speaking Properties* (Newark, DE: University of Delaware Press, 1991).

Tennenhouse, Leonard, *Power on Display: The Politics of Shakespeare's Genres* (New York: Methuen, 1986).

Thomson, A. J. P., *Deconstruction and Democracy: Derrida's Politics of Friendship* (New York: Continuum, 2005).

Toynbee, M. R., 'Charles I and the King's Evil', *Folklore* 61.1 (March 1950): 1–14.

Turner, Henry S., 'The Problem of the More-than-One: Friendship, Calculation, and Political Association in *The Merchant of Venice*', *Shakespeare Quarterly* 57.4 (2006): 413–42.

Uman, Deborah and Sara Morrison (eds), *Staging the Blazon in Early Modern English Theater* (Burlington, VT: Ashgate Publishing, 2013).

van Mill, David, *Liberty, Rationality, and Agency in Hobbes's Leviathan* (Albany, NY: SUNY Press, 2015).

Vatter, Miguel, *Between Form and Event: Machiavelli's Theory of Political Freedom* (Dordrecht: Kluwer, 2000).

Vaughan, Virginia, '*King John*', in Richard Dutton and Jean Howard (eds), *A Companion to Shakespeare's Works:*

The Histories, vol. 2 (London: John Wiley & Sons, 2003), pp. 379–94.

Vaughan, Virginia, '*King John*: Subversion and Containment', in Deborah T. Curren-Aquino (ed.), *King John: New Perspectives* (Newark, DE: University of Delaware Press, 1989), pp. 62–75.

Vickers, Nancy, 'Members Only: Marot's Anatomical Blazons', in David Hillman and Carla Mazzio (eds), *The Body in Parts: Fantasies of Corporeality in Early Modern Europe* (London: Routledge, 1997), pp. 2–21.

Watson, Emily, *Mocked with Death: Tragic Overliving from Sophocles to Milton* (Baltimore: Johns Hopkins University Press, 2004).

Weber, Max, *From Max Weber: Essays in Sociology*, ed. and trans. H. Gerth and C. Mills (New York: Oxford University Press, 1946).

Weimann, Robert, 'Mingling Vice and "Worthiness" in *King John*', *Shakespeare Studies* 27 (1999): 109–33.

Weinstock, Stefan, *Divus Julius* (Oxford: Clarendon Press, 1971).

Wenman, Mark, *Agonistic Democracy: Constituent Power in the Era of Globalisation* (Cambridge: Cambridge University Press, 2013).

Wilcox, Lance, 'Katherine of France as Victim and Bride', *Shakespeare Studies* 17 (1985): 61–76.

Williams, Penry and G. L. Harriss, 'A Revolution in Tudor History?', *Past & Present* 25 (1963): 3–58.

Williamson, Marilyn, 'The Courtship of Katherine and the Second Tetralogy', *Criticism* 17 (1975): 326–34.

Willis, Deborah, 'The Monarch and the Sacred: Shakespeare and the Ceremony for the Healing of the King's Evil', in Linda Woodbridge and Edward Berry (eds), *Sacred Rites and Maimed Rites: Ritual and Anti-Ritual in Shakespeare and his Age* (Urbana and Chicago: University of Illinois Press, 1992), pp. 147–68.

Wills, David, *Dorsality: Thinking Back through Technology and Politics* (Minneapolis: University of Minnesota Press, 2008).

Wills, David, 'Full Dorsal: Derrida's *Politics of Friendship*', *Postmodern Culture* 15.3 (2005), <http://pmc.iath.virginia.edu/text-only/issue.505/15.3wills.txt> (last accessed 22 February 2016).

Wills, David, *Prosthesis* (Stanford: Stanford University Press, 1995).

Wilson, Richard, 'The Statue of our Queen: Shakespeare's Open Secret', in *Secret Shakespeare: Studies in Theatre, Religion and Resistance* (Manchester: Manchester University Press, 2004), pp. 246–70.

Wilson-Okamura, David Scott, 'Republicanism, Nostalgia, and the Crowd', *Spenser Studies* 17 (2003): 253–73.

Witmore, Michael, *Pretty Creatures: Children and Fiction in the English Renaissance* (Ithaca, NY: Cornell University Press, 2007).

Wolin, Sheldon S., 'Fugitive Democracy', *Constellations* 1.1 (1994): 11–25.

Wolin, Sheldon S., 'Political Theory as Vocation', *American Political Science Review* 63.4 (1969): 1,062–82.

Wolin, Sheldon S., *Politics and Vision: Continuity and Innovation in Western Political Thought*, expanded edition (Princeton: Princeton University Press, 2004).

Wolin, Sheldon S., 'What Revolutionary Action Means Today', *Democracy* 2.4 (1982): 17–28.

Womack, Peter, 'Imagining Communities: Theatres and the English Nation in the Sixteenth Century', in David Aers (ed.), *Culture and History, 1350–1600: Essays on English Communities, Identities, and Writing* (Detroit: Wayne State University Press, 1992), pp. 91–145.

Woodbridge, Linda, *Vagrancy, Homelessness, and English Renaissance Literature* (Chicago: University of Illinois Press, 2001).

Wootton, David, 'Oxbridge Model', *Times Literary Supplement*, 23 September 2005, p. 7, pp. 9–10.

Wynne-Davies, Marion, '"The Swallowing Womb": Consumed and Consuming Women in *Titus Andronicus*', in Valerie Wayne (ed.), *The Matter of Difference: Materialist Feminist Criticism of Shakespeare* (Ithaca, NY: Cornell University Press, 1991), pp. 129–51.

Xenos, Nicholas, 'Momentary Democracy', in Aryeh Botwinick and William E. Connolly (eds), *Democracy and Vision: Sheldon Wolin and the Vicissitudes of the Political* (Princeton: Princeton University Press, 2001), pp. 25–38.

Ziarek, Ewa, 'Bare Life', in Henry Sussman (ed.), *Impasses of the Post-Global: Theory in the Era of Climate Change*, vol. 2 (Ann Arbor: Open Humanities Press, 2012), pp. 194–211.

Ziarek, Ewa, *An Ethics of Dissensus: Postmodernity, Feminism, and the Politics of Radical Democracy* (Stanford: Stanford University Press, 2001).

Zimmerman, Susan, *The Early Modern Corpse in Shakespeare's Theatre* (Edinburgh: Edinburgh University Press, 2005).

Žižek, Slavoj, *Event: Philosophy in Transit* (London: Penguin, 2014).

Žižek, Slavoj, *The Ticklish Subject: The Absent Centre of Political Ontology* (New York: Verso, 2000).

INDEX